Creating Fast, Responsive and Energy-Efficient
Embedded Systems
using the Renesas RL78 Microcontroller

Alexander G. Dean
North Carolina State University

James M. Conrad
University of North Carolina at Charlotte

Micriµm Press
1290 Weston Road, Suite 306
Weston, FL 33326
USA

www.micrium.com

Library of Congress subject headings:

1. Embedded computer systems
2. Real-time data processing
3. Computer software—Development

For bulk orders, please contact Micrium Press at: +1 954 217 2036

ISBN: 978-1-935772-98-9

Please report errors or forward any comments and suggestions to agdean@ncsu.edu

Preface

When Renesas asked us to create a book on the RL78 microcontroller family, we jumped at the chance. It gave us the opportunity to present embedded systems as built upon concepts from critical areas (such as computer architecture and microarchitecture, memory systems, compilation methods, software engineering, kernels and operating systems, inter-process communication, and real-time systems) in a way which applies to traditional embedded systems. Many embedded texts present these concepts as they are applied to resource-rich PC-like devices such as smartphones — the trade-offs and resulting outcomes are quite different. We hope we have succeeded.

This book can be used on its own for an Introduction to Embedded Systems class or as a graduate level Embedded System Design, Analysis and Optimization class. It can also be used as a supplement in other types of classes where a microcontroller-based implementation is necessary.

This book would not have been possible had it not been for the assistance of numerous people. Several students and educators contributed to some of the chapters, including: Adam Harris (2), Suganya Jebasingh (2, 7), Michael Plautz (8), Sunil Gurram (11), Aswin Ramakrishnan (11), Vivek Srikantan (12), and Paul Mohan Das (12).

Thanks go to the compositor, Linda Foegen, and especially to June Hay-Harris, Rob Dautel, and Todd DeBoer of Renesas for their help in getting this book produced and published (and for their patience!). Many, many thanks go to the reviewers who offered valuable suggestions to make this book better, especially Mitch Ferguson and Anthony Harris.

Alex Dean: I would like to thank Bill Trosky and Phil Koopman for opening the doors into so many embedded systems through in-depth design reviews. I would like to thank my students in my NCSU embedded systems courses for bringing their imagination, excitement, and persistence to class projects. I would also like to thank my wife Sonya for sharing her passion of seeking out and seizing opportunities, and our daughters Katherine and Jacqueline for making me smile every time I leave work to head home. Finally, I would like to thank my parents for planting the seeds of curiosity in my mind.

Jim Conrad: I would like to personally thank my parents, the Conrads, and my in-laws, the Warrens, for their continued assistance and guidance through the years while I worked on books. Also, I would especially like to thank my children, Jay, Mary Beth, and Caroline, and my wife Stephanie, for their understanding when I needed to spend more time on the book than I spent with them.

Alexander G. Dean and James M. Conrad
March 2012

Foreword

The world of MCU-based embedded designs can be divided into those that take advantage of existing code and MCUs, and those that require leading edge MCU architectures and implementations. Dr. Dean, with assistance from Dr. Conrad, spent more than a year internalizing the inner workings and surrounding ecosystem of the newly-developed RL78 architecture, and have generated a book showcasing the RL78 line which has a level of ultra low power and performance that has not been seen before. Indeed, by taking the best DNA of both the ex-NEC 78K MCU core and the Renesas R8C peripherals, and combining them into a new breed of MCU, the RL78 line enables design approaches that were previously spread across the low power or high performance camps and inaccessible in one device line.

The authors leverage the capabilities of the RL78 and demonstrate their own expert grasp of all the dynamics that differentiate successful end solutions from those of the "me-too" variety. They recognize that successful embedded systems require more than just good hardware and software engineering. Alex and Jim have masterfully applied RL78 capabilities to real world challenges using examples, applications and approaches that will surely empower individuals and teams of designers.

Readers aspire to find books that have the right balance between depth and breadth. Where there is too much detail, the relevance can be obscured; while a broad brush approach may trivialize the essence of key topics. This is especially true of books relating to embedded designs that must achieve a utilitarian purpose. Here, Alex and Jim skillfully navigate from topic to topic, knowing exactly when to throttle for maximum utility.

Whether you are a university student preparing for the real world, a design engineer looking for leading edge approaches to time-critical processes, or a manager attempting to further your risk management techniques, you will find Alex's approach to embedded systems to be stimulating and compelling.

Ali Sebt
Renesas
March 8, 2012

Contents

viii   CONTENTS

CHAPTER THREE

RL78 CPU Core and Interrupts   37

CHAPTER FOUR

Software Engineering for Embedded Systems   67

CHAPTER SEVEN

CHAPTER ELEVEN

CHAPTER TWELVE

Optimizing for Program Speed

CHAPTER THIRTEEN

Power and Energy Optimization

Chapter One

Introduction to Embedded Systems

1.1 LEARNING OBJECTIVES

In this chapter the reader will learn:

- What an embedded system is
- Why to embed a computer
- What functions and attributes embedded systems need to provide
- What constraints embedded systems have

1.2 CONCEPTS

An embedded system is an application-specific computer system which is built into a larger system or device. Using a computer system rather than other control methods (such as non-programmable logic circuits, electro-mechanical controls, and hydraulic control) offers many benefits such as sophisticated control, precise timing, low unit cost, low development cost, high flexibility, small size and low weight. These basic characteristics can be used to improve the overall system or device in various ways:

- Improved performance
- More functions and features
- Reduced cost
- Increased dependability

Because of these benefits, billions of microcontrollers are sold each year to create embedded systems for a wide range of products.

1.2.1 Economics and Microcontrollers

Microcontrollers are remarkably inexpensive yet offer tremendous performance. The microprocessor for a personal computer may cost $100 or more, while microcontrollers typically cost far less, starting at under $0.25. Why is this so?

Microcontrollers provide extremely inexpensive processing because they can leverage **economies of scale.** MCUs are programmable in software, so a chipmaker can design a single type of MCU which will satisfy the needs of many customers (when combined with their application-specific software). This reduces the per-chip cost by amortizing the design costs over many millions of units.

The cost of an integrated circuit (such as a microcontroller or a microprocessor) depends on two factors: non-recurring engineering (**NRE**) cost and **recurring** cost. The **NRE** cost includes paying engineers to design the integrated circuit (IC) and verify through simulation and prototyping that it will work properly. The **recurring cost** is incurred by making each additional IC, and includes raw materials, processing, testing and packaging.

The IC's area is the major factor determining this recurring cost. As the IC design gets smaller, more copies of the circuit will fit onto a silicon wafer, reducing the recurring cost. Microcontrollers are much smaller than microprocessors for personal computers, so they will cost less (given the same number of ICs sold). The NRE cost must be divided across each IC sold. As the number of ICs sold rises, the NRE adder falls, and so each IC's price falls as well. Low-volume chips are more expensive than high-volume chips.

1.2.2   Embedded Networks

Some embedded systems consist of **multiple embedded computers** communicating across an **embedded network,** and offer further benefits. Each embedded computer on the network shares a set of wires to communicate with in which a communication protocol is utilized to share the wires, instead of dedicating a set of communication wires for each possible route. Several advantages come from having fewer wires:

- Lower parts cost, as fewer wires are needed.
- Lower labor costs, as it is faster to assemble.
- Greater reliability, as it has fewer connections to fail.

Other advantages come from allowing separate nodes to share information. New features may be possible, or the system efficiency may be improved through better coordination of activities among different nodes.

1.3   TYPICAL BENEFITS OF EMBEDDED SYSTEMS _____

As an example, let's examine how embedded systems have affected automobiles. A typical modern car has dozens of microcontrollers embedded within it. Let's see why.

1.3.1   Greater Performance and Efficiency

Computer control of automobile engines lowers pollution and increases fuel efficiency, reducing operating costs.

Burning gasoline with air in internal combustion engines is a tricky business if we want to maximize efficiency yet minimize pollution. The main factor affecting emissions is the ratio of air mass to fuel mass. The ideal ratio is 14.7 to 1, and the catalytic converter is designed to operate most efficiently at this ratio. If there is too little air (a rich mix), then excessive carbon monoxide (CO) and hydrocarbons (HC) will be produced. If there is too much air (a lean mix), then large amounts of oxides of nitrogen (NOx) will be created. So we would like for each fuel injector to add just the right amount of fuel. This depends on the mass of the air inside the cylinder, which depends on factors such as air temperature and air pressure. These in turn depend on altitude and weather, as well as whether the engine is warmed up or not.

Another factor is the timing of the sparkplug firing. If it fires early, then there is more time for combustion within the cylinder before the exhaust valve opens. This raises the average temperature within the cylinder and changes the combustion process, affecting CO, HC, and NOx concentrations.

It would be quite impractical to design a mechanical control system that considered all of these factors and opened the fuel injectors at just the right instant for the right amount of time. Thankfully, an inexpensive microcontroller is quite effective at these kinds of calculations and control.

1.3.2   Lower Costs

There are various ways in which an embedded system can reduce the costs associated with a device.

- **Component costs:** Embedded software can compensate for poor signal quality, allowing the use of less-expensive components. For example, a low-cost pressure sensor may be very temperature-dependent. If ambient temperature information is already available, then it is a simple matter to compensate for the temperature-induced error.
- **Manufacturing costs:** Many vehicles use the Control Area Network (CAN) protocol to communicate across an in-car network. The embedded network reduces assembly and parts costs because of the simpler wiring harness.
- **Operating costs:** As mentioned above, an embedded system enables automobile engines to operate more efficiently, reducing the amount of gasoline needed and hence lowering operating costs.
- **Maintenance costs:** Some vehicles predict oil life by monitoring engine use history, notifying the driver when an oil change is needed.

1.3.3   More Features

An MCU running application-specific software offers tremendous opportunities for features and customization. These features can make your company's products stand out from the competition.

- **Cruise control** keeps the car running at the same speed regardless of hills, wind, and other external factors.
- **Smart airbags** reduce injuries by adjusting inflation speed based on passenger weight.
- **Power seats** move to each driver's preferred position automatically, based on whose keyless entry fob was used to open the car.
- **Headlights and interior lights** shut off automatically after a time delay if the car is not running, and prevent the lights from draining the battery.

1.3.4   Better Dependability

Embedded systems and networks offer many opportunities to improve dependability.

- An engine controller (and other controllers) can provide various "limp-home modes" to keep the car running even if one or more sensors or other devices fail.
- A warning of an impending failure can be provided.
- Diagnostic information can be provided to the driver or service personnel, saving valuable trouble-shooting time.

1.4   EMBEDDED SYSTEM FUNCTIONS

There are several common functions which embedded systems typically provide.

- **Control systems** monitor a process and adjust an output variable to keep the process running at the desired set point. For example, a cruise control system may increase the throttle setting if the car's speed is lower than the desired speed, and reduce it if the car is too fast.
- There is often **sequencing** among multiple states. For example, a car engine goes through multiple states or control modes when started. During **Crank and Start,** the fuel/air mix is lean and depends on the engine coolant temperature. Once the engine has started, the controller switches to the **Warm-Up** mode in order to raise the engine and exhaust system temperatures to their ideal levels. Here the fuel/air mixture and ignition timing are adjusted, again based in part on the engine coolant

temperature. When the engine has warmed up it can switch into **Idle** mode. In this mode the controller seeks to minimize the engine's speed, yet still run smoothly and efficiently despite changes in loads due to air conditioning, power steering, and the electrical system.

- **Signal processing** modifies input signals to eliminate noise, emphasize signal components of interest, and compensate for other factors. For example, a hands-free speakerphone interface may use multiple microphones, beam-forming, and active noise cancellation to filter out low-frequency road noise. Other sensors may have spark-plug noise filtered out.

- **Communications and networking** enable different devices on the same network to exchange information. For example, the engine controller may need to send a message indicating speed. To do this, the speed value must be formatted according to the communication protocol and then loaded into the network interface peripheral for transmission.

1.5   ATTRIBUTES OF EMBEDDED SYSTEMS

Embedded systems are designed so that the resulting device behaves in certain desirable ways.

- Embedded systems need to **respond to events** which occur in the environment, whether a user presses a button or a motor overheats. A system which is not sufficiently responsive is not likely to be a successful product. For example, when we press a channel select button for the radio, we would like for it to respond within some reasonable time.

- For **real-time systems,** the timing of the responses is **critical** because late answers are wrong answers. Igniting the fuel in a cylinder is time-critical because bad timing can damage or destroy engine components (to say nothing of reducing power, or the efficiency and pollution concerns mentioned previously).

- Embedded systems typically require sophisticated **fault handling and diagnostics** to enable safe and reliable operation. Often the fault handling code is larger and more complex than the normal operation code. It is easy to design for the "everything goes right and works fine" case. It is far more difficult to determine how to handle the exceptional cases. What is likely to fail? Which failures can lead to dangerous conditions? How should the system handle failures? How will you test that the system handles the failures correctly?

- Embedded systems may be expected to **operate independently** for years without operator attention such as adjustment or resetting. The system is expected to operate robustly and always work. Given that it is very difficult and expensive to write perfect, bug-free software, developers build in mechanisms to detect faulty behavior and respond, perhaps by restarting the system.

1.6   CONSTRAINTS ON EMBEDDED SYSTEMS

Embedded systems often have **constraints** which limit the designer's options and can lead to creative and elegant solutions. These constraints are typically different from those for general-purpose computers.

- **Cost** is a common constraint. Many applications which use embedded systems are sold in very competitive markets, in which price is a major factor. Often a manufacturer will hire subcontractors to design and build individual sub-systems. This then allows manufacturer to pit potential subcontractors against each other, keeping prices down.
- There may be **size** and **weight** limits for portable and mobile applications. An embedded system for an automotive remote keyless entry transmitter must fit into a small fob on a key ring which fits easily into a pocket. Both the transmitter and the receiver must not be too heavy. A heavier car will have worse acceleration, braking, cornering, and fuel efficiency. Aircraft and spacecraft are especially sensitive to weight since a heavier craft requires more fuel to achieve the same range.
- There may be limited **power** or **energy** available. For example, a battery has a limited amount of energy, while a solar cell generates a limited amount of power. High temperatures may limit the amount of cooling available, which will limit the power which can be used.
- The **environment** may be harsh. Automotive electronics under the hood of a car need to operate across a wide range of temperatures ($-40°C$ to $125°C$, or $-40°F$ to $193°F$), while withstanding vibrations, physical impact, and corroding salt spray. Spark plugs generate broadband radio frequency energy which can interfere with electronics.

1.7   DESIGNING AND MANUFACTURING EMBEDDED SYSTEMS

Embedded systems are designed with a central microcontroller and other supporting electronic components mounted on a printed circuit board (PCB). PCBs provide the means to connect these integrated circuits to each other to make an operational system. The PCB provides structural support and the wiring of the circuit. The individual wires on the PCB are called traces and are made from a flat copper foil. While many circuit designs may use the same standard components, the PCB is often a custom component for a given design.

Designing a PCB requires a completed schematic for the circuit. This schematic is sometimes different than the schematic seen in textbooks. It often contains extra information about the components and construction of the board. For example, a textbook schematic may only show a battery for the power supply, while the production schematic would show the battery case, the number of cells, the rating of the battery, and the manufacturers of the components.

From the schematic, a designer will use their computer-aided design tools to identify the size of the PCB, and then place the electronic components on their board drawing. The designer will also place the wiring between the components on the PCB.

The physical PCB is manufactured from a fiberglass-resin material that is lightweight and inexpensive. A manufacturer will add copper wiring traces to the surfaces of the board and the appropriate insulation and white silk screening. The final manufacturing steps are applying solder, placing the components, and heating/cooling the solder. Figure 1.1 shows an example of a finished board.

Figure 1.1   EIN GreenEval Zigbee Module.

The completed boards are electrically tested for functionality. Any board failing the test is inspected in more detail to find the problems. These boards are repaired to increase the passing rate acceptable to the manufacturer. The boards are wrapped in anti-static materials and shipped to the next location for the next stage of production, or immediately installed in a mechanical enclosure (like the mechanical shell of a mobile phone).

1.8   AN EXAMPLE OF AN EMBEDDED SYSTEM: THE EIN GREENEVAL ZIGBEE MODULE

The EIN GreenEval Zigbee[1] module is one example of a Renesas MCU-based embedded system. This device has thirty-four digital I/O lines that are controlled by a Zigbee radio.

Figure 1.1 shows the main board of the EIN GreenEval Zigbee Module. As seen in this example, taking off the shielding provides a good look at the internal circuitry. Six of the main components are visible. Starting from left to right; the large cylindrical device hanging off the left edge of the board is an antenna for the 2.4 GHz radio.

The chip labeled 5PE20V (the small 8-pin chip at the top left of the image) is a page-erasable serial Flash chip.[2] This chip communicates with the Renesas MCU through the SPI bus. This chip is also used to hold more data than the MCU. Since the MCU can only handle 8 kilobytes of data, it is quickly filled. This extra flash chip can hold an additional 256 kilobytes.

The square chip on the lower left is a Skyworks 2.4 GHz Front-End Module (FEM),[3] which amplifies and switches radio signals between the antenna and the MCU. It is controlled by three output pins of the MCU. One pin controls putting the FEM to sleep to save power, another pin selects whether the FEM will send or receive data, and the last pin actually transmits and receives data to and from the FEM.

The large chip in the center is a Renesas R5FF36B3 from the M16C family of chips with 256 KB + 24 KB of ROM, 20 KB of RAM, and 8 KB of data.[4] Thirty-four I/O pins are used to interface with external pins on the module. This processor is running at 4 MHz (controlled by the small metal chip which is actually a temperature compensated crystal oscillator). This chip has an RF radio built in.

The pins at the far right are a programming and interface header. They are used to communicate with and program the Renesas MCU.

1.9   SUMMARY OF BOOK CONTENTS

This book is structured as follows:

- Chapters 2 and 3 present basic microcontroller and interfacing concepts and the specifics of the RL78 architecture.
- Chapters 4, 5, and 6 show how software is built. At the high level they present software engineering concepts and practices. In the middle they show how programs are compiled and downloaded. Finally, at the low level they show how C code is implemented in the MCU's native language.
- Chapters 7, 8, and 9 present how to use peripherals to interface with the environment and simplify programs.
- Chapter 13 presents additional peripherals which can increase system robustness (the watchdog timer and voltage brown-out detector) and accelerate data transfer speed (direct memory access).
- Chapters 11, 12, and 13 present how to optimize embedded software for predictable responsiveness, speed, energy, and power.

1.10   RECAP

An embedded system is an application-specific computer system which is built into a larger system or device. Using a computer system enables improved performance, more functions and features, lower cost, and greater dependability. With embedded computer systems, manufacturers can add sophisticated control and monitoring to devices and other systems while leveraging the low-cost microcontrollers running custom software.

1.11   REFERENCES

Envisionnovation. *EININC Products*. Ontario: Envisionnovation, 2010. Web. Accessed at http://www.eininc. net/products.html

Numonyx MP25PE20 datasheet http://www.micron.com//get-document/?documentId=5965&file=M25PE20_ 10.pdf

RENESAS MCU: M16C Family/M16C/60 SERIES. Renesas Electronics America, Inc., 2010. Web. Accessed at http://am.renesas.com/products/mpumcu/m16c/m16c60/m16c6b/m16c6b_root.jsp

SKYWORKS Solutions, Inc. *SKYWORKS Products: SKY65352–11*. Woburn, MA: SKYWORKS Solutions, Inc., 2009. Web. Accessed at http://www.skyworksinc.com/Product.aspx?ProductID=752

Chapter Two

Microcontroller Concepts, Infrastructure, and Interfacing

2.1 LEARNING OBJECTIVES

Embedded systems consist of computers which are embedded in larger systems. Additional circuitry such as power supplies, clock generators, and reset circuits, are required for the computer to work. Transducers (devices that convert one type of energy into another) are also used to connect microcontrollers to the outside world. There are two classes of transducers: inputs and outputs. Inputs (sensors) include devices such as switches, temperature sensors, keypads, and buttons. Output transducers include devices such as LEDs, motors, and coils.

In this chapter the reader will learn general information about:

- The infrastructure needed for powering, clocking, and controlling any embedded system
- Configuring general purpose input/output ports using software
- Using digital signals to control LEDs and motors, and to monitor switches and keypads
- Converting analog signals to digital (and back) to interface with analog devices

2.2 MICROCONTROLLER-BASED EMBEDDED SYSTEM HARDWARE BASICS

Figure 2.1 shows an example of the components in a generic microcontroller-based embedded system. The gray box shows what is contained in (integrated with) a typical microcontroller, but this is not definitive for every MCU. In this chapter we will examine several of these components. In the next chapter we will examine the details of the processor itself.

- A power supply is necessary to power the circuit.
- An oscillator is required to drive the system's digital logic.
- A processor is required to execute program instructions.
- A reset circuit is required to ensure the processor starts correctly on power-up or when a reset is requested.
- Nonvolatile memory is required to hold the program and fixed data.

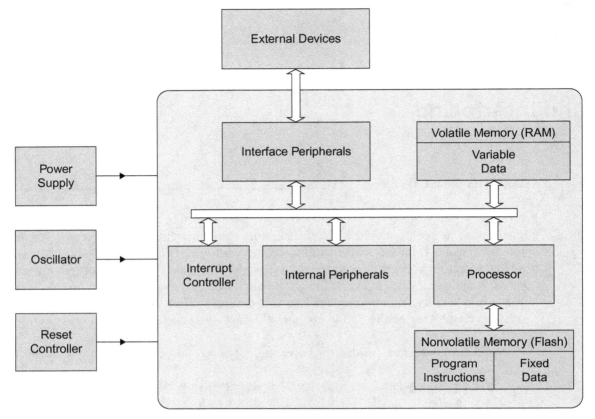

Figure 2.1   Block diagram of a generic embedded system.

- Volatile memory is typically used to hold data which changes as the program runs.
- Interface peripherals communicate with external devices to sense the values of input signals and control the output signals.
- Internal peripheral devices provide additional functions without the need for external interfacing.

2.3   INFRASTRUCTURE: POWER, CLOCK, AND RESET

2.3.1   Power Supply

A microcontroller requires electrical power to run. The MCU data manual indicates the range of acceptable voltages and typical current drawn across those voltages, often under the title of *Recommended Operating Conditions* or *Electrical Characteristics*. For example, the RL78G13 MCU has a recommended operating voltage range from 1.6 V to 5.5 V. **Below this range** the MCU is not guaranteed to operate correctly. Faults may come from transistors switching too slowly, capacitors charging or discharging too slowly, memory cells losing their data, and other such malfunctions. **Above this range** the MCU will draw excessive power and grow hotter than necessary. Continuing to higher voltages and currents, one reaches the *Absolute Maximum Ratings* (also detailed in the data manual). Beyond these ratings, the IC will be damaged due to excessive current, excessive heat, insulation (oxide) breakdown and other such faults.

To ensure that the chip will operate as expected, a system should never be designed to operate too close to the absolute maximum ratings. The data manual indicates that the Absolute Maximum voltage for any pin is 6.5 V. Fluctuations in the power supply may cause the values to go over the absolute maximum ratings of the chip, which can damage the microprocessor. The power supply should be designed with a safety factor to account for these fluctuations.

Within the safe operating range, the clock speed at the lower voltages may be limited. Oscillators may only run at low frequencies with lower voltages. Also, transistor switching speed falls as $V_{\text{supply}} - V_{\text{threshold}}$ falls, so a longer clock period is needed to allow signals to propagate through the slower logic. For example, the RL78G13's main clock system oscillator can run at up to 4.0 MHz with a 1.6 to 1.8 V supply, up to 8 MHz with a supply above 1.8 V but below 2.7 V, and up to 20 MHz with a supply above 2.7 V. MCUs typically have built-in circuitry for dividing or multiplying the oscillator frequency to derive a different final operating frequency for the internal logic.

2.3.2   Clock Signal Generation

Microprocessors are synchronous circuits that require a clock to work. This clock allows data to be pushed through the stages of the instruction pipeline and helps the microprocessor coordinate tasks. When selecting a clock generator, the microcontroller datasheet must be used. This datasheet gives the values of the different clocks that a particular microprocessor can accept.

There are two major types of clock signal generators: those that work on purely electrical principles, and those that work on mechanical vibration (resonance of a quartz element). The signal generators for the electrical driven clock can be simple resistor-capacitor (RC) or inductor-capacitor (LC) circuits. Generally, these clocks aren't very accurate on their own, and their design can become quite complicated when precision is required. Many microprocessors offer signal generators with an internal clock that consists of an RC circuit inside the chip, which can be configured. These clocks should not be used when precise timing is required. Figure 2.2 shows the connection of an RC oscillator to the clock input of a microprocessor.

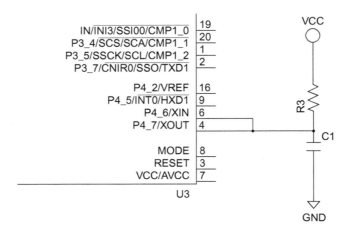

Figure 2.2   RC Clock Generator

Clock signal generators that are mechanically driven use a quartz crystal to produce a steady signal. These oscillators rely on the piezoelectric effect of the crystal. This method of clocking is accurate (around 30 parts per million or about 0.003% error), cheap, and widely available. Generally, two small load capacitors are required between each lead of the crystal and ground, as shown in Figure 2.3. The values of these capacitors are based on the crystal characteristics and are listed in the crystal's datasheet.

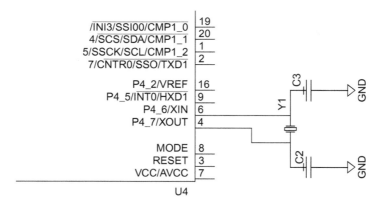

Figure 2.3   Connection of a crystal or ceramic resonator clock generator.

Ceramic resonators are growing in popularity for use as a clock generator. The resonators use a piezoelectric ceramic element that is not as accurate as quartz, yet more accurate than RC circuits. They may also contain the appropriate load capacitors built in so they do not require any additional components to work.

External clock generator integrated circuits can also be used. These clocks use a quartz or RC circuit as a resonant oscillator, but also contain an amplifier. The frequency can be changed by reprogramming the clock generator. The duty cycle may also be selectable for use in cases where a 50 percent duty cycle cannot be used. These circuits are usually more expensive when compared to other oscillators.

2.3.3   Reset Circuit

Resetting a microcontroller puts it in a predictable state and stops all of its operations. This is needed for two reasons. First, when a system is powered up, it takes time for the supply voltage to rise to the recommended operating range. The MCU needs to be held in reset until the voltage is high enough for the circuit to operate correctly. Second, the processor may need to be reset if certain serious conditions are detected, or if the user presses a reset switch.

The processor needs to start off in a predictable state. For example, the program counter must hold the address of the first instruction in the program. It is extremely helpful to have the other aspects of the system configured in a safe and well-defined way (e.g., interrupts disabled, outputs, and unnecessary peripherals disabled).

When the reset signal is asserted, the microprocessor loads predefined values into the system control registers. All microprocessors designate a pin that is solely used for resetting the chip. Characteristics such as polarity (active high or active low) and minimum duration are specific to the microprocessor being used and can be found in the manufacturer's datasheet.

2.4   INTERFACING WITH DIGITAL SIGNALS _____

2.4.1   General Purpose Digital I/O Basics

Embedded systems consist of computers embedded in larger systems. The processor needs to sense the state of the larger system and environment, and control output devices. The most basic way to do this is through one or more discrete signals, each of which can be in one of two states (on or off). General purpose digital I/O **ports** are the hardware which can be used to read from or write to the system outside the microcontroller.

The RL78 has multiple I/O ports, numbered starting at P0. Each port typically has eight bits, with each bit connected to a specific pin on the MCU package. For most ports, each bit can be configured individually as an input or output, although there are some limited-function port bits which have partial configurability such as input-only.

A port pin may serve several purposes; for example, one might be used as a general purpose I/O pin, as an A/D converter input, or as an interrupt input, based on how it is configured. Depending on the purposes these pins serve, they might have extra registers.

2.4.1.1 Control Registers

There are multiple registers used to control and monitor ports. We can find the details of these registers in the User's Manual (Renesas Electronics Corporation 2011) chapter on Port Functions.

- The Port Mode register (PM) controls whether a particular port bit is an input (selected with 1) or an output (0).
- The Port register (P) holds the data value for the port. For example, if port 0 is configured as all inputs, then reading from register P0 will indicate what binary input values are present on the pins of port 0. If port 1 is configured as all outputs, writing to register P1 will cause those binary values to appear on the pins of port 1.
- The Pull-Up resistor option register (PU) controls whether an internal pull-up resistor is connected (selected with 1) to that input bit or not (0).
- The Port Input Mode register (PIM) controls which type of voltage threshold (TTL or CMOS) is used to determine whether an input is a 1 or a 0. The CMOS thresholds (normal, selected with 0) are proportional to the supply voltage V_{DD}, while the TTL thresholds (1) are fixed voltages.
- The Port Output Mode register (POM) controls whether an output can be driven up or down (push-pull mode, selected with 0), or just down (N-channel open-drain, selected with 1). This is useful for applications such as sharing a bus which may be driven by other devices.
- The Port Mode Control register (PMC) controls whether an input is used for analog (selected with 1) or digital (0) purposes.
- The Peripheral I/O Redirection register (PIOR) allows certain peripheral signals to be routed to one of two possible port pins, simplifying circuit design.

2.4.1.2 C Code Support for Accessing Control Registers

The 'ior5f100le.h' file has C code constructs that make it easy to access each port with C code. Each port is defined as a *structure* and each register of the port is defined as a *union* of variables within that structure. An example of how the special function register P0 (the port register for port 0) is defined as follows.

First, a new data type called __BITS8 is defined. This allows easy C-level access to individual bits within a byte. Each field in the structure provides access to the corresponding bit. The C compiler will generate appropriate assembly code to ensure that only the bit of interest is accessed.

```
typedef struct {
    unsigned char no0:1;
    unsigned char no1:1;
    unsigned char no2:1;
```

```
    unsigned char no3:1;
    unsigned char no4:1;
    unsigned char no5:1;
    unsigned char no6:1;
    unsigned char no7:1;
} __BITS8;
```

Second, a union is declared which consists of two components, one of type unsigned char and the other of type __BITS8. Since a union *overlaps* all of the internal fields, this gives us two ways of accessing the same data—a byte at a time (via P0) or a bit at a time (via P0_bit). The @ 0xFFF00 is a non-standard compiler-specific directive used to indicate to the compiler that the register in question is located at address 0xFFF00. Finally, the directives __saddr and __no_init provide additional information to the compiler.

```
    __saddr __no_init volatile union {
    unsigned char P0;
    __BITS8 P0_bit;
} @ 0xFFF00;
```

Let's see an example of how to use these code constructs. First, let's configure port 0 to be all outputs. To do this we need to load all bits in PM0 with zero. We can do this with a single operation by setting it to zero.

```
    PM0 = 0;
```

Next let's set port 0's even bits to zero and odd bits to one. Note that port 0 only has seven bits (no0 through no6). We can do this by accessing the bits individually:

```
    P0_bit.no0 = P0_bit.no2 = P0_bit.no4 = P0_bit.no6 = 0;
    P0_bit.no1 = P0_bit.no3 = P0_bit.no5 = 1;
```

We can also do this by pre-computing the byte which needs to be loaded into P0. Binary 0101010 is 2A in hexadecimal, so our code is as follows:

```
    P0 = 0x2A;
```

2.4.1.3 Automatic Code Generation

Figure 2.4 shows the tools and files typically used for software development. The developer creates source code files (e.g., in C) which are compiled and assembled to create corresponding object files. These object files are then linked together to create an executable file which is programmed into a microcontroller's program memory.

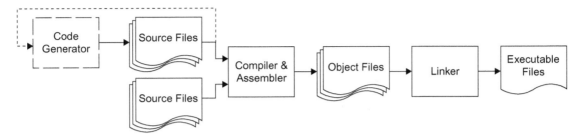

Figure 2.4   Software toolchain processes source and intermediate files to create executable file.

Some MCU makers and software tool vendors provide code generation tools which simplify the developer's job of writing software for accessing peripherals (device drivers). This device driver code is typically specific to a processor family, so its development is typically quite time-consuming until the coder has mastered the devices. In order to use the code generator, the programmer specifies the peripheral configuration using a graphical user interface and then invokes the "Generate Code" command. The tool creates C code and header files containing software to configure the SFRs as specified graphically. Some tools will also generate access functions, interrupt service routines and data structures to further simplify the developer's job.

Renesas provides a code generator called Applilet ("Application Leading Tool") for the RL78 family and others as well. We will examine Applilet in more detail in a later chapter, and we will examine how to use it to support the examples presented. Let's start off by seeing how we use it to configure the port in the previous example. Figure 2.5 shows the interface Applilet provides to the developer. The left window pane holds a tree view of the different peripherals which can be configured: system, port, interrupts, serial, A/D, timer, watchdog timer, real-time clock, interval timer, and so on. There are also corresponding icons arranged horizontally in the right pane. The "Generate Code" button allows the user to generate updated code based on the specified settings. A valuable feature of Applilet is that it provides "round-trip engineering" in that you can generate code with Applilet, add in your own code, and read it back into Applilet for further modification without deleting or breaking your additions.

First, we wish to configure port 0 as an input port. Figure 2.5 shows the default port configuration screen for port 0. All port bits are specified as unused. In order to configure them all as outputs, we need to **check "Out" for each port bit.**

Note that some of the bits have an N-channel open-drain output mode available, as indicated by the "N-ch" check box for those bits. We also see that pull-up resistors can be enabled on each bit, and some offer a TTL-level buffer input mode. Finally, we can specify the initial value of the output bits as one (by checking the "1″ box) or zero (by leaving it unchecked). We will use this to **set the even bits to zero and the odd bits to one.** The resulting screen appears in Figure 2.6. If we check the "Change I/O by software" box, Applilet will generate a pair of functions for us to change the direction of a port bit to input or output.

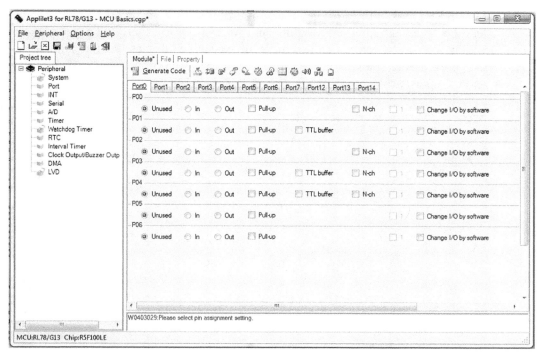

Figure 2.5   Applilet's default port configuration screen.

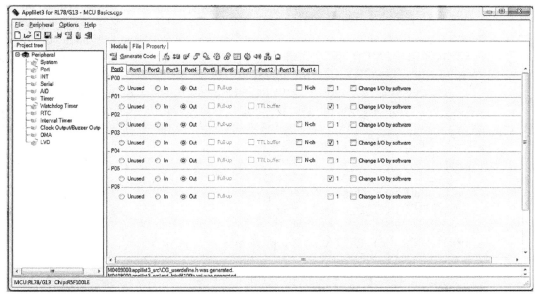

Figure 2.6   Configuring port 0 to all outputs, and odd bits to ones.

Let's take a look at the code generated by Applilet after we press "Generate Code". We select the "File" tab next to "Module" and we can see in Figure 2.7 a tree view of the files which we just generated. The Port item has three files associated with it: CG_port.c, CG_port_user.c, and CG_port.h. We see that the CG_port.c contains function PORT_Init and CG_port_user.c contains function PORT_UserInit.

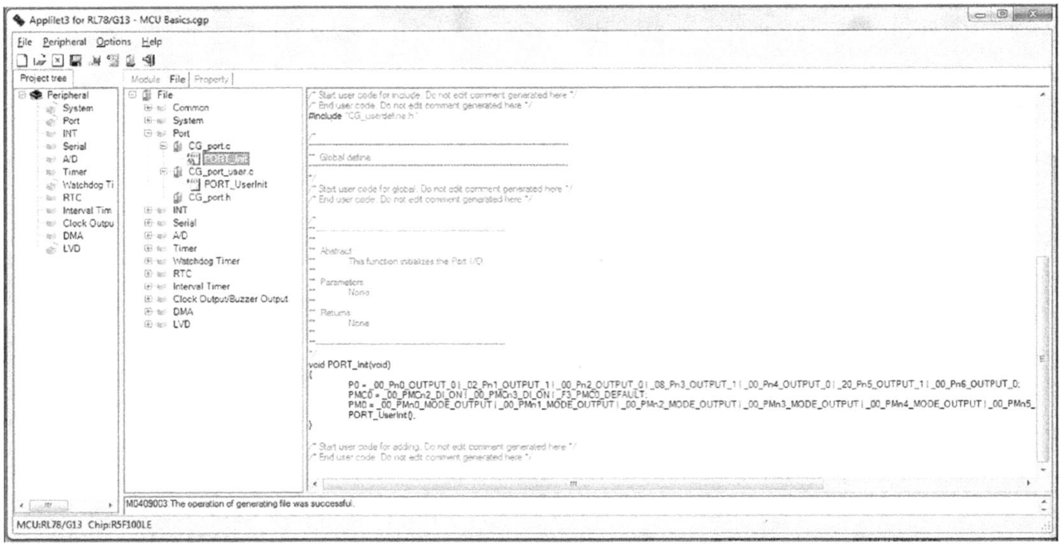

Figure 2.7   File CG_port.c generated for configuring ports.

Port 0 is configured by assigning initialization values to the port register P0, the port mode control register PMC0, the port mode register PM0, and then calling the user-defined (and currently empty) PORT_UserInit function.

The code generator creates constants to make it easier to understand the specific bits written to the ports. For example, the output data value for the port is created by ORing together multiple output bits. Each bit is defined as a symbol with multiple fields. For example _00_Pn0_OUTPUT_0 represents:

- _00: the actual value of the symbol (0x00)
- _Pn0: port n bit 0
- _OUTPUT_0: output value of 0

Similarly, _02_Pn1_OUTPUT_1 represents:

- _02: the actual value of the symbol (0x02)
- _Pn1: port n bit 1
- _OUTPUT_1: output value of 1

In the program, when we wish to access the port bits, we can do it directly, as above:

```
P0_bit.no0 = P0_bit.no2 = P0_bit.no4 = P0_bit.no6 = 0;
P0_bit.no1 = P0_bit.no3 = P0_bit.no5 = 1;
```

or as:

```
P0 = 0x2A;
```

For some peripherals Applilet will generate additional access functions to avoid the need to directly control the bits (which typically requires a side trip to the reference manual).

2.4.2   Using LEDs as Outputs

Now let's look at how we can use the general-purpose I/O ports to interface with simple devices such as LEDs, switches, keypads, and motors. Along the way we will examine how to use some of the control registers listed above.

One common output device is a light-emitting diode (LED). Figure 2.8 and Figure 2.9 show two ways of connecting LEDs to a microprocessor. Most microcontrollers I/O pins can sink more current than they can supply, so LEDs are typically connected with cathode to the microcontroller pin. This requires writing a zero to the port pin to turn on the LED.

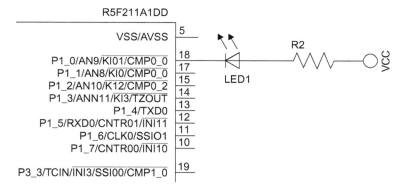

Figure 2.8   The microprocessor is sinking current from the LED. Turning on the LED requires a logical LOW on the output pin.

LEDs require a current-limiting resistor so that they do not draw too much current from the I/O pin to which they are connected. The resistor can be placed on either side of the LED. The formula following Figure 2.9 on the next page shows how to calculate the value of the current limiting resistor. V_{LED} is the forward voltage of the LED at the desired current I_{LED} and it can be determined by examining the LED's datasheet.

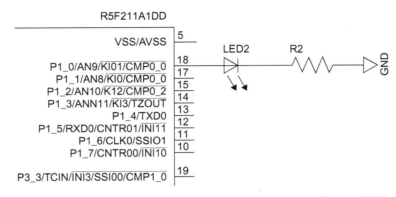

Figure 2.9   The microprocessor is sourcing current to an LED. Turning on this LED requires a logical HIGH signal on the output pin.

$$R = \frac{V_{CC} - V_{LED}}{I_{LED}}$$

Let's look at the code to drive an LED with its cathode connected to port 1 bit 0, as in Figure 2.8. First we configure the port as an output by writing 0 to the port mode register bit:

```
PM1_bit.no0 = 0;
```

Now we can write to the port bit to turn the LED on:

```
P1_bit.no0 = 0;
```

We can also turn the LED off:

```
P1_bit.no0 = 1;
```

2.4.3   Driving a Common Signal with Multiple MCUs

Sometimes we would like to have multiple devices drive the same signal wire. For example, consider an MCU-based thermometer which drives its alarm output signal low if the temperature is too high or too low, and drives it high otherwise. This alarm signal controls a loud warning siren. How can we monitor multiple temperatures and use a single centrally-located alarm LED? We cannot simply connect all of the alarm outputs together.

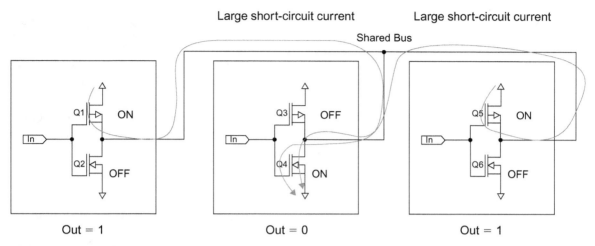

Figure 2.10   Push-pull driver circuits driving same line with different values will destroy at least one output transistor.

Figure 2.10 shows the "push-pull" output used by the MCU GPIO ports. If one thermometer tries to drive its output low, then its lower transistor (Q2) will be turned on and will pull the output line to ground with a very low resistance (e.g., 0.1 Ω). If another thermometer tries to drive its output high, then its upper transistor (Q1) will be turned on and will pull the output line to V_{CC} with a very low resistance (e.g., 0.1 Ω). With both transistors on, there is a low-impedance path from V_{CC} to ground, and a large amount of current flowing through the two transistors. The current will create heat and destroy one or both transistors.

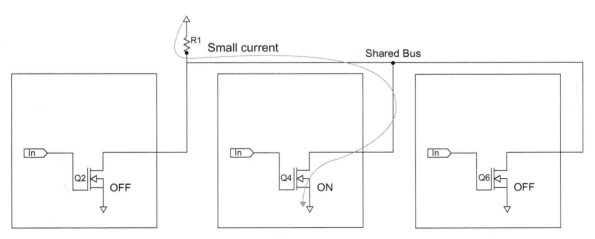

Figure 2.11   Open drain driver circuits driving same line with different values will not damage any components.

To solve this problem, some GPIO ports outputs allow an "open drain" configuration, in which the upper MOSFET is absent (or is merely disabled). This is also called "wired-OR." The resulting circuit is shown in Figure 2.11. This circuit allows multiple open drain outputs to be connected together safely without risk of a short-circuit from V_{CC} to ground. A pull-up resistor may be needed on the output if a floating signal is unacceptable.

Some RL78 output port drivers can support open drain mode. It is enabled when the corresponding port output mode register bit (POM) is set to 1.

2.4.4   Using Switches as Inputs

One common input device is a single-pole single-throw (SPST) switch. We can connect it as shown in Figure 2.12. The resistor will pull the voltage on that pin to logic HIGH until the button connects to ground. When the button is pressed, the voltage at that pin will drop to zero (logic LOW). Let's look at the code to use port 1 bit 1 for this input.

First we configure the port as an input by writing 1 to the port mode register bit.

```
PM1_bit.no1 = 1;
```

Now we can read from the pin, keeping in mind that a 0 indicates the switch is pressed, and a 1 indicates it is released. In this case we will turn off an LED whenever the switch is pressed, and turn it on when the switch is released.

```
if (P1_bit.no1 == 0) {
   //switch is pressed, so turn off LED
   P1_bit.no0 = 1;
} else {
   //switch is not pressed, so turn on LED
   P1_bit.no0 = 0;
}
```

Contact bounce is a worry with any mechanical switch. When the switch is closed, the mechanical properties of the metals in the switch cause the contacts to literally bounce off of one another. Often the microcontroller is fast enough to read each of these bounces as an individual switch press, resulting in unexpected and probably incorrect system behavior. Your design should take this into account with either a hardware or software *debouncing* solution. A hardware approach may use digital logic or analog circuitry (e.g., resistors and a capacitor). Hardware debouncing circuits are very useful for interrupt pins. Software debouncing works by not recognizing a changing input until the input has stabilized for a certain period of time.

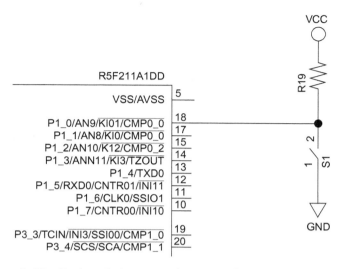

Figure 2.12   Basic switch connection to a microprocessor input pin.

We can simplify this circuit by eliminating pull-up resistor R19 using the MCU's built-in pull-up resistor. We do this by adding the following code to the initialization sequence:

```
PU1_bit.no1 = 1;
```

2.4.5   Scanning Matrix Keypads

Using one input pin per switch works well for a small number of switches. However, using this approach for a large number of switches (for example for a keypad or even a keyboard) is inefficient, since we would need to use an MCU with many inputs, raising its cost.

Instead we can use matrix scanning to reduce the number of inputs required. This works by connecting multiple switches to a single input, and reading just a single switch at a time. We use output pins to control which switch in the input is read. For instance, Figure 2.13 shows a keypad matrix. The top three signals are configured as outputs, and are used as the columns of the matrix. The three pins connected as the rows of the matrix are all input pins. A switch is placed in the circuit at each intersection of a column and row.

When no switches are pressed, the row inputs are all disconnected and floating. We will use pull-up resistors to pull each of them to logic HIGH.

When a switch is pressed, it will connect the row input to the column output. We want our code to drive one column output to logic LOW at a time.[1] Our code will then determine

---

[1] If we used pull-down resistors, our code would need to drive the column output to a logic HIGH instead.

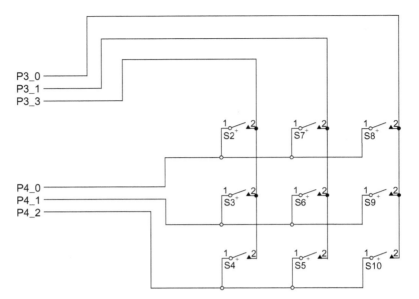

Figure 2.13   Keypad switch matrix.

which row input is LOW and therefore which switch in the keypad is pressed. For example, if the microprocessor noted a LOW input in the middle row pin at the time when middle column output was logic LOW, then the center switch must have been pressed.

Let's look at some code to make this happen. Assume that the columns in Figure 2.13 are connected to port 3 bits 0, 1, and 2 respectively, and the rows are connected to port 4 bits 0, 1, and 2 respectively. First we need to configure the columns bits as outputs and the rows bits as inputs:

```
PM3_bit.no0 = PM3_bit.no1 = PM3_bit.no2 = 0;    //columns are outputs
PM4_bit.no0 = PM4_bit.no1 = PM4_bit.no2 = 1;    //rows are inputs
```

Next we need to enable the pull-up resistors for row inputs:

```
PU4_bit.no0 = PU4_bit.no1 = PU4_bit.no2 = 1;
```

Now we are ready to drive the first column low and read the keypad rows:

```
P3_bit.no0 = 0;    //Set the output of the first column to 0
P3_bit.no0 = 1;    //Set the output of the second column to 1
P3_bit.no0 = 1;    //Set the output of the third column to 1
```

```
if (P4_bit.no0 == 0) {
   //Conditional code for Row 0, Column 0
} else if (P4_bit.no1 == 0) {
   //Conditional code for Row 1, Column 0
} else if (P4_bit.no2 == 0) {
   //Conditional code for Row 2, Column 0
}
```

We could repeat this process for the remaining columns, but the code would be rather messy and hard to maintain. It is better practice to take advantage of loops and variables to simplify the code structure.

2.4.6   Driving Motors and Coils

Embedded systems often need to cause physical movement, and motors and solenoids (a type of coil) are typical output devices. For example, a valve may be closed by a motor, or a door lock may be driven by a solenoid. Motors and solenoids usually draw far more current than a MCU's output circuits can provide, and may also require higher voltages. The MCU's output limits are found in the datasheet. Buffer circuits are used to provide the needed output current and voltage.

Direct Current (DC) motors can be driven with simple transistor drivers or H-bridges (shown in Figure 2.14). If the left input of the circuit is connected to port 1 bit 2 and the right input of this circuit is connected to port 1 bit 3, then we configure the port bits as outputs:

```
PM1_bit.no2 = PM1_bit.no3 = 0;
```

The code to turn the motor one direction is:

```
P1_bit.no2 = 1;
P1_bit.no3 = 0;
```

The code to turn the motor in the other direction is:

```
P1_bit.no2 = 0;
P1_bit.no3 = 1;
```

Finally, we can stop the motor by setting both outputs to the same value:

```
P1_bit.no2 = 1;
P1_bit.no3 = 1;
```

Note that a real circuit would include protection diodes across each transistor to the inductive voltage spike when shutting off the motor.

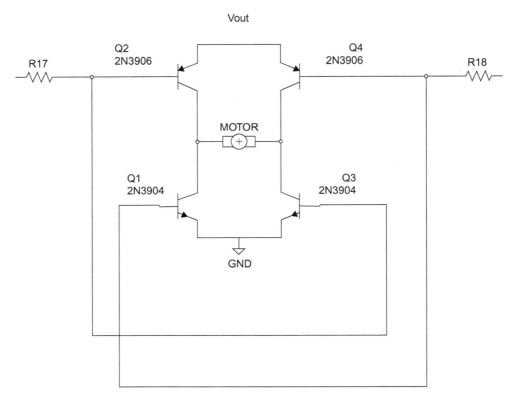

Figure 2.14 H-bridge motor driver. Two if the microprocessor's outputs are connected to the resistors. The motor will not turn if both inputs are the same value.

Stepper motors can be driven with transistors or stepper motor driver ICs. Some ICs such as the L293 or the 754410 are specifically designed to drive the DC motors and interface directly with a microcontroller. **Servos** are motor/gearbox combinations with built-in motor control circuitry. These devices can often connect their control pins directly to a microprocessor as their internal circuitry handles driving the motor itself. We will examine how to control a servo motor in Chapter 9.

   Relays are controlled by energizing their coil, and are treated similarly to motors. Figure 2.15 shows a basic coil driving circuit. The code to drive a coil is the same as for driving an LED.

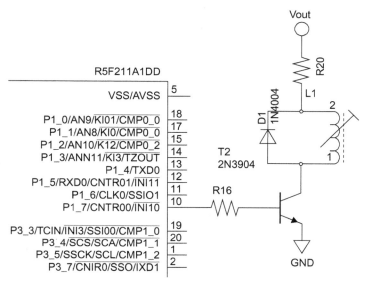

Figure 2.15   A simple coil driver.

There are other methods of controlling large loads with a microprocessor, such as using relays or triacs. The main goal for all load driving circuits is to keep the source and sink currents of the microprocessor within the manufacturer's recommendations.

2.4.7   Voltage Level Shifting

Some sensors may require different voltages than what the microprocessor requires. Care should be taken when interfacing these sensors. If the microprocessor runs at 5 V and the sensor runs at 1.8 V, the microprocessor will not be able to read a HIGH logic signal on the sensor output. Circuits for interfacing with higher voltage sensors can be designed using transistors or by using level converter ICs, which convert the signals between the microcontroller and the sensor either uni-directionally or bi-directionally (in case the microprocessor needs to communicate to the sensor.) The use of a flyback diode is very important when interfacing inductive loads, to safely dissipate the voltage spike when the voltage to the load is removed.

2.5   INTERFACING WITH ANALOG SIGNALS

The world is not digital; it is analog. Microphones, thermometers, speakers, light sensors, and even video cameras are all analog sensors. As a result, the signals from these sensors must be converted to digital values so that the microcontrollers can process them.

2.5.1   Analog Comparison

The simplest analog to digital conversion operation is a single comparison: Is the input voltage greater than a reference voltage? It compares an analog voltage input with an analog reference voltage, determines if the input is larger than the reference, and indicates the result with a single bit (1 means yes and 0 means no). A comparator can be used to determine if a battery voltage is too low, a temperature is too high, a pressure is too high, and so forth.

The circuit needed to perform this operation is called an analog comparator and is quite simple. Some microcontrollers contain one or more comparator circuits.

2.5.2   Multi-bit Analog to Digital Conversion

For many applications, a single yes-no answer is inadequate and a more precise measurement is needed. In this case, an *Analog to Digital Converter* (also referred to as ADC, A/D, A-to-D, and A2D) is used to produce a more precise multi-bit binary number which indicates how large an input voltage is relative to a known reference voltage. This measurement process is called *quantization.*

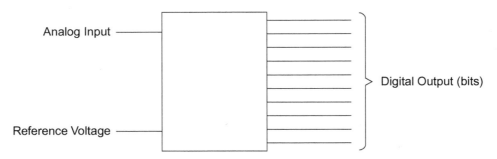

Figure 2.16   Analog to digital converter (ADC) block diagram.

A block diagram for a simple ADC is shown in Figure 2.16. The number of bits N in the digital output is called the *resolution* of the ADC.

The digital approximation n for a particular analog input voltage V_{in} can be found mathematically. V_{+ref} is the upper end of the input voltage range, V_{-ref} is the lower end of the input voltage range, and N is the number of bits of resolution in ADC. V_{-ref} is often connected to ground (0 V), resulting in the basic equation[2]:

$$n = \text{int}\left(\frac{V_{in}}{V_{+ref}} * 2^N\right)$$

For example, consider a two-bit ADC with a reference voltage V_{+ref} of 3.3 V. What output code will result for an input voltage of 3.1 V?

$$n = \text{int}\left(\frac{3.1\ V}{3.3\ V} * 2^2\right) = \text{int}\,(3.75) = 3 = 11_b$$

What is the output code for an input value of 1.5 V will result in an output of 01?

$$n = \text{int}\left(\frac{1.5\ V}{3.3\ V} * 2^2\right) = \text{int}\,(1.8) = 1 = 01_b$$

Figure 2.17 plots the transfer function which is used to convert an analog voltage (measured on the horizontal axis) to its digital output code representation (on the vertical axis). It shows that 3.1 V maps to 11, and 1.5 V maps to 01.

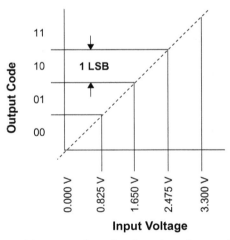

Figure 2.17   A plot of the 2-bit ADC's transfer function shows the range of input voltages which maps to each output code.

---

[2] This equation is extended in the chapter on analog interfacing to include other factors.

Note that a single code (e.g., 01) represents an entire range of input voltages (0.825 V to 1.65 V). The ADC will not be able to distinguish or *resolve* different voltages within this range; both 0.9 V and 1.5 V will be converted as 01. The next code (10) represents the next range of voltages (1.65 V to 2.475 V). The range of voltages represented by a single code is called the *voltage resolution* of the ADC. The voltage resolution of the conversion is determined by the reference voltage and the number of bits in the conversion result:

$$\text{Resolution} = \frac{V_{\text{Ref}}}{2^N}$$

We can calculate the resolution of this ADC:

$$\text{Resolution} = \frac{V_{\text{Ref}}}{2^N} = \frac{3.3 \ V}{2^2} = 0.825 \ V$$

If we need to resolve the two voltages closer than 0.825 V, we need an ADC with better resolution (more bits). For example, a four bit ADC with a 3.3 V reference will have a resolution of 0.206 V and will produce different result codes for 0.9 V and 1.5 V.

Once the raw ADC value is known, the application software can use the reverse of this formula to calculate the actual possible range of voltages on that pin. Since the datasheet for most sensors provides a formula for converting the voltage to the unit the sensor is measuring (be it degrees Celsius, distance in centimeters, pressure in kilopascals, etc.), this formula can be inserted into the firmware to make sense of the data.

More advanced analog sensors use a communication protocol such as RS-232, RS-485, I^{2}C, or SPI. These sensors generally convert a physical parameter (temperature, pressure, magnetic field strength, etc.) into an analog voltage, convert that voltage it a digital value, and then send it to the microcontroller for processing using a communication system. These communication systems often use protocols which allow multiple sensors to be connected to the same pins of the microcontroller.

2.5.3   Digital to Analog Conversion

Just as we must convert analog signals to digital to process them, sometimes there is a need to convert digital signals to analog. In systems that control audio, speed, or even light levels; digital output from a microprocessor must be converted into an analog signal. There are several different methods for converting digital signals to analog.

2.5.3.1 *Resistor Networks*

Resistor networks allow a very simple solution for converting digital signals to analog. There are many methods of using resistor networks for DACs, but two designs are most common.

2.5.3.1.1   Binary Weighted DACs: Resistor networks are another simple method for DAC conversion. Several different methods are available for using resistor networks, and again it is up to the designer to decide which method is best for a particular design. *Voltage-Mode Binary Weighted DACs* are commonly used with microcontroller circuits. In this design, resistors are connected together on one end (the analog output), and the other ends are connected directly to the pins of a microcontroller port. The resistor values are selected so that the each bit's contribution to the output voltage corresponds to the bit's binary weight (e.g., 2^0, 2^1, 2^2). Figure 2.18 shows an example of a 4-bit Binary Weighted DAC. The LSB is connected to R4, which has value R. R5 has resistance R/2, R6 has resistance R/4, and R7 has resistance R/8.

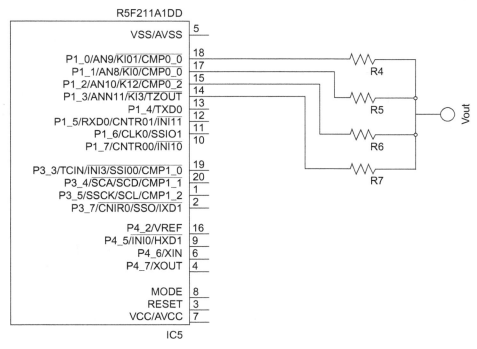

Figure 2.18   Four-bit binary weighted network DAC.

2.5.3.1.2   R-2R DAC:

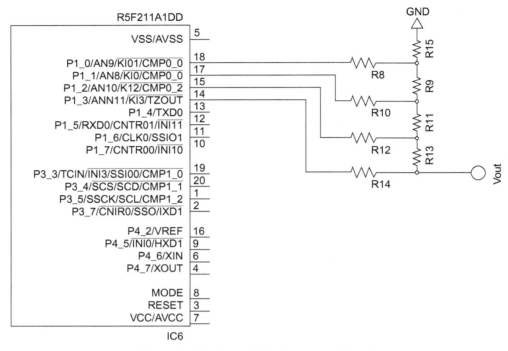

Figure 2.19   Four bit R-2R network DAC.

Another method of using resistor networks to design a DAC is called the *R-2R* or *R/2-R Network*. It consists of resistors of only two values. One resistance value is twice the other. For instance, if the R resistors are 1 kΩ, then the 2R resistors are 2 kΩ.

Figure 2.19 shows an example R-2R network. Resistors R9, R11, and R13 each have resistance R (e.g., 1kΩ) while resistors R8, R10, R12, R14, and R15 each have resistance 2*R (e.g., 2 kΩ). The LSB is connected to R8.

As with the binary weighted DAC, the output voltage corresponds to the binary code on the port.

$$V_{\text{out}} = \frac{\text{binary code}}{2^N} * V_{\text{ref}}$$

Let's consider an example. This is valid for both R-2R as well as Binary Weighted DACs. If the V_{ref} is 5 V and there is a 4-bit binary value 1001 (decimal number 9) on the microcontroller pins, we would expect the output voltage to be:

$$V_{\text{out}} = \frac{9}{2^4} * 5 \ V = 2.8125 \ V$$

2.5.3.2 Pulse Width Modulation

A common method for controlling the speed of a simple DC motor or the brightness of an LED is *Pulse Width Modulation*. Pulse Width Modulation works as a DAC by changing the duty cycle of an oscillating digital output as shown in Figure 2.20. In the case of an LED, the more time the duty cycle is HIGH, the brighter the LED. This method works in cases where the oscillating frequency is so fast that the resulting output seems smooth. The LED is actually turning on and off many tens of times per second; however, the human eye cannot detect the independent flashes of the LED due to their speed. Motor speed can be controlled this way because the inertia of the spinning armature carries the motor forward through the moments when no power is applied. A PWM signal is typically generated by a timer peripheral which sets or clears the output signal when the internal counter reaches configurable count values.

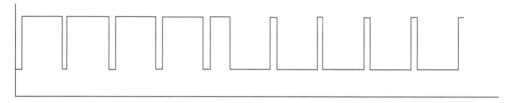

Figure 2.20 An example PWM signal. If this were controlling an active-high LED, the LED would be brighter during the first half of the graph and dimmer over the second half.

2.6   RECAP

It should now be easier to understand how the embedded systems you encounter in your everyday life actually operate and communicate with the outside world. It should also be easier to break some of these systems down into their component parts, given the knowledge of sensor and actuator interfacing presented in this chapter.

2.7   REFERENCES

Renesas Electronics Corporation. *RL78/G13 16-Bit Single-Chip Microcontrollers User's Manual: Hardware.* 2011.

2.8   EXERCISES

1. Name ten devices that use an embedded system.
2. Write the C code to set port 4, bits 0 through 3 to be input pins, and port 4, bits 4 through 7 to be output pins.

3. Write the C code to read the data on port 4, bits 0 through 3 and write the read data to port 4, bits 4 through 7.

4. What resistor value should be used to connect an LED with a forward voltage of 3.1 volts and a forward current of 20 mA to the input pin of a microcontroller that outputs 5 volts?

5. Is it generally safe to connect a coil or motor directly to a microcontroller I/O pin? Why or why not?

6. Is it generally safe to connect a servo control input directly to a microcontroller I/O pin? Why or why not?

7. How many volts per ADC step are in a system with an ADC resolution of 10 bits, and a reference voltage of 3.3 V?

8. How many volts per ADC step are in a system with an ADC resolution of 12 bits, and a reference of 5 V?

9. An analog input has a voltage of 1.37860. What value will the ADC return if it has an 8-bit resolution and a reference of 4.25 volts?

10. An analog input has a voltage of 7.61245. What value will the ADC return if it has a 12-bit resolution and a reference of 10 volts?

11. Using a binary-weighted DAC, using 8 bits and a reference of 4.35 volts, what is the voltage of the output if the 8-bit value is 01011010?

12. Modify the keypad matrix scanning code to support a matrix with NC columns and NR rows. Assume NC and NR are each less than or equal to 8. Your code must use loops to minimize code duplication.

Chapter Three

RL78 CPU Core and Interrupts

3.1 LEARNING OBJECTIVES

In this chapter the reader will learn about:

- Basic organization of a CPU core within a microcontroller
- The RL78 architecture's instruction set, register set, data types, addressing modes, and instruction processing pipeline
- Concepts and mechanisms for interrupts
- The RL78 architecture's interrupt mechanisms, and how to use external interrupts

We tackle interrupts in this early chapter because they are a key mechanism for creating responsive systems with simple a software structure. They provide the illusion of concurrency without requiring an operating system.

3.2 CPU CONCEPTS

A microcontroller consists of a processor core (for executing instructions), memory (for storing data), and supporting peripheral components which add functionality or improve performance. Figure 3.1 shows the block diagram of a 64-pin RL78 MCU, of which the G13 is one example. The figure shows how instruction execution is just a small part of a microcontroller's responsibility. Notice the four small boxes in the center labeled "RL78 CPU Core," "RAM," "Code Flash Memory," and "Data Flash Memory." These are the parts which are used to store and execute instructions. The rest of the MCU consists of peripherals which make it much easier to embed the MCU in a device by tackling hardware and software complications.

Figure 3.2 shows the CPU core from the instruction-processing point of view. The program's instructions are stored in code flash memory at the top of the diagram. The program counter (PC) specifies which memory location to read in order to fetch the next instruction

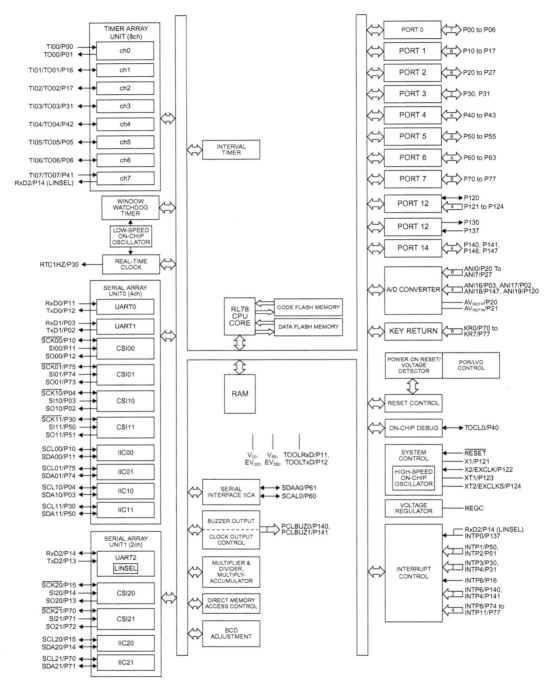

Figure 3.1 Block diagram for 64-pin RL78 MCUs (from RL78 Hardware Manual.)

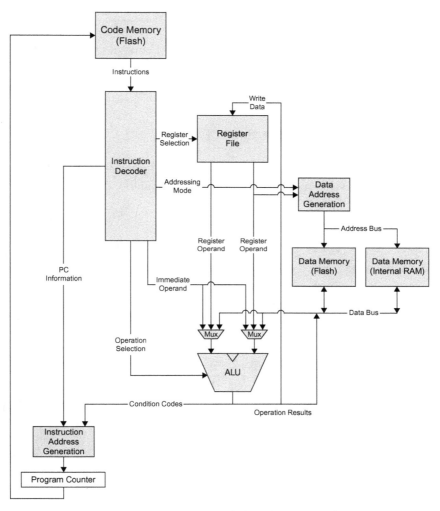

Figure 3.2 Simplified instruction and data flow through the CPU core.

from flash memory. This instruction is then decoded into various control and data signals which are sent to other parts of the CPU to control their operation:

- Whether to access the register file for instruction operands, and which registers to read or write
- Whether to access memory for instruction operands, and how to generate the address
- Whether to provide an immediate operand to the ALU, and how to generate it
- Which operation the ALU should perform (add, subtract, move, etc.)
- How to modify the PC to determine the next instruction's address

3.3   RL78 CPU CORE

We now examine the different parts of the CPU core shown in Figure 3.1. First we briefly discuss the types of instructions available, and then we see how an instruction proceeds through the RL78 CPU core.

3.3.1   RL78 Instruction Set Architecture

A processor's instruction set architecture (or programmer's model) defines the data types, registers, addressing modes, and instructions available to an assembly language programmer or compiler's code generator.

3.3.1.1   Data Types

The native data types for a CPU core are those directly supported by the processors hardware and not requiring emulation in software (typically provided by library functions or generated by the compiler). Native data types can be processed much more quickly than emulated data types, resulting in faster code. The RL78 ISA supports multiple data types: **bit, byte** (eight bits), and **word** (16 bits).

3.3.1.2   Instruction Set

The RL78 ISA provides a variety of instructions, shown in Table 3.1. There are **general instructions** for data movement and loading, addition and subtraction, increment and decrement, logical operations, shift and rotate, conditional and unconditional branching, subroutine call and return, and data stack manipulation. There are also **processor-control instructions** for selecting the register bank, enabling or disabling interrupts, and halting or stopping the processor.

There are also various **specialized instructions** available:

- **Bit-oriented instructions:** These allow the program to perform various operations (move, and, or, exclusive ore, set, clear, invert) on an individual bit. These can eliminate some masking operations and enable faster and smaller code.
- **Skip instructions:** These are like conditional branches with an implicit target—they skip the next instruction ($N + 1$) and continue by executing the following instruction ($N + 2$). These skips can eliminate some jump operations and enable faster and smaller code, as they are much faster than conditional branches.
- **Multiply and divide instructions:** In addition to the standard MULU instruction, some RL78 cores may also support operations such as 16×16 multiply or multiply/accumulate (with a 32-bit accumulator), and 16/16 and 32/32 bit divides.

TABLE 3.1.   RL78 Instruction Set Summary

INSTRUCTION TYPE	1-BIT	8-BIT	16-BIT
Data Transfer	MOV1	MOV, XCH, ONEB, CLRB, MOVS	MOVW, XCHW, ONEW, CLRW
Operations	AND1, OR1, XOR1, SET1, CLR1, NOT1	ADD, ADDC, SUB, SUBC, AND, OR, XOR, CMP, CMP0, CMPS	ADDW, SUBW, CMPW
Increment/ Decrement		INC, DEC	INCW, DECW
Shift and Rotate		SHR, SHL, SAR, ROR, ROL, RORC, ROLC	SHRW, SHLW, SARW, ROLWC
Call and Return	CALL, CALLT, BRK, RET, RETI, RETB		
Multiply/Divide		MULU	*Optional: MULHU, MULH, DIVHU, DIVWU, MACHU, MACH*
Stack			PUSH, POP, MOVW
Branches	BT, BF, BTCLR	BR, BC, BNC, BZ, BNZ, BH, BNH	
Skip	SKC, SKNC, SKZ, SKNZ, SKH, SKNH		
CPU Control	SEL RBn, NOP, EI, DI, HALT, STOP		

3.3.2   Program Memory, Instruction Fetch, and Decode

Microcontrollers typically have flash program memory integrated on-chip to simplify system design, reduce costs and improve performance. As shown in Figure 3.3, the RL78G13 has 64 kB of flash program memory located at addresses 00000H to 0FFFFH. Other processors in the RL78 family have from 16 kB to 512 kB of flash program memory, but it always starts at address 00000H.

The program counter (PC) register holds the address of the next instruction to execute. The CPU drives the program memory address bus with the PC and reads the instruction. Long instructions may require multiple cycles to read. The instruction is then decoded to determine how to control other subsystems in the CPU core.

The program counter is updated to point to the next instruction. This depends on whether the current instruction is a control-flow instruction (e.g., jump, conditional branch, subroutine call, return) or if the CPU needs to jump to or return from an interrupt service routine.

3.3.3   General Purpose and Special Registers

There are various registers in the CPU core. Some are general-purpose registers for data processing and can be accessed by common instructions. Others are specialized registers which are used to improve performance, simplify programing, or provide control over specific processor features.

The instruction decoder provides information on whether to access an operand in a register, and if so, how.

3.3.3.1   General Purpose Registers

The RL78 ISA has four banks of general purpose registers. Two bits in the program status word (PSW) register specify which bank to use. The general purpose registers are used for sources and destinations of ALU operations and some may also be used as pointers to memory. Each bank can be accessed as:

- 8-bit registers: X, A, C, B, E, D, L, H. Also referred to as registers R0, R1, R2, R3, R4, R5, R6, and R7.
- 16-bit registers: AX, BC, DE, HL. Also referred to as register pairs RP0, RP1, RP2, and RP3.

3.3.3.2   Special Registers

There RL78 ISA also has multiple special-purpose registers.

- Registers **CS** and **ES** are 4 bits long each and can be used to extend 16-bit registers to 20 bits, allowing access to the full 1 MB of address space. CS is used for instruction addresses while ES is used for data addresses.
- Control registers
  - The stack pointer **SP** is used for the stack-based addressing mode. It is 16 bits long, and bit 0 is always cleared to 0 so only even addresses can be accessed. SP points to the last used memory location (top) of the stack. The stack grows toward smaller addresses.
  - The program counter **PC** is 20 bits long and specifies the address of the next instruction to execute.
- The program status word **PSW** is 8 bits long and has control flags and status flags.

❑   Control flags

Figure 3.3   Program Status Word register

- **IE** controls the masking (enabling) of maskable interrupts. When set to 1, maskable interrupts can be serviced. When cleared to 0, maskable interrupts cannot be serviced.
- **RBS0** and **RBS1** select one of the four register banks.
- **ISP0** and **ISP1** control the priority of acknowledgeable maskable vectored interrupts.

❑   Status flags
- **Z** (zero) is set to 1 if the previous operation result was zero, or else it is cleared to 0.
- **CY** (carry) is set to 1 by an add (or subtract) instruction which overflows (or underflows). A rotate instruction loads CY with the shift-out value. Bit manipulation instructions use it as an accumulator.
- **AC** (Auxiliary carry) is set if an operation resulted in a carry from or a borrow to bit 3.

3.3.4   Data Memory

The RL78 has a unified 1 MB address space (shown in Figure 3.4) which provides access to physically separate memories, special function registers, vector tables, and other such items. A memory map shows where in the memory space these different items are located. For example, the code flash memory (which holds the program) is created as a separate module so that it can be accessed at the same time as other parts of the memory (e.g., RAM holding data).

The instruction decoder provides information on whether to access an operand in memory, and if so, how. In particular, it specifies whether to read or write from memory, which address to access, and how long the operand is.

How to compute the address depends upon the addressing mode used, and may consist of:

- a fixed memory address
- a shortened memory address with missing bits filled in with default values
- a register as used a pointer
- a register added to a constant and used as a pointer
- two registers added and used as a pointer

3.3.4.1   Memory Map

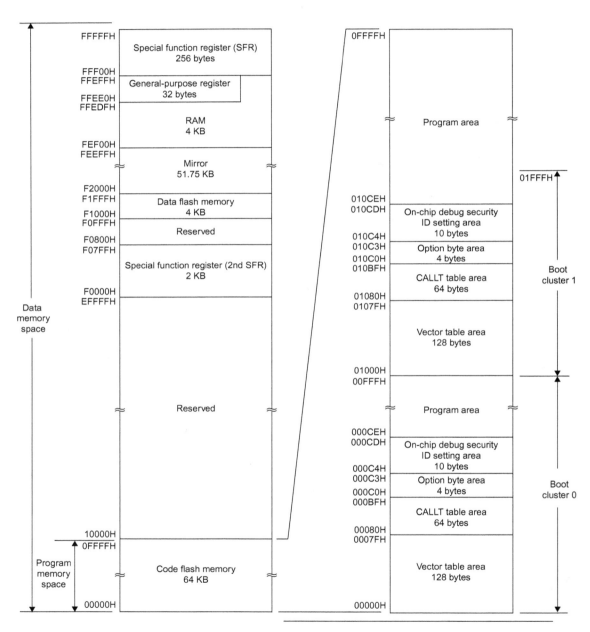

Figure 3.4   Memory map for RL78G13 (R5F100LE) MCU (Figure 3.4 from RL78/G13 Hardware Manual)

3.3.4.2 Addressing Modes

We see from the memory map in Figure 3.4 that the MCU could have up to 1 MB of memory, which requires 20 bits to address (2^{20} bytes = 1 MB). Consider an instruction which adds a memory operand (e.g., located at address FEFEEH) to register A and stores the result in register A. If we specify the memory operand with its full 20-bit address, then the instruction will require 20 bits just for that operand address, or 2 and 1/2 bytes. We also need to specify the add operation and register A, so we will need at least three bytes and perhaps four. This will be a long instruction which wastes memory. Furthermore, **fetching** all of these bytes will take multiple cycles (e.g., two cycles across a 16-bit wide bus), slowing down the instruction's execution speed. In order to reduce average instruction size and processing time, the RL78 ISA provides various addressing modes for data and instructions. These addressing modes **reduce instruction size** in part to speed up the program and reduce program memory requirements. The addressing modes also make it easier to generate assembly code.

3.3.4.2.1   Data Addressing Modes:

The RL78 ISA has multiple addressing modes for accessing data, generally ordered from fastest/smallest to slowest/largest: See Figure 3.5 on page 46 for details.

- **Implied** addressing uses the opcode rather than a register specifier to identify the register (e.g., an accumulator).
- **Register** addressing uses a general purpose register, which is specified with two bits (register pair) or three bits (single byte register).
- **Short direct** addressing specifies the address of the data using an 8-bit immediate value (SADDR). Only 256 bytes in the address range FFE20H to FFF1FH are accessible. The SADDRP mode accesses only register pairs, which are located at even addresses.
- **Direct** addressing specifies the address of the data using a 16-bit immediate value (ADDR16) in the instruction word. Only the 64 kB with addresses in the range F0000H to FFFFFH are accessible. This value may be extended to 20 bits using the ES register (ES:ADDR16), in which case the entire 1 MB address space is accessible.
- **SFR** addressing specifies the 8 bit address of a special function register. SFRP accesses 16-bit words at even addresses.
- **Register indirect** addressing specifies a 16-bit register pair (DE or HL) to use as a pointer to the location in the top 64 kB of memory. The ES register can be used to extend DE or HL to 20 bits, allowing the entire 1 MB address space to be accessed.
- **Based** addressing adds a register (B, C) or register pair (HL, DE, SP, BC) and an immediate offset (8 or 16 bits) in the instruction word and possibly the ES register to create the 16- or 20-bit address of the memory to be accessed. There are several variants of based addressing which are described in further detail in the software manual (Renesas Electronics, 2011).

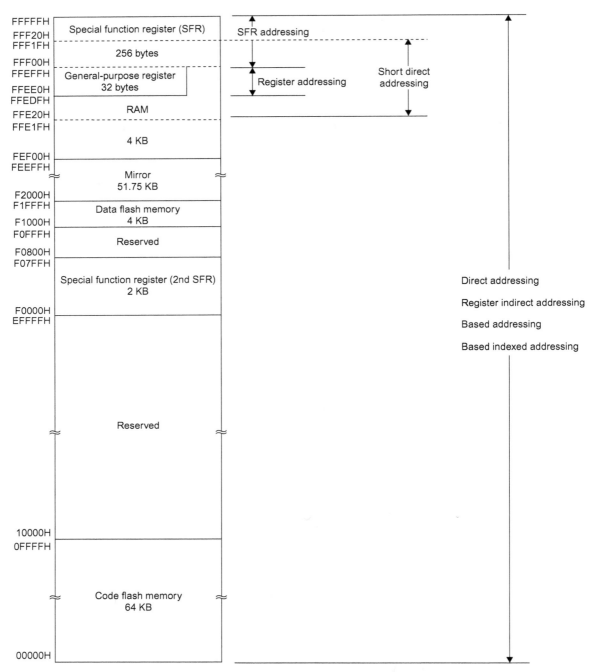

Figure 3.5   Correspondence between data addressing modes and memory map (Figure 3.15 from RL78/G13 Hardware Manual.)

- **Based indexed** addressing adds a register (B or C) and a register pair (HL) and possibly the ES register to create the 16- or 20-bit address of the memory to be accessed.
- **Stack addressing** uses the stack pointer SP as to push and pop data.

3.3.4.2.2   Instruction Addressing Modes: The RL78 ISA has the following addressing modes for accessing instructions. These are used for branch, call, and similar instructions. The resulting address is placed into the PC register to specify the next instruction to read.

- **Relative** addressing adds a signed 8- or 16-bit displacement to the current program counter value to update the PC.
- **Immediate** addressing loads the PC with a 16- or 20-bit absolute address specified in the instruction word.
- **Table indirect** addressing loads the PC with one of 32 16-bit addresses stored in the call table area of memory (CALLT).
- **Register direct** addressing loads the PC with the CS register concatenated with a register pair (AX, BC, DE, HL).

3.3.5   Arithmetic/Logic Unit

The ALU (arithmetic/logic unit) is the heart of the CPU, as it performs the actual data processing operations such as addition, subtraction, comparison, and so on. The ALU may receive its operands from the register file, memory, or other subsystem in the memory map. The instruction decoder specifies which operation the ALU should perform.

3.3.6   Instruction Processing Pipeline

Pipelined instruction processing *overlaps* the execution of different parts of multiple instructions. This increases the instruction throughput (instructions per second), but does not reduce the time taken to execute an individual instruction. Pipelining reduces the amount of time needed to execute code.

Examining the CPU diagram in Figure 3.2 shows how an instruction propagates through the circuit from top to bottom and does not need to use all of components at the same time. A pipelined processor starts handling the next instruction at the top before the current instruction has made it all the way through the logic and completed. Latches which hold intermediate results between pipe stages are added in order to ensure proper operation.

A pipeline of N stages can reduce the execution time of a program by a factor of approximately N in the ideal case. This neglects delays due to pipeline fill and drain, and stalls due to hazards.

3.3.6.1   RL78 Pipeline Structure

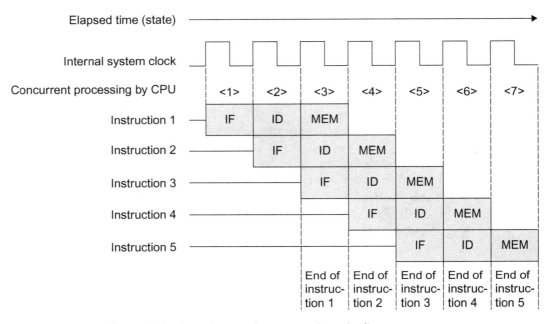

Figure 3.6   RL78 instruction processing pipeline sequence.

The RL78 CPU pipeline has three stages, as shown in Figure 3.6:

- The IF (Instruction Fetch) stage fetches the instruction from memory and increments the fetch pointer.
- The ID (Instruction Decode) stage decodes the instruction and calculates operand address.
- The MEM (Memory access) stage executes the instruction and accesses the specified memory location.

Many but not all RL78 instructions take one cycle to execute once the pipeline is full. The **RL78 Family Users Manual: Software** (Renesas Electronics, 2011) presents execution times for each instruction in Table 5.5.

3.3.6.2   RL78 Pipeline Hazards

There are various situations in which instructions cannot flow smoothly through the pipeline due to *hazards*. For example, a *data hazard* occurs when necessary data has not been computed yet. A *structural hazard* occurs when the resource is busy with other processing. A *control hazard* occurs because the program's control flow may change (e.g., due to a conditional branch). In this case the target address is unknown and therefore next instruction to execute is also unknown. In all of these cases the pipeline stalls for one or more clock cycles until the hazard is resolved. The following situations lead to hazards which stall the pipeline:

- Accessing data from flash or external memory (rather than internal RAM.)
- Fetching instructions from RAM rather than from internal flash ROM.
- Current instruction using memory addressed by register written in previous instruction (e.g., indirect access.)
- Changing the control flow of the program with instructions such as calls, branches and returns. Conditional branches are not resolved until the MEM stage, so the target address is not known until two cycles later. Because instruction fetching proceeds sequentially, branches are essentially predicted to be not taken. As a result, taken conditional branches take two more cycles than not-taken conditional branches.

3.4   INTERRUPTS

An interrupt is a mechanism which causes the processor to execute a specific function (an *interrupt service routine,* or *ISR)* in response to a specified event occurring, regardless of what part of the program is currently being executed (i.e., *asynchronously).* This scheduling mechanism is built into configurable hardware, so it responds quickly yet is flexible. After the ISR completes, the processor resumes executing the program where it left off.

Interrupts make it much easier for a developer to create software which can respond quickly to multiple events yet still keep a simple program structure which is easy to develop and debug. Microcontrollers typically use interrupts to indicate events such as input signal changes, timer expiration, analog conversion completion, low voltage, serial message reception, and others. If we do not have interrupts, we need to rely on *polling* to determine if an event has occurred. We will see that this approach quickly grows inefficient, unwieldy, and slow.

Complex computer systems rely on an operating system to link events with function execution (and often rely in part upon interrupts), but embedded systems often do not need such a heavy-weight and resource hungry solution to be responsive. Instead, embedded systems rely on the interrupt mechanisms built into most microcontrollers.

3.4.1   Breakfast with Polling vs. Interrupts

Consider the task of preparing breakfast, including brewing a pot of coffee. We need to boil the water for the coffee, which takes roughly three minutes. The exact time depends on factors such as the burner setting, which kettle is used, the quantity of water and its temperature, and air temperature and pressure. So we don't know exactly when the water will boil. Without interrupts, we will need to examine (poll) the water to see if it has started boiling yet. Let's put in a step where we wait until the water is boiling before proceeding with coffee preparation (turning off the burner, pouring the water into the coffee, etc.).

The breakfast program looks like this:

```
Put water in kettle, place on stove, and turn on burner
Grind coffee beans
Put ground coffee in filter in cone
Put cone on coffee mug
Wait until water is boiling
Turn off burner
Pour boiling water into coffee cone
Get bowl from cabinet
Get cereal box from cabinet
Pour cereal into bowl
Put cereal box back in cabinet
Get milk out of fridge
Pour milk into bowl
Put milk back in fridge
Get spoon
```

With this approach we may waste a large amount of time in the "Wait until water is boiling" stage. We can use this time to perform other work which we interleave with our boiling checks:

```
Put water in kettle, place on stove and turn on burner
Grind coffee beans
Put ground coffee in filter in cone
Put cone on coffee mug
if water is boiling {
   Turn off burner
   Pour boiling water into coffee cone
}
Get bowl from cabinet
Get cereal box from cabinet
Pour cereal into bowl
Put cereal box back in cabinet
if water is boiling {
   Turn off burner
   Pour boiling water into coffee cone
}
Get milk out of fridge
Pour milk into bowl
```

```
Put milk back in fridge
if water is boiling {
    Turn off burner
    Pour boiling water into coffee cone
}
Get spoon
if water still hasn't boiled {
    Wait until water boils
    Turn off burner
    Pour boiling water into coffee cone
}
```

Notice that now we have to check several times, and the amount of time before we see the water is boiling depends on the other things we are doing.

How quickly do we need to respond to the water boiling? This is our *response time requirement*. Boiling water with nothing in it (e.g., for coffee) is not very time-critical; after a long time the water will boil away. However, boiling water with pasta in it for too long will lead to the pot overflowing and making a mess.

How quickly we notice the water is boiling depends on the polling frequency. The more often we poll, the sooner we will notice the water is boiling. However, we will also waste more time performing polling, and we will complicate the program structure. So, for boiling water with pasta we would need to insert many more boiling water checks.

Using polling to detect events is easy for simple systems but quickly grows unwieldy. The field of real-time system scheduling examines better approaches and is discussed further in the Chapter 10.

Now let's see how the system looks if we use an interrupt, indicating the water is boiling. We will rely on a kettle which whistles when the water boils. Now our program will consist of two parts: the main preparation and the response to the boiling water.

The main preparation is as follows:

```
Put water in kettle, place on stove and turn on burner
Grind coffee beans
Put ground coffee in filter in code
Put cone on coffee mug
Get bowl from cabinet
Get cereal box from cabinet
Pour cereal into bowl
Put cereal box back in cabinet
Get milk out of fridge
Pour milk into bowl
Put milk back in fridge
Get spoon
```

The response to the boiling water is as follows:

```
Put down whatever is in our hands
Turn off burner
Pour boiling water into coffee cone
Pick up whatever we put down
```

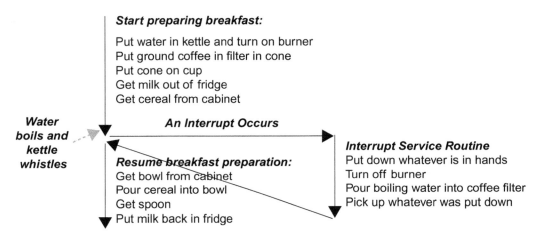

Figure 3.7 Sequence of events when preparing breakfast.

The system will behave as shown in Figure 3.7 and work well regardless of when the water starts boiling. This approach has several benefits:

- Efficient preparation since we don't need to keep checking on the water.
- Easily maintained preparation sequence (e.g., code), since the two independent activities are kept separate and not duplicated.
- Fast response to boiling water.

3.4.2   RL78 Interrupt Mechanisms

The RL78 architecture supports interrupts from many possible sources, both on- and off-chip. When a interrupt is requested, the processor saves some of its execution state (program counter and program status word), executes the ISR corresponding to the interrupt request, and then resumes the execution of the interrupted program.

The address of each ISR is listed in the interrupt vector table in memory. Whenever an interrupt occurs, the processor uses this table to determine the location of the ISR.

3.4.3   Interrupt Processing Activities

3.4.3.1   *Hardware Activities Acknowledging an Interrupt*

The CPU has a hard-wired response to interrupts and does not require any software execution or intervention.

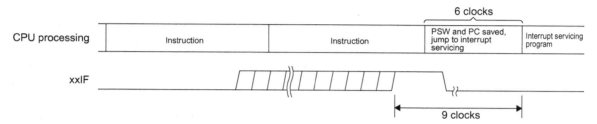

Figure 3.8   Best-case interrupt response time.

1.   When an interrupt is requested, the CPU will finish executing the current instruction (and possibly the next instruction[1]) before starting to service the interrupt. Figure 3.8 shows a best-case example, in which the ISR begins executing 9 cycles after the interrupt is requested. In the worst case (with a long instruction and an interrupt request hold situation) this can take up to 14 cycles.

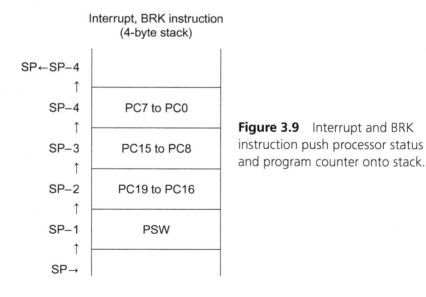

Figure 3.9   Interrupt and BRK instruction push processor status and program counter onto stack.

---

[1] Certain instructions (called interrupt request hold instructions) delay interrupt processing to ensure proper CPU operation.

2. The CPU pushes the current value of the PSW and then the PC onto the stack, as shown in Figure 3.9. Saving this information will allow the CPU to resume processing of the interrupted program later without disrupting it.
3. The CPU next clears the IE bit. This makes the ISR non-interruptible. However, if an EI instruction is executed within the ISR, it will become interruptible at that point.
4. If the interrupt source is a maskable interrupt, the CPU next loads the PSW PR field with the priority of the ISR being serviced (held in the bits ISP0 and ISP1). This prevents the processor from responding to lower-priority interrupts during this ISR.
5. The CPU loads the PC with the interrupt vector for the interrupt source.
6. The ISR begins executing.

3.4.3.2   *Software Activities during ISR Execution*

The ISR must be written to prevent it from corrupting system state. Note that only a small portion of the state is saved automatically: the PC and the PSW. Since interrupts are asynchronous to the executing program, we can't tell which registers (e.g., A) are being used by that program and which are free. An ISR needs to be conservative and save the state of all of the registers it will modify, and then restore them on ISR exit.

Compilers will generate the save and restore code automatically for functions designated as ISRs.

- The standard method is to push the registers to use onto the stack upon ISR entry (in the prolog), and pop them off just before exit (in the epilog). The IAR compiler relies on the __interrupt keyword to indicate if a function is an ISR and needs this special treatment.
- Some processors (including the RL78) provide extra register banks. Compilers support this feature by allowing developers to specify which register bank an ISR will use. For example, the IAR Embedded Workbench C Compiler recognizes the directive #pragma bank=*bank#*. The ISR will execute code to switch to a separate register bank upon ISR entry. This can dramatically reduce context switch time. The original bank is restored when the return from interrupt pops the PSW from the stack. A designer must ensure that ISRs are not reentrant and do not share any register bank.

3.4.3.2.1   ISR Code Example #1   Consider an ISR which calls a subroutine IICA0_Master-Handler if a special function register IICS0 has the most significant bit set. We examine the assembly code generated by the IAR C compiler and find the following in the listing (.lst) file:

```
 180              __interrupt void MD_INTIICA0(void)
\                     MD_INTIICA0:
 181          {
\   000000 C1                   PUSH      AX
```

```
\   000001 C7                        PUSH      HL
\   000002 AEFC                      MOVW      AX, 0xFFFFC
\   000004 C1                        PUSH      AX
 182            if ((IICS0 & _80_IICA_STATUS_MASTER) == 0x80U)
\   000005 8E51                      MOV       A, 0xFFF51
\   000007 5C80                      AND       A, #0x80
\   000009 D1                        CMP0      A
\   00000A 61E8                      SKZ
 183                {
 184                    IICA0_MasterHandler();
\   00000C FD....                    CALL      IICA0_MasterHandler
 185                }
 186            }
\                          ??MD_INTIICA0_0:
\   00000F C0                        POP       AX
\   000010 BEFC                      MOVW      0xFFFFC, AX
\   000012 C6                        POP       HL
\   000013 C0                        POP       AX
\   000014 61FC                      RETI
```

The AX, HL, and CS (accessed through address 0xFFFFC) registers are saved on the stack in the prolog and restored in the epilog. The RETI instruction is a return from interrupt and ends the ISR. If we examine the RL78 software manual we will see that the PUSH, MOVW, and POP instructions in the prolog and epilog each take one clock cycle. Hence the ISR spends a total of eight cycles to save and restore the context of the three registers (AX, HL, and CS).

3.4.3.2.2 ISR Code Example #2 Some processor architectures (register-memory architectures) support operations on operands located in memory, without requiring that they be loaded into registers. This simplifies ISRs as they need not save and restore as much context. The RL78 is one such architecture. For example, consider an interrupt service routine which toggles an output port bit and increments a global variable. We examine the assembly code generated by the IAR C compiler and find the following in the listing (.lst) file:

```
 61             __interrupt void MD_INTP2(void)
\                          MD_INTP2:
 62             {
 64                 P5_bit.no5 ^= 1;
\   000000 7A0520                    XOR       S:0xFFF05, #0x20
 65                 int_count++;
\   000003 A2....                    INCW      N:int_count
 67             }
\   000006 61FC                      RETI
```

This code is quite efficient, consisting of merely three instructions. Details on these instructions can be found in the RL78 software manual. Both the exclusive or (XOR) and the increment word (INCW) operate on data stored in memory, eliminating the need to load the data into registers for modification.

The XOR and INCW instruction each take **two clock cycles** because they each need to perform two memory accesses for the read/modify/write operation. If the operands were already in registers, each of these instructions would only take **one clock cycle** each.

More complex ISRs may benefit from having data loaded into registers for manipulation. In choosing which approach to follow, the compiler needs to balance the **cost of loading and storing operands** from memory into registers (and the **additional context save/restore cost** required to support this) against the benefit of **faster data processing** instructions.

3.4.3.3 Hardware Activities upon ISR Exit

A maskable interrupt's ISR must end with a RETI instruction, while a software interrupt must end with a RETB instruction. This will pop the PC and then PSW from the stack to resume prior program execution.

3.4.4 Interrupt Characteristics

3.4.4.1 Maskable vs. Non-Maskable Interrupts

Interrupts may be *Maskable* or *Non-Maskable*.

- Maskable interrupts can be disabled. For example, we may not want to use a specific interrupt source in our system, so we should mask that source to ensure it never is activated. We may wish to have the processor ignore serial port activity before the port is correctly initialized, to avoid spurious errors. Once the port and the supporting data structures are initialized we would unmask the interrupt.
- Non-maskable interrupts are interrupts that cannot be ignored by the processor. When such an interrupt occurs, the processor will service the interrupt unconditionally because of its criticality. Some examples of causes of non-maskable interrupts are reset signal assertion, low supply voltage, illegal instructions, and memory errors.

3.4.4.2 Software Interrupt

Executing a BRK instruction will trigger a software interrupt. This interrupt is not maskable and is not prioritized.

3.4.5   Controlling the CPU's Response to Interrupts

The PSW register has two fields which allow a program to define how to respond to interrupts. The IE bit allows all maskable interrupts to be ignored, while the ISP field allows lower-priority interrupts to be ignored while still responding to higher priority interrupts.

3.4.5.1   IE: Interrupt Request Acknowledgement Enable or Disable

The **IE bit** in the PSW register controls the **masking** (disabling) of maskable interrupts. When set to 1, maskable interrupts can be serviced. When cleared to 0, maskable interrupts are **masked** and are not serviced. The EI and DI instructions set and clear the IE flag, respectively.

3.4.5.2   ISP1 and ISP0: Interrupt Service Priority

The ISP field in the PSW (ISP1 and ISP0) specifies the current interrupt priority level of the CPU. 00 represents the highest priority and 11 the lowest. The CPU will service interrupts with a priority level (set by PR1 and PR0, described below) which is the same as is the ISP or higher priority (and therefore numerically smaller).

3.4.6   Configuration of Maskable Interrupts

All maskable interrupts share certain common configuration and status features, as detailed in this section. Figure 3.10 shows configurable bits and processing. Note that the IE bit in the figure is the Interrupt Enable flag in the PSW register.

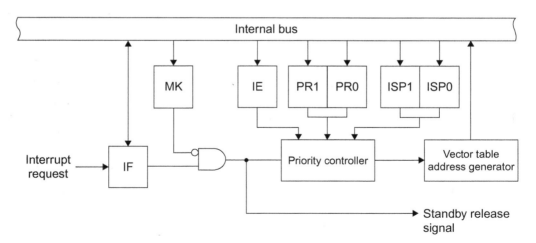

Figure 3.10   Structure of Internal Maskable Interrupt Circuitry.

3.4.6.1 IF: Interrupt Request Flag

An interrupt request flag (IF) indicates whether an interrupt source has requested an interrupt. The flag is set when an interrupt source requests an interrupt, and is cleared when the processor acknowledges the interrupt. It can also be accessed by software to determine if a specific interrupt has been requested or clear a pending request.

The interrupt flags are located in the registers IF0L and IF0H, through IF3L and IF3H. Each interrupt request flag has a specific name consisting of the interrupt source name combined with IF (e.g., PIF5, DMAIF1, TMIF04).

3.4.6.2 MK: Interrupt Mask Flag

Maskable interrupts are masked (disabled) by setting the source's MK flag to one. They are unmasked (enabled) by clearing the source's MK flag. The mask flags are located in the registers MK0L and MK0H through MK3L and MK3H. Each interrupt mask flag has a specific name consisting of the interrupt source name combined with MK (e.g., PMK5, DMAMK1, TMMK04).

3.4.6.3 PR1 and PR0: Interrupt Priority Specification Flags

The priority of each interrupt source can be set to one of four levels using the PR1 and PR0 flags. 00 specifies the highest priority.

The interrupt priority specification flags are located in the registers PR00L and PR00H through PR13L. Each interrupt request flag has a specific name consisting of the interrupt source name combined with IF (e.g., PIF5, DMAIF1, TMIF04).

3.4.7 Interrupt Vector Table

The **interrupt vector table** holds the 16-bit address (vector) of each ISR.[2] The CPU uses this table to load the PC with the correct ISR address. Figure 3.11 shows an example of part of the interrupt vector information for the RL78G13 MCU. In some cases a vector is used by multiple interrupt sources. For example, the reset vector (located at 00000H) is used when the RESET pin is asserted, for power-on-reset, when a low operating voltage is detected, when the watchdog timer overflows, or when an illegal instruction is executed.

---

[2] This means the interrupt service routine must be located within the first 64 kB of memory.

Interrupt Source List (1/4)

INTERRUPT TYPE	DEFAULT PRIORITY	INTERRUPT SOURCE NAME	INTERRUPT SOURCE TRIGGER	INTERNAL/ EXTERNAL	VECTOR TABLE ADDRESS	BASIC CONFIGURATION TYPE	20-PIN	24-PIN	25-PIN	30-PIN	32-PIN	36-PIN	40-PIN	44-PIN	48-PIN	52-PIN	64-PIN	80-PIN	100-PIN	128-PIN
Maskable	0	INTWDTI	Watchdog timer interval (75% of overflow time)	Internal	0004H	(A)	✓	✓	✓	✓	✓	✓	✓	✓	✓	✓	✓	✓	✓	✓
	1	INTLVI	Voltage detection		0006H		✓	✓	✓	✓	✓	✓	✓	✓	✓	✓	✓	✓	✓	✓
	2	INTP0	Pin input edge detection	External	0008H	(B)	✓	✓	✓	✓	✓	✓	✓	✓	✓	✓	✓	✓	✓	✓
	3	INTP1			000AH		✓	✓	✓	✓	✓	✓	✓	✓	✓	✓	✓	✓	✓	✓
	4	INTP2			000CH		—	✓	✓	✓	✓	✓	✓	✓	✓	✓	✓	✓	✓	✓
	5	INTP3			000EH		✓	✓	✓	✓	✓	✓	✓	✓	✓	✓	✓	✓	✓	✓
	6	INTP4			0010H		—	✓	✓	✓	✓	✓	✓	✓	✓	✓	✓	✓	✓	✓
	7	INTP5			0012H		✓	✓	✓	✓	✓	✓	✓	✓	✓	✓	✓	✓	✓	✓
	8	INTST2/ INTCSI20/ INTIIC20	UART2 transmission transfer end or buffer empty interrupt/CSI20 transfer end or buffer empty interrupt/ IIC20 transfer end	Internal	0014H	(A)	—	—	—	✓	✓	✓	✓	✓	✓	✓	✓	✓	✓	✓

Figure 3.11 Interrupt sources and vector addresses.

3.4.8   Concurrent Interrupts

There are several possible interrupt sequences which can arise if interrupts are requested close in time or even simultaneously.

3.4.8.1   Interrupts Disabled in ISRs

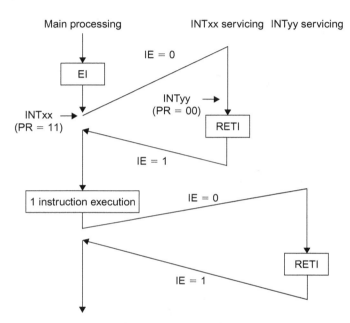

Figure 3.12   Sequential ISR processing due to disabled IE bit in ISR.

In the default case, shown in Figure 3.12, ISRs do not re-enable interrupts until executing their RETI instruction. When responding to INTxx, the CPU clears the IE bit to 0 and this prevents the CPU from responding to INTyy. In this case, interrupts are sequentialized (INTxx finishes before INTyy starts) and not nested.

Note that this is the safest practice and should be followed unless you have an extremely good reason to re-enable interrupts and understand the hazards of data races. "My ISRs take too long to run" is almost never a valid reason for re-enabling interrupts in ISRs, and instead an indication of bad software architecture and design.

3.4.8.2   Interrupts Enabled in ISRs

What happens if our ISR executes an EI instruction to set the IE bit? This depends on the priority of the second interrupt (INTyy) relative to the first interrupt (INTxx).

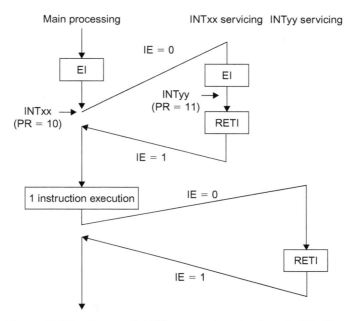

Figure 3.13   Sequential ISR processing due to prioritization.

If the second interrupt is the same or lower priority (PR is an equal or larger value), then the first ISR will finish executing, as shown in Figure 3.13.

However, if the second interrupt is higher priority (PR is a smaller value), then the second ISR will interrupt the first ISR, as shown in Figure 3.14.

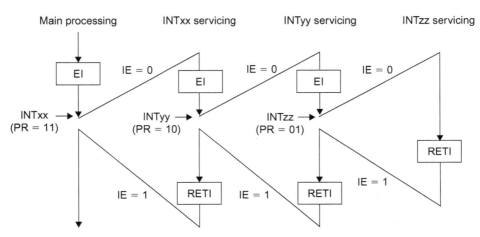

Figure 3.14   Nested ISR processing due to prioritization.

3.4.8.3 *Simultaneous Interrupt Requests*

If multiple interrupts are requested simultaneously then the interrupts are prioritized. The interrupt with the highest priority (as defined by the smallest value of PR bits) is serviced first and the requests for lower priority interrupts are held pending. If there are multiple interrupts with the highest PR-bit-defined priority, then the interrupt with the highest *default priority* (smallest value, see Figure 3.11) is serviced first and other interrupt requests are held pending.

3.4.9   External Interrupts (Pin Input)

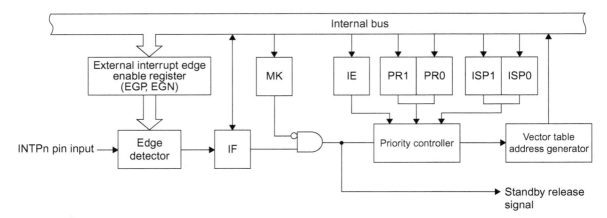

Figure 3.15   External maskable interrupt (INTPn.)

The RL78 interrupt system supports *external interrupts*—these are triggered by an external signal which is fed to a specific input. The RL78G13, for example, has thirteen external interrupts.

The external interrupts sources can be configured to trigger on a rising edge, a falling edge, or both edges. This is done using the EGP and EGN registers, for rising and falling edges respectively.

3.4.9.1 *External Interrupt Example*

In this program we will configure an external interrupt INTP0 (on port 13 bit 7) to respond to falling edges. Each falling edge will result in an ISR toggling an LED connected to port P5 bit 5 and also increment a variable called *counter.*

In Figure 3.16 we use Applilet to set INTP2 to trigger on the falling edge, and assign it a low priority (3).

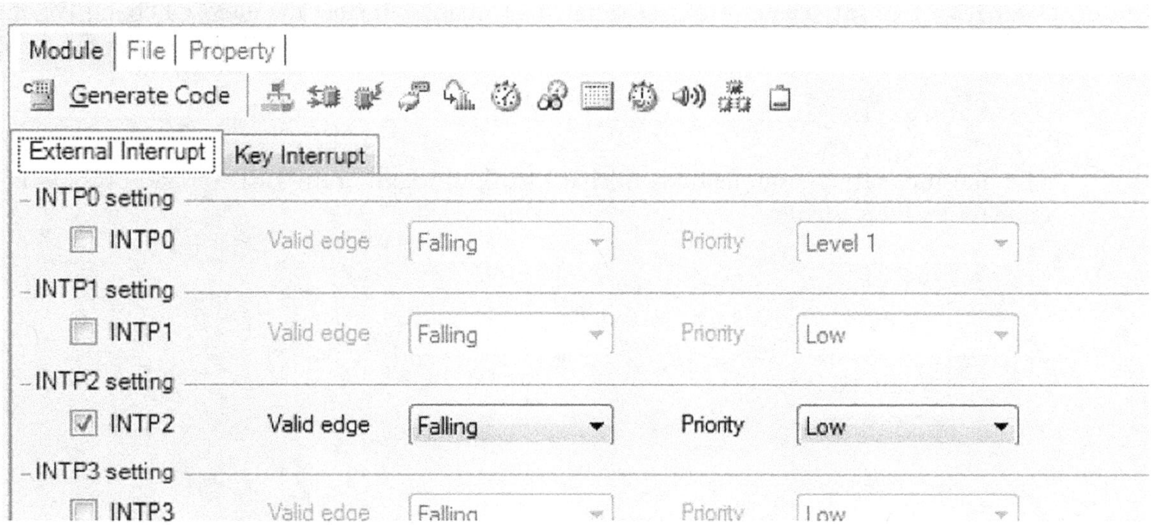

Figure 3.16   Configuring INTP2 with Applilet.

In Figure 3.17 we use Applilet to configure the port to drive the LED.

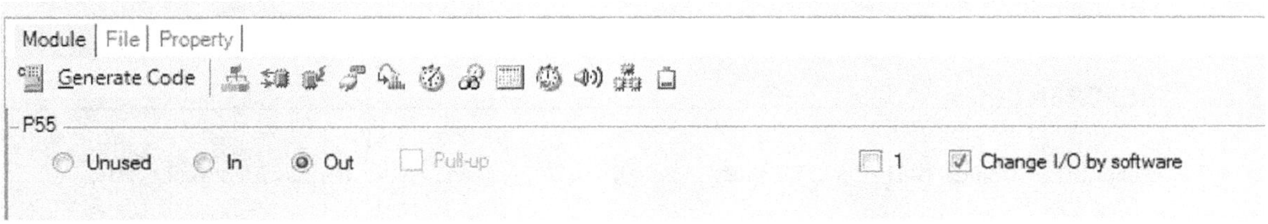

Figure 3.17   Configuring port 5 bit 5 as an output.

3.4.9.1.1   CG_main.c The main function initializes the peripherals, enables the interrupt, and then does nothing.

```
extern unsigned int_count;
void main (void) {
    __low_level_init();   /* Initialize peripherals */
    INTP2_Enable();       /* Enable the mute button interrupt */
    while (1)
        ;
}
```

3.4.9.1.2   CG_int_user.c A global variable int_count will store the interrupt count. We define it in CG_int_user.c. The variable is incremented by the ISR and read by the main function.

```
unsigned int_count = 0;
```

The interrupt service routine does the hard work of toggling the LED on and off, and incrementing the variable.

```
#pragma vector = INTP2_vect
__interrupt void MD_INTP2(void)
{
    P5_bit.no5 ^= 1;
    int_count++;
}
```

3.5   RECAP

This chapter presented an overview of how a processor core within a microcontroller is organized and how it operates. The RL78 instruction set architecture was presented and examined in detail. Concepts of interrupts were introduced and then demonstrated using the RL78's interrupt system. An example using external interrupts is presented.

3.6   REFERENCES

Renesas Electronics. (2011). *RL78 Family User's Manual: Software,* USA: Renesas Electronics, 2011.

3.7   EXERCISES

1. Examine the RL78 software user's manual. Which instruction takes the longest time to execute?
2. Compile the following program and calculate the average IPC (cycles per instruction) based on the total number of cycles to execute and the total number of instructions.

```
void main(void) {
    volatile int a = 3, b = 5, c;
    c = a*b;
}
```

3. Write an assembly language program to calculate the 16-bit checksum of ten words located in memory.
   a. Use the register indirect addressing mode. How many clock cycles will the program take to execute?
   b. Use the based addressing mode. How many clock cycles will the program take to execute?
   c. Use the based indexed addressing mode. How many clock cycles will the program take to execute?

4. Assume an RL78 MCU is executing a 2-byte-long instruction starting at address 01200H when an interrupt is requested. Assume the stack pointer is pointing to FF000H and is not modified by the instruction. Draw a diagram of the stack (including address and known contents) upon entry into the interrupt service routine.

5. Consider the ISR from example #2 and assume the RL78 processor is running at 32 MHz.
   a. What is the maximum frequency at which this ISR can execute?
   b. What would the maximum frequency be if the processor had to load operands into register A (or AX) before it could perform the XOR and INCW operations?

6. What are the minimum and maximum amount delays between an interrupt being requested and the ISR beginning to execute, assuming interrupts are enabled and the RL78 MCU is running at 32 MHz?

7. Is it possible to configure the interrupt system so that a lower priority interrupt can delay the response of a higher priority interrupt? Explain and provide an example.

8. Write a program using **one ISR** to implement a quadrature shaft encoder. Determine rotation direction by sampling the quadrature signal.

9. Write a program using **two ISRs** to implement a quadrature shaft encoder. This will require some creativity.

Chapter Four

Software Engineering for Embedded Systems

4.1   LEARNING OBJECTIVES

We have tremendous flexibility when creating software; we make many decisions going from an idea to a final working system. There are technical decisions, such as which components we use to build a system, their internal structure, and how we interconnect them. Some of the technical decisions will lead to a product that works, but not all will. There are also process decisions, such as how we plan to build the system, and how to select those components. Similarly, some process decisions can lead to an easier or more predictable development effort, while others will lead to project delays or cancellation, or can even bankrupt the company. A good software process will evolve over time, incorporating lessons learned from each project's successes and failures. Hence a good process will make it easier to do the technical work. The goal of this chapter is to show how both process and technical issues need to be considered to successfully create a product on time and on budget.

In this chapter we try to present just the most critical concepts to help the reader understand that "does the code work?" is **one question,** but **not the only question** to answer. There are many excellent books and articles which go into great depth on software engineering for embedded and general purpose software; a few are listed in the references section. For example, Jack Ganssle has a "top ten list" of why embedded systems projects get into trouble (2006). In this chapter we discuss how a good software engineering process addresses eight of them. Phil Koopman presents a detailed and practical book on embedded software development processes and issues (2010). We will refer the reader to specific chapters in the latter text periodically in order to keep this chapter short and readable.

4.2   INTRODUCTION

4.2.1   Risk Reduction

Reducing risks is a driving force behind software engineering and project management. A software development organization can benefit by constantly refining its processes as it learns both what it does well, and how to improve what it does poorly.

Developing embedded software is usually **unpredictable.** For example:

- What if there is a bug in our code? What if the compiler sometimes seems to generate buggy code?
- What if the code we need to write actually turns out to be a lot more complex than we thought?
- What if we don't have enough memory for our program or its data? What if the processor can't run our code fast enough?
- What if activating a motor resets the processor due to a weak power supply?
- What if that external A/D converter peripheral doesn't seem to work the way the datasheet said it would?
- What if the lead developer wins the lottery and quits a month before the product deadline?
- What if the new developer we hired turns out to be incompetent, lazy, or both?
- What if half of our development team gets sick, is laid off, or is reassigned?
- What if the customer adds new requirements every week, or wants the product done two months early?

If any of these risks actually occur they will increase the amount of development work needed. Whether it affects the product development deadlines depends on how much overtime the development team is willing to put in, whether other developers can help out, whether anything in the development process turns out to be faster than expected, and so forth. Missing deadlines will have negative financial impacts: project costs will increase and income from product sales will be delayed. Some of these risks also have other impacts: higher power consumption, fewer features, board redesign, and so forth.

Ganssle identifies "Unrealistic Schedules" as the number one reason for embedded system project problems. Successful software organizations create a **development plan** for the project to show development tasks and output products as well as risk management approaches. Koopman discusses development plans in detail in Chapters 2 through 4 of his book *Better Embedded System Software* (2010).

4.3   SOFTWARE DEVELOPMENT STAGES

4.3.1   Development Lifecycle Overview

The embedded product lifecycle has multiple steps, as shown in Figure 4.1.

The software development process consists of multiple steps within that embedded product lifecycle. One example process model is the V model, shown in Figure 4.2. It consists of:

- Defining system requirements.
- Creating an architectural or high-level design, deciding on the general approach to build the system, and then creating appropriate hardware and software architectures.

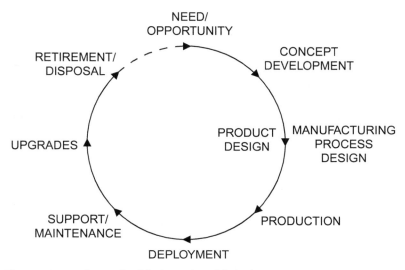

Figure 4.1   The embedded product lifecycle. (Courtesy P. Koopman, 2010.)

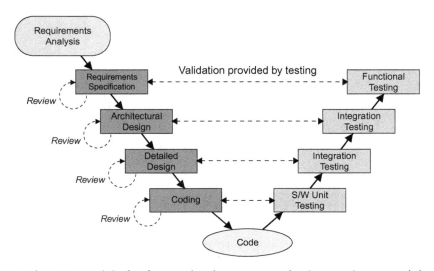

Figure 4.2   The "V" model of software development emphasizes testing at each level of design detail.

- Creating detailed designs.
- Implementing code and performing unit testing.
- Integrating the code components and performing integration testing.
- Changing the code after "completion" to fit custom deployment requirements, fix bugs, add features, etc.

The process breaks a problem into smaller easier problems through the process of **top-down design** or **decomposition.** Each small problem is solved and the solutions are combined into a software solution. There are many approaches possible:

- Do we design everything up front, and then code it? This is called a **big up-front design.**
- Do we have a prototype or a previous version which we can build upon?
- Do we design and build a little at a time?
- What do we work on first, the easy or the hard parts?

Which model we should use depends on the types and severity of risks. Some industries may be required to follow a specific development process in order for the product to receive certification. Ganssle identifies "Poorly Defined Process" as reason number six for embedded system project troubles (2006).

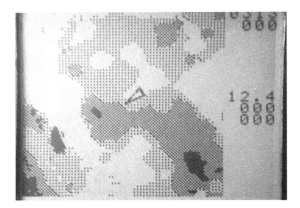

Figure 4.3 Chartplotter screen with boat icon overlaid on depth chart.

Figure 4.4 Chartplotter screen with numerical depth and speed information.

In this chapter we will use an example embedded system to illustrate the issues involved. Our target system is an electronic chartplotter for boats. The chartplotter can display a depth chart on a graphical LCD with an icon superimposed to show the boat's current position and direction, as shown in Figure 4.3. This helps the user steer the boat to avoid shallow water. Alternatively, we may choose to have a numerical display and omit the chart, as shown in Figure 4.4. The chartplotter receives position, direction, and speed information from a GPS receiver, and depth and battery voltage information from a depth sounder.

4.3.2 Graphical Representations

There are many graphical forms of diagrams we can use to describe a system's **structure** or **behavior.** We will examine several forms in this chapter. UML (Unified Modeling Language) has many types, shown in Figure 4.5. These diagrams are useful throughout the development process to present **requirements, architecture, and detailed design.**

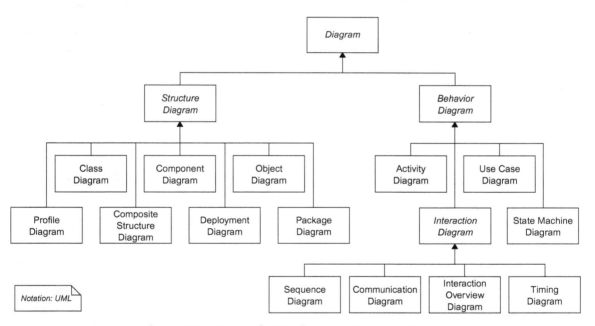

Figure 4.5 Types of UML diagrams (Courtesy Wikipedia).

4.3.3 Requirements

A system design begins with functional requirements. Ganssle identifies "Vague Requirements" as reason number five for projects getting into trouble. Koopman presents an excellent discussion of software requirements (Chapters 5 through 9, 2010) so we will just present a high-level view here.

- Requirements should be **written down.** This helps everyone have the same picture of what needs to be accomplished, and makes omissions easier to spot.
- There are three types of requirements. **Functional** requirements define what the system needs to do. **Nonfunctional** requirements describe emergent system behaviors such as response time, reliability, and energy efficiency. **Constraints** define the limits on the system design, such as cost and implementation choices.
- There are multiple ways to **express requirements,** both in text and graphically. The most appropriate and convenient method should be used. Graphical methods such as state charts, flow charts and message sequence charts should be used whenever possible because (1) they concisely convey the necessary information, and (2) they often can be used as design documents.
- Requirements should be **traceable to tests.** How will the system be tested to ensure that a requirement is met? Requirements should be quantified and measurable.
- The requirements should be **stable.** Frequent changes to requirements ("churn") often have side effects and disrupt the ideal prioritization of work tasks. It is easy for the latest changed requirement to be interpreted as the most important requirement, when in fact this is rarely the case.

4.3.4   Design Before Coding

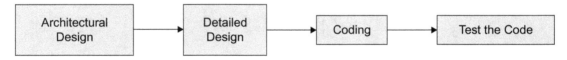

Figure 4.6   Basic stages in development.

There are various development models which we will discuss later in this chapter. At this point, it is sufficient to understand that there are different ways to "slice and dice" the work to be done, keeping in mind that we should develop each sub-system in the order **architect-design-implement.** For example, don't start writing code if you haven't designed the algorithm yet. This sequencing is quite important so we discuss it further.

One of the most effective ways to reduce risks in developing software is to **design before writing code.**[1] Ganssle identifies "Starting Coding Too Soon" as reason number nine

---

[1] There is related prior work in carpentry: Think thrice, measure twice, cut once.

for projects getting into trouble (2006). We refer to high-level design as the architecture, and the low-level design as the detailed design. Figure 4.6 shows an overview of the development process.

- **Writing code locks you in to specific implementations** of an algorithm, data structure, object, interface method, and so forth. If this happens before you understand the rest of the system, then you probably haven't made the best possible choice, and may end up having to make major changes to the code you've written, or maybe even throw it away.

- Designing the system before coding also gives you an **early insight** into what parts are needed, and which ones are likely to be complex. This helps prevent the surprises which slow down development. One of the best ways of reducing schedule risk is to understand the system in depth before creating a schedule, and then add in extra time buffers for dealing with the risky parts. **Estimation** is the process of predicting how long it will take to create the system.

- Designs should include graphical documents such as flowcharts and state machines when possible. The goal is to have a **small and concise set of documents** which define how the system should do its work. Graphical representations are easier to understand than code because they abstract away many implementation details, leaving just the relevant items.[2] This makes it easy for others to understand your design and identify risks. It also helps bring new hires up to speed on the project and reduces the chances they'll break something when they start maintaining or enhancing the code.

4.3.5   Peer Reviews of Design Artifacts

It is very helpful to have other team members review artifacts before proceeding to the next phase of development. First, having another perspective on an issue brings in greater experience and helps detect oversights. Ganssle identifies "Bad Science" as reason number seven for projects getting into trouble (2006). Second, if you know that someone else will be reviewing what you are creating, you are likely to be more careful and professional. Peer reviews should be applied to all development artifacts: **requirements, test plans, architecture, detailed designs,** and **code.** We refer the reader elsewhere for more details on peer reviews (Koopman, 2010).

---

[2] Different businesses may have differing levels of formality (e.g., UML), but do not underestimate the benefit of a simple diagram (whether hand-written or created in Visio).

4.3.6   System Architecture and Design Approach

The system architecture defines your approach to building the system. What pieces are there, and how are they connected? What type of microcontroller and peripherals will be used? What major pieces of software will there be? How do they communicate? What will make them run at the right time? We present a summary of architectural concepts here, and encourage the reader to dig deeper in the referenced text (see Chapters 10 and 11 in Koopman).

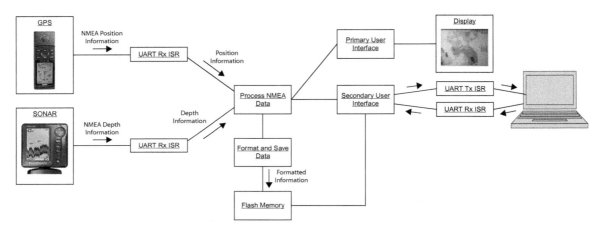

Figure 4.7   Communication diagram for chartplotter emphasizes data flow through tasks.

Figure 4.7 presents a UML communication diagram which emphasizes how data flows through the different subsystems within the chartplotter, as well as to and from external devices. Sonar and GPS information is delivered through two serial ports to the system. We will use interrupt service routines and queues to buffer the data between the serial ports and the main application task code. There are four separate tasks in the system:

- The Process NMEA Data task will receive the data from the sonar and GPS, decode it, and update the relevant variables which indicate current depth, position, and so forth.
- The Primary User Interface task will update the display.
- The Format and Save Data task will convert the depth and other variables into a human-readable text format and write them to flash memory.
- The Secondary User Interface task will provide a serial console interface so we can read the logged data from flash memory, erase it, and perform other system maintenance functions.

We can look at the timing of a series of interactions between elements over time using a sequence diagram. For example, Figure 4.8 shows how both the GPS and SONAR send data to the chartplotter, which processes each message. Time progresses downwards, so the events higher in the diagram occur earlier in time.

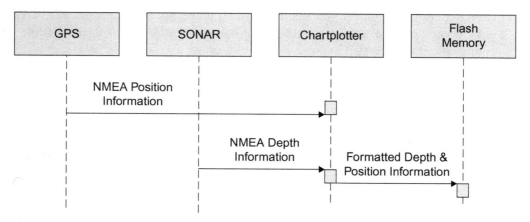

Figure 4.8   Sequence diagram showing communication between different system elements.

A communication diagram, shown in Figure 4.9, corresponds more to a data flow diagram, replacing the timeline with numbered communication labels.

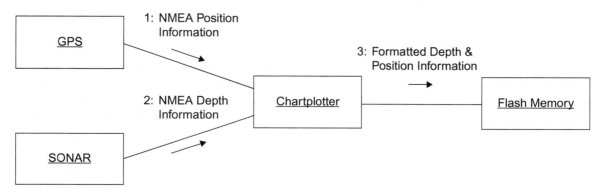

Figure 4.9   High-level communication diagram for chartplotter.

We can look at the system with a layered point of view. For example, data arriving from the GPS is buffered and then decoded by an NMEA-0183 parser before being provided to the application for use.

4.3.7   Architectural Design to Meet Critical Properties

How does this architecture meet the most critical aspects of the requirements? These may be related to time, safety, robustness, or something else which is application-specific. In any case it is important to convey these concepts.

4.3.7.1   Time-Critical Processing

It is quite helpful to have a section in the architecture document which describes **which processing is time-critical,** and **how the system is architected** to ensure the timing requirements are met. For example, consider a light dimmer controller:

The system must switch power outputs within 50 microseconds of a zero-crossing of the AC power line. Failure to switching within this time will lead to electrical noise and interference with other devices. The system is designed so that a hardware analog window comparator detects zero crossings and triggers a non-maskable interrupt. All power output switching is performed by the ISR, which controls its outputs based on flags set by the main code which indicates which outputs to enable. Hence interrupts must not be disabled for longer than x microseconds.

The system must shut down within 10 ms of an overcurrent or overvoltage condition occurring. Failure to shut down within this time can lead to equipment damage and failure. We plan to use a periodic interrupt running at 1 kHz in order to sample dedicated analog hardware comparators which detect these conditions. Because of the 1 kHz interrupt rate, interrupts must not be disabled for longer than 8 ms, in order to allow a 1 ms safety margin.

Further information on real-time system design is available in Chapter 14 of the referenced text (Koopman, 2010).

4.3.7.2   Safety-Critical Processing

It is quite helpful to have a section in the architecture document which describes **which processing is safety-critical,** and **how the system is architected** to ensure the safety requirements are met. For example:

The software tasks X, Y, and Z are safety-critical. They cannot be modified without triggering recertification. In order to ensure real-time performance, we use a preemptive scheduler and assign X, Y, and Z priorities higher than all other tasks. In order to minimize the chances of data corruption, all critical variables used by X, Y, and Z are protected by storing them with complements or with a block CRC.

Again, there is further detailed information in the referenced text (Chapters 26–30 in Koopman, 2010) cover critical system properties).

4.3.8   Detailed Design

After we have decided upon an architecture for the system we can work on designing the subsystems within it. Again, graphical representations can be quite useful, especially if the corresponding requirements are graphical, as in this and similar cases they can be reused.

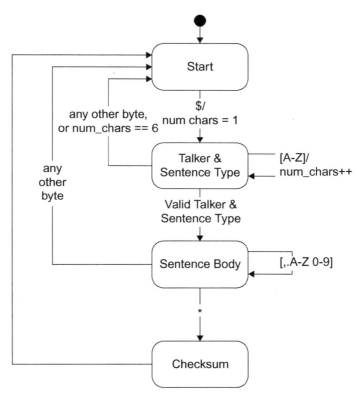

Figure 4.10   State chart design for recognizing NMEA-0183 messages.

For example, state-based system behavior is best presented graphically. Figure 4.10 shows a finite state machine design for a UART Receive data ISR (the two circles labeled "UART Rx ISR" in Figure 4.7) which recognizes certain valid NMEA-0183 messages and enqueues them for later decoding. Corrupted or unneeded messages are discarded, saving buffer space in RAM and processor time. These messages have a specific format which includes the talker type (GPS, depth sounder, etc.), the message type, multiple data fields (often with each followed by engineering units), and a checksum for error detection. The statechart in Figure 4.10 shows how the decoder moves from state to state as specific characters (e.g., $, *, letters A through Z) are received on the serial port, possibly in conjunction with other conditions.

We use an FSM-plus-ISR combination for two reasons. First, we want to minimize the amount of time spent in the ISR. Structuring the problem as an FSM allows us to write code which doesn't waste any time waiting for things to happen. The ISR is only executed when the UART has received a byte of data. Second, parsing structured data is a good match for FSMs as it allows us to define rules to step through the different fields in a message and validate them.

Figure 4.11 shows a flowchart design for the task "Process NMEA GGA" which decodes a received GGA message. This code is much less time-critical, so it is implemented in a task which the scheduler runs after being notified that the queue holds at least one valid message. The diagram emphasizes the consecutive and conditional processing nature of the activity.

There are various other representations available beyond these two workhorses, so we direct the reader other texts (see Chapters 12 and 13 of Koopman).

4.3.9   Implementation

Now that we have a detailed design it should be straightforward to proceed to the actual implementation of the code. C is the dominant programming language for embedded systems, followed by C++ and assembly language. C is good enough for the job, even though there are some languages which are much safer. The risk with C is that it allows the creation of all sorts of potentially unsafe code. Ganssle identifies "The Use of C" (or "The Misuse of C") as reason 8 for projects getting into trouble. There are a few points to keep in mind as you develop the code (2006):

- Three fundamental principles should guide your decisions when implementing code: simplicity, generality, and clarity (Kernighan & Pike, 1999).
  - □ Simplicity is keeping the programs and functions short and manageable.
  - □ Generality is designing functions that can work, in a broad sense, for a variety of situations and that require minimum alterations to suit a task.
  - □ Clarity is the concept of keeping the program easy to understand while remaining technically precise.
- Code should conform to your company's **coding standards** to ensure that it is easy to read and understand. See Koopman's Chapter 17 for more information on why coding style matters (2010). There are many coding standards examples available (Ganssle, J., 2008). The rules we have seen broken most often, and which have the biggest payoff, are these:
  - □ Limit function length to what fits onto one screen or page.
  - □ Use meaningful and consistent function and variable naming conventions.
  - □ Avoid using global variables.
  - □ If you find yourself writing the same code with minor variations, it may be worth parameterizing the code so only one version is needed.

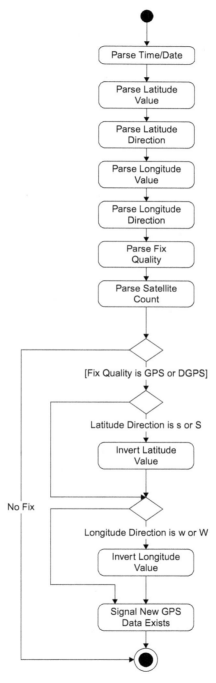

Figure 4.11   Activity diagram for parsing "GGA" NMEA-0183 message

- Data sharing in systems with preemption (including ISRs) must be done very carefully to avoid data race vulnerabilities. See Chapter 11 of this text and Koopman's Chapters 19 and 20 for more details.
- **Static analysis** should be used to ensure that your code is not asking for trouble. Most (if not all) compiler warnings should be turned on to identify potential bugs lurking in your source code. Tools such as LINT are also helpful and worth considering.
- **Magic numbers** are hard-coded numeric literals used as constants, array sizes, character positions, conversion factors and other numeric values that appear directly in programs. They complicate code maintenances because if a magic number is used in multiple places, and if a change is needed then **each location** must be revised and it is easy to forget about one. Similarly, some magic numbers may depend on others (e.g., a time delay may depend on the MCU's clock rate). It is much better to use a **const variable** or a **preprocessor #define** to give the value a meaningful name which can be used where needed.
- It is important to **track available design margin** as you build the system up. How much RAM, ROM, and nonvolatile memory are used? How busy is the CPU on average? How close is the system to missing deadlines? The Software Gas Law states that software will expand to fill all available resources. Tracking the resource use helps give an early warning. For more details, see Koopman's discussion on the cost of nearly full resources (2010).
- **Software configuration management** should be used as the code is developed and maintained to support evolving code and different configurations as well.

4.3.10 Software Testing

Testing is an important part of software development. It is essentially impossible to develop error-free non-trivial software in a single try. It is especially difficult to design upfront a system which will handle all possible input conditions (including failures) correctly. Ganssle identifies "Inadequate Testing" and "Writing Optimistic Code" as reasons number three and two for projects getting into trouble. Koopman covers verification and validation of systems in detail.

Testing the developed software ensures that the product meets the requirements defined. That is, **testing proves that the software does what it is supposed to do.** A corollary is that **testing identifies the software's weaknesses.** These defects are typically prioritized based on their criticality.

Although one can never completely test a program, some tests are more useful and important than others. Hence, it makes sense to think while planning the tests in order to get the biggest return. Testing should be a logical, disciplined and systematic process, rather than a rote and mechanical process. As with other subjects covered here, there are many excellent texts on software testing for further information (Phillips, 2004).

There are several independent dimensions of testing to consider:

- Software tests may or may not depend on the internal details of how the module is built. **Black box testing** assumes no knowledge about the internal structure, and focuses instead on functionality. **White box (or clear box)** testing takes advantage of such knowledge, so it can be more efficient in finding faults.
- Software testing should be done at **various phases** of the development process. **Unit tests** are performed during coding on a per-module basis. **Integration tests** are performed as the system is assembled (integrated) from modules.
- **Regression testing** ensures that past bugs which were fixed have not been re-introduced.

4.3.10.1 Do We Know How the System is Built?

Black Box Testing tests the functionality of the software by treating it like a black box with unknown contents. **How** the software performs a task **is unknown and unimportant** to the test. The only needed thing to pass the test is for the software to do what it should. There are many types of black box testing. Among them are tests for readiness, finite state machine, cause-effect graphing, boundary value testing, and user profile:

- Readiness: This test checks if a function is present and functional, and ready for testing. Black box testing should always begin with this form of testing.
- Finite state machine: Much software can be considered as finite state machines that transit between different states based on different events. This form of testing tests the transitioning between states and for errors that may occur with them.
- Cause effect graphing: This form of testing helps to organize the concepts in other black box techniques. For this test, the tester organizes all possible inputs and outputs of a program. This results in a form of a complete software test and helps to systematically organize test cases.
- Boundary value testing: In this form of testing the inputs to the test system are divided into meaningful sets and then tested in groups. One value from each set is then input to the system rather than the whole set. This helps save time.
- User profile: This form of testing focuses on how the user intends to use the software and which errors are important to their proper functioning while using the software. This minimizes the amount of time needed to be put into testing. However, learning what part of the program is used often is the difficult part of the test.

White Box Testing relies on knowledge of the structure of the software. It is also known as clear box testing. **How** the software performs a task **is known** to the testers, enabling them to identify probable errors. Important elements of white box testing are coverage and branch and conditioning testing.

- Coverage: The aim of white box testing is to cover every statement, state, and path in a program within the constraints of time and money. This can be a daunting task, especially if the program has a magnitude of conditional statements.
- Branch and condition testing: The goal of branch testing is to traverse every path through the program. One way to do this is to use a flow chart of the program. The first test goes through one part of the program. The next one differs from the one before. In this manner, all paths are traversed, even those that share a common part.

4.3.10.2 How Many Modules Do We Test at a Time?

Individual **unit testing** of modules is typically done by the software developer as the code is created. As the developer has intimate knowledge of the implementation of the module, this testing is typically white-box testing to maximize the effectiveness. The developer writes test harness code to run the unit under specific conditions and verify the correct responses. Unit testing is quite effective because if there is a bug, it is in that module's code, design or requirements.

With **integration testing** each module is merged into the main program and is tested to check if it works individually as well as with the rest of the program without causing any errors. There are often scenarios where a subroutine works perfectly on its own, but fails when integrated into the overall system due to unexpected dependencies, requirements, or interactions.

There are various types of integration testing: Bottom up, top down, sandwich, and build. Selecting the type of integration testing depends upon the people and product involved in development.

- Bottom up: This is one of the classic approaches for design and testing. Each problem is broken down into smaller parts and solutions are written for them, also called modules. Each module is tested individually and combined into subsystems which in turn are also tested and then combined into a larger system. This goes on until the complete solution is acquired and tested.
- Top down: The top down form of integration testing is similar to the bottom up form but starts with a fully tested main routine. Modules are added to the main routine one after the other and tested as a combination. The process thus continues until all the modules have been added to the main program and tested.
- Sandwich: The sandwich testing form combines bottom up and top down forms of testing. The top down part tests the main controlling sub systems whereas the bottom up part integrates and tests the individual modules into sub systems.
- Build: The build form of integration testing starts with a core system to which functionally related module sets are added consecutively.

There is also a "worst-practice" integration testing method known as **Big Bang** testing. With this form of testing, all modules are combined and tested as a whole. Big bang testing is not advisable with untested modules as diagnosing the error can be very difficult—which of the many modules is really causing the problem? Or is an interaction between two or more modules the cause?

4.3.10.3   *How Do We Keep from Breaking Old Bug Fixes?*

The goal of **regression testing** is to ensure that bugs which were found in past testing were fixed and are still fixed. Sometimes an effort to fix a bug introduces other bugs. Regression testing uses a suite of tests which triggered bugs in the past. Automated regression testing allows developers to verify quickly and easily that their bug fix really is a fix. Regression testing may be applied to both unit and integration testing.

4.4   SOFTWARE DEVELOPMENT LIFECYCLE MODELS

We now discuss software development lifecycle models in more detail. Recall that in Figure 4.6 we saw that design should occur before coding. Now consider a system with multiple subsystems—how should we "slice and dice" the development tasks?

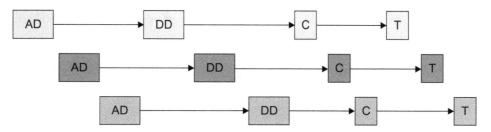

Figure 4.12   Fully interleaved subsystem development stages.

As shown in Figure 4.12, we could create all of the subsystem architectures before progressing to the detailed design of each and then implementations. This approach works better if the subsystems are relatively loosely coupled and independent.

We could instead build the subsystems more sequentially, as shown in Figure 4.13. With this approach we don't create the detailed design for a subsystem until we have completed the creation and testing of the previous subsystem. This allows us to ensure that the early subsystems are working completely before progressing to later subsystems.

Alternatively, we might feel that a critical subsystem is risky and needs to be prototyped before we can commit to the architectures (or perhaps just designs) for the other subsystems. This case is shown in **Figure 4.14.**

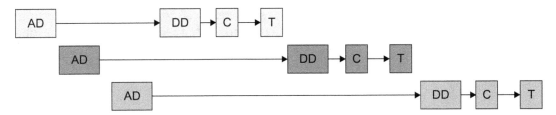

Figure 4.13 Partially sequential subsystem development stages.

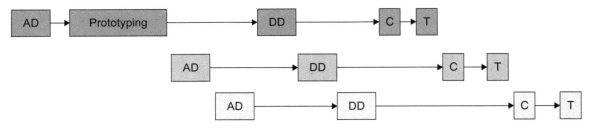

Figure 4.14 Hybrid subsystem development with up-front prototyping for risk reduction.

We can divide this scheduling of development tasks into two categories: waterfall (big up-front design) and everything else (build a piece at a time). The advantage of the latter approaches is that they deliver portions of the implementation to the customer and other stakeholders earlier. This allows problems and misconceptions to be found earlier and therefore fixed without disrupting the schedule as much. Projects with greater risks will benefit more from more iterative approaches, while less risky projects may be implemented more efficiently with a less iterative approach.

This chapter only provides a general description of these software processes. Further details can be found in the references of this chapter.

4.4.1 Waterfall Process

The waterfall model of software development is an idealized process which assumes that we know everything up front. The process gets its name because the processes flows down the steps like falling water. This process is most appropriate when the problem is very well understood so there is little risk. The following are the steps for the waterfall process:

1. Determine user needs
2. Gather requirements
3. Design
4. Build
5. Test
6. Demonstrate user product

Figure 4.15: The Waterfall Process expressed as a V-chart illustrates the waterfall process. In practice, there are often arrows jumping back up the waterfall[3] which makes this model an idealization.

Figure 4.15   The idealized waterfall process.

4.4.2   Iterative Process

The iterative process is used to deliver a product in increments. The customers define the goals of the product at the beginning of development and are always anxious to have something quickly working. The iterative process provides the product to the customer in parts and provides developers an opportunity to learn about the product and the customer while building the product. This type of process is typically used when there is enough time for developing a project in parts and the customer is eager to provide feedback on how the product functions while it is being developed. Figure 4.16 illustrates the iterative process.

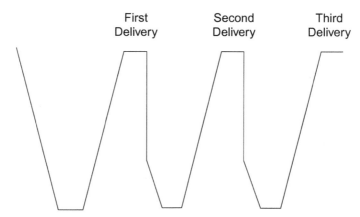

Figure 4.16   Example of an iterative process with one development team expressed as a V-chart.

---

[3] Imagine salmon leaping upstream over the rapids.

4.4.3   Spiral Process

The spiral process combines many fundamental contents of different process models into a single process. This process works best for projects that have a high risk of failure, such as research projects dealing with developing a new technology. Figure 4.17 illustrates the spiral process. Each cycle starts with the steps shown in the upper left quadrant, which are objectives (goals to achieve), constraints (limitations on resources), and alternatives (different approaches to achieve the objectives). The second quadrant (clockwise direction) shows the next steps in the process, which are risk analysis and prototyping. It begins with alternatives produced in the first quadrant. The developers then use the prototypes to analyze each alternative's risks and gain more insight. The third quadrant consists of the evaluation and decision making processes, followed by building the solution. The final quadrant consists of understanding what to do for the next cycle, which is repeated in the first quadrant. The developers revise the previous phases and create a plan for the next quadrant, review the same, and then decide whether to go ahead with the plan or stop building the project.

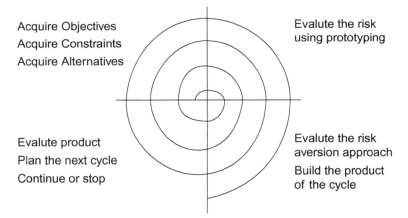

Acquire Objectives
Acquire Constraints
Acquire Alternatives

Evalute the risk
using prototyping

Evalute product
Plan the next cycle
Continue or stop

Evalute the risk
aversion approach
Build the product
of the cycle

Figure 4.17   The general spiral process.

4.4.4   Agile Development Methods

The most common agile development methods are scrum, extreme programming, and lean development. These methods seek to deliver the product to the customer in satisfactory condition as early as possible in a continuous manner.

Let's examine scrum. With scrum, development activity is divided into a series of sprints lasting two to four weeks. At the end of the sprint the team will have a working, deliverable software product. There are three main types of participants:

- The product owner speaks for the customer.
- The team delivers the product.
- The Scrum Master is responsible for eliminating obstacles from the team's path.

Each sprint begins with the team members and product owner discussing features from a prioritized feature list (the product backlog). The product owner identifies the desired features, and the team estimates which can be delivered within the sprint, adding them to a task list called the sprint backlog. The sprint backlog is frozen for the sprint, so that the team members have clear goals during that development period. Each day during the sprint there is a brief (fifteen minute) status meeting in which each team member answers three specific questions:

- What have you done since yesterday's meeting?
- What are you going to do today?
- Are there any issues keeping you from meeting your goals?

The Scrum Master then seeks to address the issues. Finally, each sprint is time-boxed. If a feature is not completed by the end of the sprint, it goes back into the product backlog. One of scrum's main strengths is the short development cycle, which improves the speed of feedback. There are aspects to scrum which we do not cover here, but further details are available in numerous texts on the subject.

4.4.5   Prototyping

Prototyping is a popular and useful software process, especially when determining the look and feel of the software has a higher priority than its basic functions. One of the drawbacks of the prototyped process is that when the waterfall model of development is used, the developer may create something completely different from what the customer expected, since the requirements are gathered only at the beginning of the development process. Thus, prototyping is better when it is performed as either an iterative or evolutionary process.

Two basic types of prototypes used are the throw away and evolutionary prototype. In the throw away prototype, developers use a demonstration tool or language. Once the customer is satisfied with the prototype, the developers throw away the prototype and build the actual product with real programming languages. In the evolutionary prototype, the developers use code from the prototype in the actual system.

4.5   RECAP

- A major risk of software development is starting coding too early. Designing the system and its components before coding reduces development risks significantly, and also provides other benefits.
- Industry follows many (and sometimes differing) processes when developing software. A process gives a directional path to developing software in an organized manner, and allows the people developing the software and using the software, to maintain expectations from the development process at regular intervals.
- Pseudo code and graphical methods to design solutions to a software programming problem allows understanding, resolving, and maintaining logical flow of a program. They can also be directly included in the documentation for the program.
- Testing is an integral part of software testing and software not subjected to testing is bound to fail. There are different techniques available for testing which should be applied as appropriate.

4.6   REFERENCES

Ganssle, J.. *The Art of Designing Embedded Systems, 2nd Edition.* Burlington, MA: Newnes, 2008.

Ganssle, J. G.. "Breakpoints: Jack's Top Ten." *Embedded Systems Design,* December, 2006: pp. 61–63.

Kernighan, B. W., & Pike, R. *The Practice of Programming.* Boston: Addison-Wesley, 1999.

Koopman, P. J. *Better Embedded System Software.* Pittsburgh: Drumnadrochit Education, 2010.

Phillips, D. *The Software Project Manager's Handbook: Principles That Work at Work.* New York: John Wiley & Sons, 2004.

4.7   EXERCISES

1. Create a set of requirements for a vending machine which accepts coins and one-dollar bills, and provides change. Assume that each type of item has its own button.
2. Create a set of requirements for a controller for an elevator in a ten-story building.
3. Create a state machine for use in a cellphone to identify local phone numbers, long-distance phone numbers, and invalid phone numbers.
4. Estimate how long it will take you to create a working program to flash the LEDs on your favorite microcontroller board at a frequency proportional to the ambient Celsius temperature. Then go ahead and create the program. Log the time spent for each development activity. Analyze the time required for each activity, the accuracy of your estimations, and finally suggest improvements.

Chapter Five

Software Development Tools

5.1 LEARNING OBJECTIVES

The goal of this chapter is to provide an overview of the tools and software support used for developing embedded software.

- The build toolchain translates a program specification written in a source language into an executable image
- The debug tools download the executable image onto the target hardware and allow the developer to control and inspect both the execution behavior and data of the program
- Software support such as code generators and support modules reduce the amount of coding required by a developer, reducing development time

5.2 SOFTWARE DEVELOPMENT TOOLCHAIN

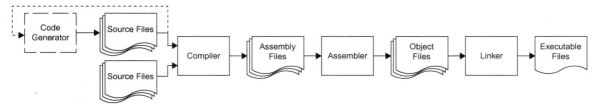

Figure 5.1 Overview of software compilation process for a C program.

Figure 5.1 shows the tools and files typically used for software development. The developer creates source code files (e.g., in C) which are compiled and assembled to create corresponding object files. These object files are then linked together to create an executable file which is programmed into a microcontroller's program memory.

5.2.1 Compiler

The compiler translates a program from a source format (e.g., C language) to a target format (e.g., RL78 assembly language). Note that this is not a one-to-one mapping, as there are many possible assembly language programs which could perform the work specified by the source code.

Compilers for embedded systems differ from compilers for general-purpose processors (GPPs). Minimizing code and data size is often critical for embedded systems since memory sizes are limited due to price pressures. This makes compiler code and data size optimizations extremely important. The tongue-in-cheek "Software Gas Law" states that a program will eventually grow to fill all available resources. Embedded system software evolves as features are added and defects are fixed, while the hardware changes much more slowly. It is much easier to reprogram an MCU than to redesign the hardware. As a result there is great value in compiler optimizations which can squeeze more code and data into the available resources.

Speed optimization is also often critical. However, it is done differently for embedded systems and GPPs. First, GPP instruction sets have evolved over time to enable extremely high clock rates (> 2 GHz) and deep instruction processing pipelines. Embedded processors with their lower clock rates do not need such deep pipelines, which leads to different code optimization trade-offs. Second, a lower clock rate means that embedded systems have a smaller performance penalty than GPPs for accessing memory instead of registers. This has two interesting effects. First, the compiler makes different optimization trade-offs with data allocation. Second, instruction sets for embedded systems can support memory-to-memory and bit-level operations rather than being forced into a load/store model. Recall the interrupt service routine from Chapter 3 which did not need to store any context—the RL78's memory-to-memory operation support eliminated the need to modify any processor registers, improving the speed of the resulting code.

5.2.2 Assembler

The assembler translates an assembly language file into an object file holding machine code. This translation is much more direct than compilation, as each assembly language instruction translates to a machine language instruction. In some cases the assembler may need to select among multiple forms of an instruction (e.g., depending on how far away a branch target is, or how long an immediate data value is).

5.2.3 Linker

The linker combines the object code from the files generated by the assembler, and may also incorporate object code from library files (e.g., sprintf). The linker organizes the different sections of the program in appropriate parts of memory and then updates references to addresses which were missing.

For example, if in our source code we call the function sprintf, the assembly code will contain an instruction **CALL sprintf.** However, the label sprintf must be translated to the address where the function sprintf actually begins. This address depends on where the module is placed in memory. The linker first lays out the different memory sections from all modules and then calculates the addresses of the cross-referenced functions and variables, and then finally patches the code with the correct addresses.

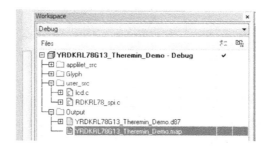

Figure 5.2   Output files created for project by linker.

The linker produces two output files, as shown in Figure 5.2. The first is the image file (with the suffix .d87) to be loaded into the MCU's flash program memory. This includes all of the code (user and library), interrupt vectors, initialization data, and other such information.

```
9 641 bytes of CODE  memory
2 369 bytes of DATA  memory (+ 104 absolute )
4 819 bytes of CONST memory

Errors: none
Warnings: none
```

Figure 5.3   End of map file.

The second output file which is created is a map file. This is a text file which describes where symbols are mapped to and how memory is used. By selecting the map file in the workspace window we can examine the file. Figure 5.3 shows an important part (at the very end of the file)—a summary of how much memory is used by our program. It is important to track how much memory we are using to ensure we don't run out of space (as predicted by the Software Gas Law).

5.2.4   Automating the Build Process

The build process is automated in order to save time and developer effort. The build control system tracks dependencies among source files so that changing one file will only result in rebuilding that module, dependent modules, and the final executable image. This speeds up builds significantly. Unix- and Linux-based systems use a program called **make** (and the associated **makefile** which defines dependencies and build actions). IAR Embedded Workbench, like other IDEs, takes care of the build process internally and automatically.

Figure 5.4   Toolbar section for controlling program building process.

Figure 5.4 shows the toolbar with options for building a single source file, building the entire project, and stopping the build process. There are typically other commands available in the project menu. For example, the clean command deletes all intermediate and output files.

5.3   PROGRAM DEBUGGING

A debugger is a software program which we run to manipulate and monitor the execution of the target system's program. It enables us to load a program, control its execution, and monitor its variables. In this section we examine C-Spy, a source-level debugger from IAR Systems which is integrated into Embedded Workbench.

5.3.1   Downloading Programs

Figure 5.5   Toolbar section for downloading the program and starting the debugger.

Figure 5.5 shows the toolbar with options for downloading the program and starting the debugger (solid triangle), or merely starting the debugger without downloading the program (empty triangle).

5.3.2 Examining Programs

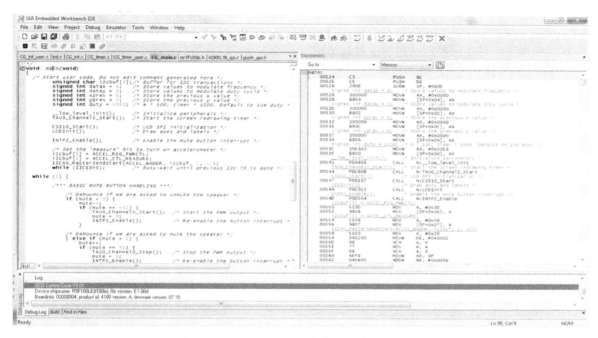

Figure 5.6 Source and object code listing.

Many debuggers can show us both the source-level C program and the disassembled object code, as shown in Figure 5.6. The currently executing statement or instruction is highlighted, allowing us to track the program execution easily. The disassembly view gives us a fine-grain view of precisely what the processor is doing, and sometimes can be quite helpful.

5.3.3 Controlling and Observing Program Execution

Figure 5.7 Toolbar for controlling program execution (when program is stopped).

Figure 5.8 Toolbar for controlling program execution (when program is running).

There are several options available for controlling the program's execution behavior. From left to right in Figure 5.7 and Figure 5.8, the buttons allow us to:

- Reset: Reset the processor and the program.
- Stop: Stop a running program.
- Step Over: Execute code until reaching a step point. If it encounters a function call, then it will step over (execute the entire function) and stop after returning from the function.
- Step Into: Execute code until reaching a step point. If it encounters a function call, it will step down into the function and stop at its first line.
- Step Out: Execute the remaining code in the function and step out of it up to the function which called this function.
- Next Statement: Execute code until reaching the next statement in the source code.
- Run to Cursor: Execute code until reaching the source statement holding the cursor.
- Go: Execute the program until stopped or a breakpoint is reached.

5.3.3.1 Breakpoints

We can set a breakpoint at a specific line in the source code or object code by right-clicking on that line to bring up a context menu. Figure 5.9 shows an example of a breakpoint which has been set in a C source file.

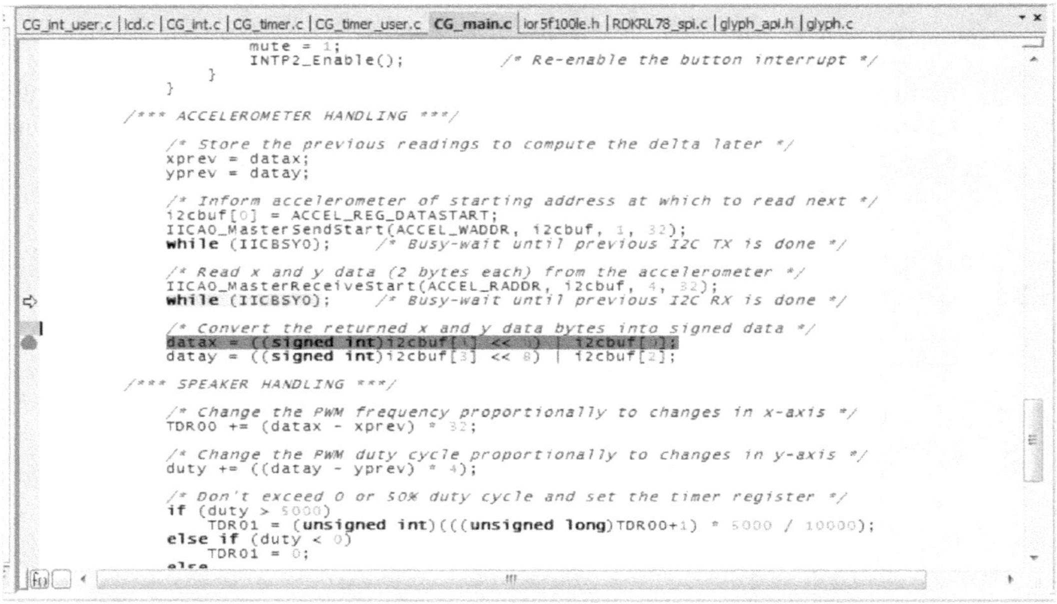

Figure 5.9   Source code window showing next line of code to execute (while . . .) and breakpoint (datax . . .).

5.3.3.2 Call Stack

Figure 5.10 Call stack viewer window.

We can examine the program's current level of subroutine call nesting by using the function call stack viewer window, as shown in Figure 5.10. In this example, the program is executing the C function **LCDDrawIndicator,** which was called by C function **main,** which was called by an instruction at address _MAIN_CALL + 0x3.

5.3.4 Examining and Modifying Data

Being able to examine and even change the value of variables in a program is extremely helpful when debugging a program. For example, Figure 5.11 shows the local variables and arguments in the current function. A variable's value can be changed by selecting it in this window. There are similar windows for examining global variables and specific "watch" variables.

```
Locals                                                     ×

Expressi...  Value      Location          Type
⊟ i2cbuf     "2"        Memory:0xFF832    unsigned char[4]
  ├─ [0]     '2' (0x32) Memory:0xFF832    unsigned char
  ├─ [1]     ' ' (0x00) Memory:0xFF833    unsigned char
  ├─ [2]     'ÿ' (0xFD) Memory:0xFF834    unsigned char
  └─ [3]     'ÿ' (0xFF) Memory:0xFF835    unsigned char
  datax      1          Memory:0xFF830    int
  datay      -3         Memory:0xFF82E    int
  xprev      1          Memory:0xFF838    int
  yprev      -3         Memory:0xFF836    int
  duty       988        Memory:0xFF82C    int
```

Figure 5.11 Local variable viewer window.

At times we may need to see the other contents of the stack. To support this we can examine the stack contents as shown in Figure 5.12. Here we see not only the local variables and arguments, but also space on the stack used for other purposes such as the return address.

This view can be especially helpful when debugging a program which crashes due to corruption of the return address by an out-of-bounds memory access.

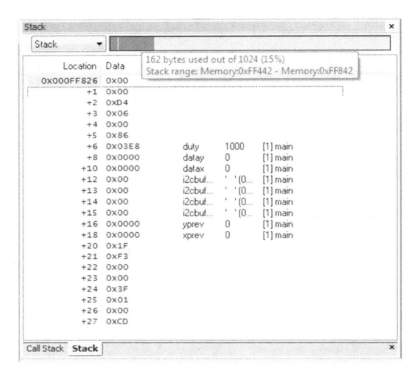

Figure 5.12   Stack viewer window.

Figure 5.12 also shows another useful feature—how much of the allocated stack space is used. Some toolchains include a calculation of maximum possible stack depth. This is helpful because we would like to allocate just enough stack space, but no more. If we don't allocate enough space, then the stack may overflow due to deeply nested subroutine calls and interrupt service routines. This leads to program crashes which are extremely hard to replicate and therefore debug. Allocating too much space means that we waste RAM, which is a limited and therefore valuable resource in microcontrollers.

There are both analytical and experimental methods for estimating maximum stack depth. A practical but unsafe experimental method called high-water marking is as follows:

- Preload the stack space with a known, fixed pattern.
- Run the program through test cases which hopefully trigger maximum stack depth requirements.

- Examine the stack space to see how much of the pattern was overwritten, and calculate the amount of stack space used.
- Multiply the amount of stack space used by a margin of safety (1.3? 1.5?) to try to compensate for the fact that we don't know if our test cases really triggered the worst case.

5.4   SOFTWARE SUPPORT FOR THE RL78

There are various additional types of software support for developers of embedded systems using the RL78 family of microcontrollers.

5.4.1   Header Files for RL78 MCUs

The 'ior5f100le.h' and 'ior5f100le_ext.h' files makes it easier to access the MCU's hardware. They provide symbolic names to access special function registers (SFRs) in the same manner as variables. This makes the code much easier to write and maintain. Each SFR is described as a union (enabling multiple views of the same data, such as one byte or eight bits) which is located in memory at the SFR's address. Symbolic names are assigned for individually addressable bits to further simplify code development. Also, symbolic names are assigned to numeric interrupt vector addresses.

The file 'intrinsics.h' specifies functions which will actually be implemented using specific RL78 instructions such as STOP, HALT, BREAK, NOP, DI, EI, and others.

5.4.2   Code Generator

Some MCU makers and software tool vendors provide code generation tools which simplify the developer's job of writing software for accessing peripherals (device drivers). This device driver code is typically specific to a processor family, so its development is typically quite time-consuming until the coder has mastered the devices. In order to use the code generator, the programmer specifies the peripheral configuration using a graphical user interface and then invokes the "Generate Code" command. The tool creates C code and header files containing software to configure the SFRs as specified graphically. Some tools will also generate access functions, interrupt service routines, and data structures to further simplify the developer's job.

Renesas provides a code generator called Applilet ("Application Leading Tool") for the RL78 family and others as well. Figure 5.13 shows the interface Applilet provides to the developer. The left window pane holds a tree view of the different peripherals which can be configured: system, port, interrupts, serial, A/D, timer, watchdog timer, real-time

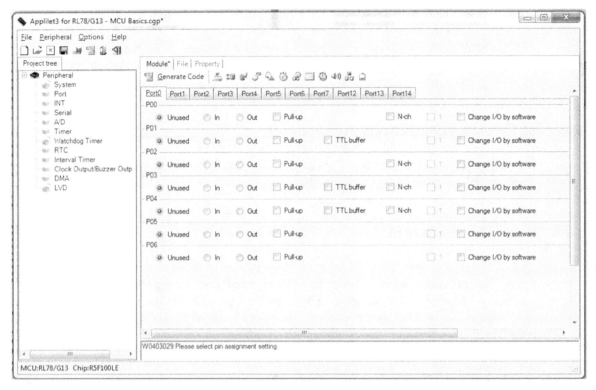

Figure 5.13   Applilet's default port configuration screen.

clock, interval timer, and so on. There are also corresponding icons arranged horizontally in the right pane. The "Generate Code" button allows the user to generate updated code based on the specified settings.

A valuable feature of Applilet is that it provides "round-trip engineering"—you can generate code with Applilet, add in your own code, and read it back into Applilet for further modification without deleting or breaking your additions.

5.4.3   LCD Support and Glyph Library

The RL78 RDK includes a monochrome graphical LCD (liquid crystal display) with a resolution of 96 by 64 pixels. Figure 5.14 shows an overview of the hardware and software components used to control the display. The LCD (at the bottom) is connected to an ST7579 LCD controller/driver IC, which is shown in Figure 5.15. The MCU communicates with the controller IC through serial three-wire communications (SPI).

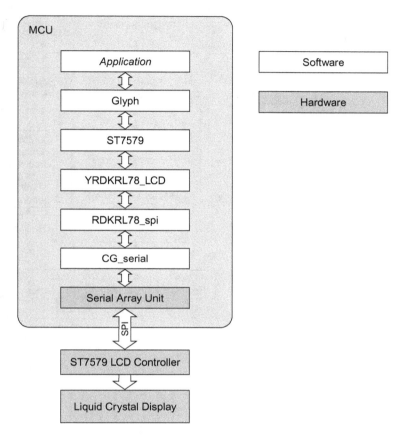

Figure 5.14   Diagram of hardware and software used for displaying text on LCD.

The ST7579 controller IC contains an internal memory buffer (display data RAM) which contains 102 by 68 bits. Each bit is used to determine whether the corresponding LCD pixel is dark or light. The Glyph module converts requests to print text (e.g., GlyphString) into a series of commands to the ST7579 controller to set or clear specific bits in the display data RAM, which then control what is displayed on the LCD.

The serial array unit (SAU) is an on-chip communication peripheral in the RL78 MCU. The CG_serial module is generated by Applilet and it contains functions to configure the SAU to perform SPI communication. The RDKRL78_spi and YRDKRL78_LCD modules provide various translation functions to support the ST7579 software driver module, which accesses the control registers within the controller IC.

Figure 5.16 shows an example with text rendered with large and small fonts using the Glyph API. There are other libraries which can be used to render text and graphics on an LCD, but we examine the Glyph library because it is included with the RL78 RDK.

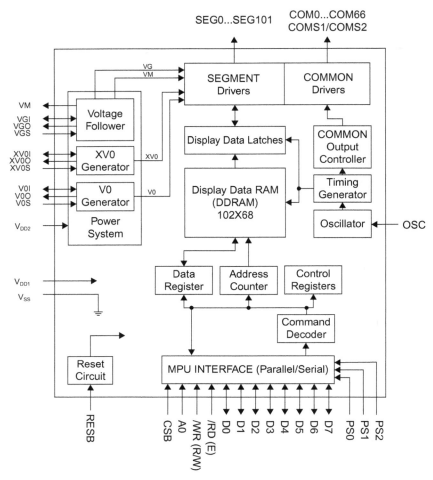

Figure 5.15   Block diagram of ST7579 LCD controller and driver IC.

Figure 5.16   Text rendered on LCD using Glyph API.

```
GlyphOpen()          GlyphSetFont()         GlyphSleep()
GlyphClose()         GlyphGetFont()         GlyphWake()
GlyphWrite()         GlyphSetDrawMode()     GlyphDrawTestPattern()
GlyphRead()          GlyphChar()            GlyphDrawBlock()
GlyphGetStatus()     GlyphString()          GlyphEraseBlock()
GlyphSetX()          GlyphGetVersionInfo()  GlyphSetContrast()
GlyphSetY()          GlyphClearScreen()     GlyphSetContrastBoost()
GlyphSetXY()         GlyphInvertScreen()
GlyphGetXY()         GlyphNormalScreen()
```

Figure 5.17   Summary of Glyph Application Program Interface.

Figure 5.17 shows a summary of the function calls which the Glyph library provides as an interface to the application program. There are functions for configuring the driver and display modes, selecting a font, positioning output, rendering text, drawing rectangles, and other activities.

5.5   RECAP

In this chapter we have learned about the tools and software support used for developing embedded software. The build toolchain translates code from a source language into an executable image to be downloaded into the MCU's memory. The debug tools enable us to control and monitor the execution of the program on the target hardware, preferably while giving a source-level view of the program and its variables. Finally, there are various support files, libraries, and code generation tools available to reduce the time and effort of writing new code.

Chapter Six

C As Implemented in Assembly Language

6.1   LEARNING OBJECTIVES

A compiler generates an assembly language program to perform the work specified by our source level (e.g., C) program. Examining the assembly code generated by the compiler helps us understand what the resulting program is really doing, and gives us insights for various optimizations and debugging.

However, it is very easy to get lost in an assembly code listing, so this chapter seeks to give the reader a basic understanding of how C is implemented in RL78 assembly language by the IAR C Compiler[1] in Embedded Workbench. Other compilers will have different details, but the concepts remain the same.

6.2   MOTIVATION

Programmers who use high-level languages[2] such as C, C++, and Java live in a make-believe world. Meaningful names for functions and variables! All the memory you could ask for! So many data types! Integers, floating point math operations (single and double precision)! So many data structures! Arrays, lists, trees, sets, dictionaries! So many control structures! Subroutines, if/then/else conditions, loops, break, and continue statements! Iterators! Polymorphism! Exception handlers with try/catch blocks!

The processor lives in the reality of its native machine language. Each memory location has its own numerical address, rather than a meaningful name. Like most embedded processors, an RL78 processor only understands how to process integers, not floating point values or even characters. It can copy data, add, subtract, multiply, divide, shift, rotate, swap, compare, and jump to a new location in the program. We rely upon a compiler and other parts of the toolchain shown in Figure 6.1 to translate from our make-believe world

---

[1] Note that there is a trade-off between code readability and optimization. We have disabled some compiler optimizations in order to make the assembly code more intelligible. When creating production code the developer would enable the optimizations in order to improve performance.

[2] Some developers may claim that C is not a high-level language, but the authors would suggest these developers try programming in assembly language for perspective.

to the reality of the processor. In this chapter we examine what assembly code the compiler generates to perform the work specified by our C source code.

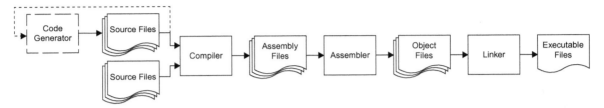

Figure 6.1   Overview of software compilation process for a C program.

6.3   WHAT MEMORY DOES A PROGRAM NEED?

```
1. int a, b;
2. const char c = 123;
3. int d = 31;
4. void main(void) {
5.     int e;
6.     e = d + 7;
7.     a = e + 29999;
8.     printf("Hello!");
9. }
```

Consider the C source code of the program fragment listed above. After it is compiled to an executable image it will contain instructions and data. It will use the microcontroller's memory various ways, so it needs different types. We are concerned with two major aspects of the information.

- ▦   Can it change as the program executes?
- ▦   How long does it need to exist?

6.3.1   Can the Information Change?

Some of the memory will contain **values which can never change as the program runs.** These go into read-only, non-volatile memory:

- ▦   Program instructions,[3] such as those to add seven to d and save the result in e's location.

---

[3] This excludes self-modifying code.

- Constant character strings ("Hello!") and constant data variables (c).
- Constant operands which are represented as immediate data values in an instruction (7, 29999).
- Data values for initializing variables (31).

Other memory will contain **values which may change as the program runs.** These go into RAM, which is read/write memory.

- Variables (a, b, d, e);
- Other information which is needed at run time (e.g., intermediate computations, return address for a subroutine, function arguments).

More information is available in the Segment Reference of the C Compiler Manual.

6.3.2   How Long Does the Information Exist?

We need to differentiate between instructions and data, as they are used differently.
How long does the **program instruction** exist?

- In **statically-linked** programs all needed functions are present for the entire execution of the program. For the RL78 and many other microcontroller families, this is the norm.
- General-purpose operating systems and some embedded operating systems support **dynamically-linked** programs to allow code modules to be loaded and unloaded as needed. This reduces memory requirements and provides other benefits at the expense of greater operating system and software toolchain complexity.

How long does the **data** exist? There are three common **storage classes** of data, classified by **lifetime:**

- **Statically allocated** data (also called **static**) exists as long as the program is running. Each variable has its own permanent location in memory.
- **Automatically allocated** data (also called **automatic**) exists only as long as the procedure which declared it exists. There is no space allocated for the data before the procedure begins execution, or after the procedure completes execution.
- **Dynamically allocated** data exists from when it is explicitly created to when it is explicitly destroyed.

One could write a program where all data is static, but this would waste a tremendous amount of memory. Instead, high-level languages **reuse memory.** The system's memory is divided into up to three sections: one for static data, one for the call stack, and one for the memory heap.

Automatic data is called that because space is **automatically allocated** in the **call stack** by the program upon beginning the procedure and **automatically deallocated** upon completing the procedure. **Dynamically allocated memory** is handled by the programmer through calls to allocate and deallocate memory from the **heap.**

6.3.3 Example of Memory Allocation

Now we are ready to see how the program listed above uses memory. The details are shown in Figure 6.2.

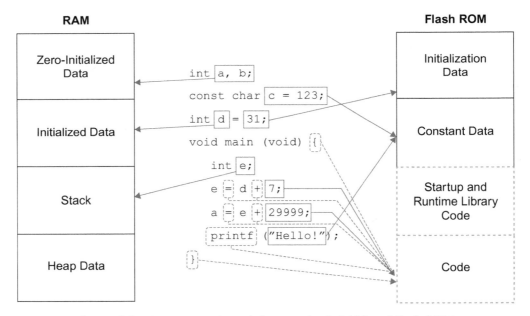

Figure 6.2 Program code and data use both RAM and flash ROM.

- Variables a and b are static, so each is given its own fixed location in RAM. Since they are not given initial values in the C program, they are allocated in the zero-initalized data section. Later we will see that the C run-time start-up module takes care of copying this data.
- Variable d is static, so it is given its own fixed location in RAM. It is given an initial value of 31, which is stored in ROM in the initialization data section. Later we will see that the C run-time start-up module takes care of copying this data.

- Variable e is declared in a function, so it is an automatic variable. It will only exist while the function main exists. The compiler will generate code to allocate and deallocate its space in the stack as the function main begins ({) and ends (}). Of course, this code is placed in the code section of ROM.
- Instructions for the additions and storing the results in variables are located in the code section of flash ROM.
- The literal values 7 and 29999 are encoded as immediate operands which are part of the RL78 machine instructions. Hence they are stored in the code section of flash ROM.
- The instructions for calling the **printf** subroutine (and instructions for the **printf** subroutine itself) are stored in the code section flash ROM.
- The string literal "Hello!" is stored in the constant data section of flash ROM.
- If we dynamically allocated memory with **malloc** or **calloc** it would be located in the heap data section of RAM.

6.3.4   Type and Class Qualifiers

The automatic classifications of data provided above are usually just what we need, but sometimes we need to provide a bit more information to the compiler so it generates better code. Other times, we wish to specify that variables must be handled carefully during optimization to ensure correct program behavior. There are several keywords we can use to modify the variable types (**const, volatile**) and storage class (**static**).

6.3.4.1 Const

A **const** variable is never written by the program. It is only read by the program. Marking a variable as const may enable the compiler to place it in ROM, saving space in valuable RAM. Some compilers are able to determine if variables are actually consts, but using this qualifier guarantees the variable will be handled as a const.

6.3.4.2 Volatile

A **volatile** variable can be changed by something outside of normal program flow. For example, an ISR could change the variable, or this could actually be a hardware register which changes in response to external signals. Compilers treat volatile variables carefully, disabling optimizations which could lead to not getting the latest version of the variable.

6.3.4.3 Static

A **static** variable which is declared within a function is only visible within the function in which it is declared (like an automatic variable), but it retains its value from one invocation to the next (like a static variable). If the variable is initialized, that initialization only occurs the first time the function executes. After that the static variable retains its most recent value.

6.3.5   Program Linking

The last tool in the toolchain of Figure 6.1 is the linker. It combines all of the necessary object files to create an executable file image which can be downloaded into the MCU's flash memory. The linker takes care of arranging data in memory and resolving addresses. The linker creates an output file called a map file to describe each compilation module's memory requirements and allocations, along with other detailed information. We will examine this map file in the chapter on speed optimization. We can access this file in IAR Embedded Workbench as shown in Figure 6.3.

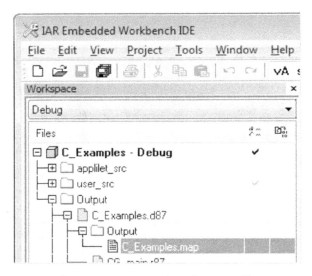

Figure 6.3   Accessing the map file.

```
7 303 bytes of CODE  memory
1 857 bytes of DATA  memory (+ 104 absolute )
1 747 bytes of CONST memory
```

Figure 6.4   Map file summary of memory requirements.

A very useful part of the map file (located at the end) is the summary of the memory requirements, grouped into CODE and CONST (which are located in Flash ROM) and DATA (which is located in RAM). In the example of Figure 6.4, we see that the program requires 1857 bytes of RAM and 7303 + 1747 = 9050 bytes of Flash ROM.

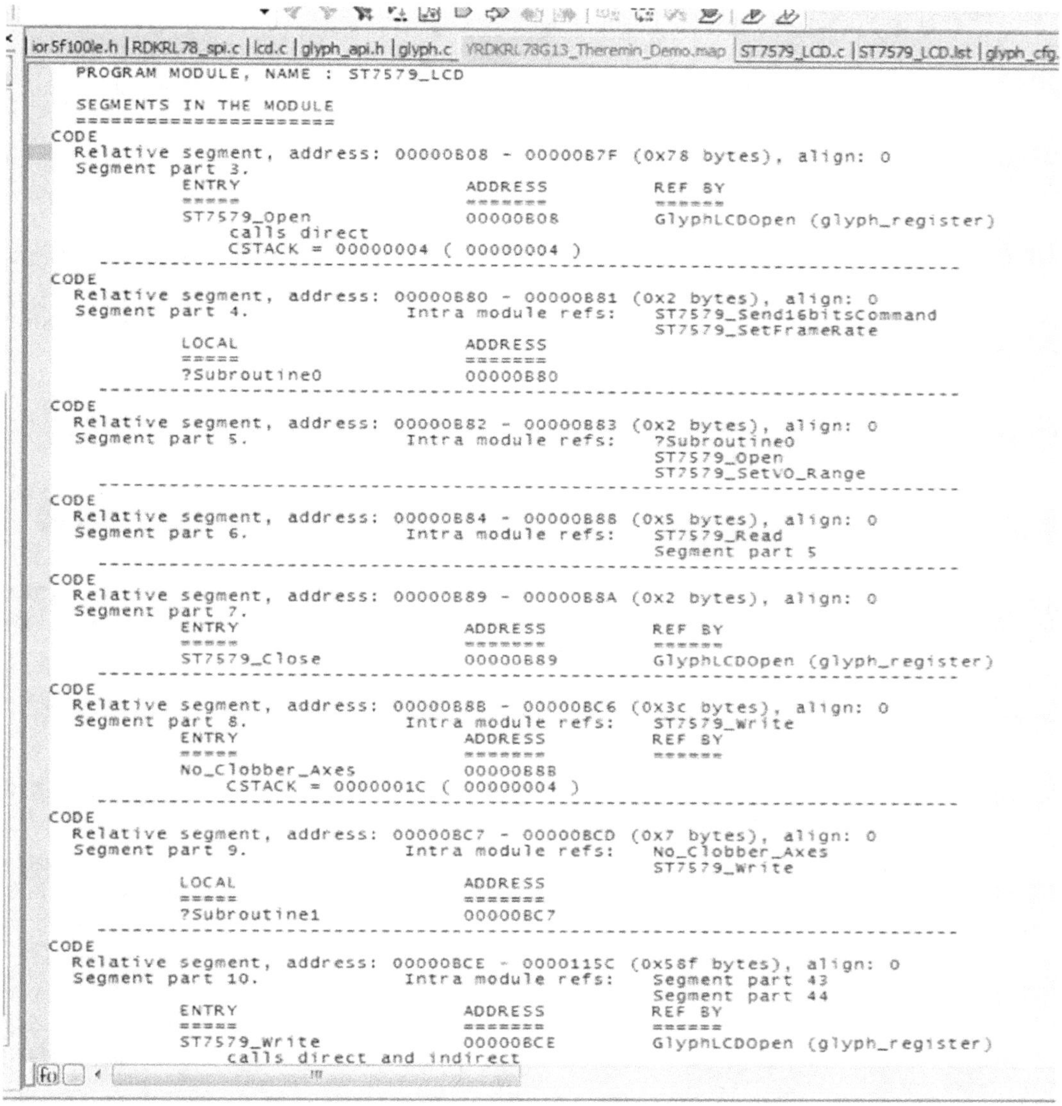


```
    PROGRAM MODULE, NAME : ST7579_LCD

    SEGMENTS IN THE MODULE
    ======================
  CODE
    Relative segment, address: 00000808 - 0000087F (0x78 bytes), align: 0
    Segment part 3.
              ENTRY                    ADDRESS               REF BY
              =====                    =======               ======
              ST7579_Open              00000808              GlyphLCDOpen (glyph_register)
                  calls direct
                  CSTACK = 00000004 ( 00000004 )
    ---------------------------------------------------------------------------
  CODE
    Relative segment, address: 00000880 - 00000881 (0x2 bytes), align: 0
    Segment part 4.              Intra module refs:    ST7579_Send16bitsCommand
                                                       ST7579_SetFrameRate
              LOCAL                    ADDRESS
              =====                    =======
              ?Subroutine0             00000880
    ---------------------------------------------------------------------------
  CODE
    Relative segment, address: 00000882 - 00000883 (0x2 bytes), align: 0
    Segment part 5.              Intra module refs:    ?Subroutine0
                                                       ST7579_Open
                                                       ST7579_SetVO_Range
    ---------------------------------------------------------------------------
  CODE
    Relative segment, address: 00000884 - 00000888 (0x5 bytes), align: 0
    Segment part 6.              Intra module refs:    ST7579_Read
                                                       Segment part 5
    ---------------------------------------------------------------------------
  CODE
    Relative segment, address: 00000889 - 0000088A (0x2 bytes), align: 0
    Segment part 7.
              ENTRY                    ADDRESS               REF BY
              =====                    =======               ======
              ST7579_Close             00000889              GlyphLCDOpen (glyph_register)
    ---------------------------------------------------------------------------
  CODE
    Relative segment, address: 0000088B - 00000BC6 (0x3c bytes), align: 0
    Segment part 8.              Intra module refs:    ST7579_Write
              ENTRY                    ADDRESS               REF BY
              =====                    =======               ======
              No_Clobber_Axes          0000088B
                  CSTACK = 0000001C ( 00000004 )
    ---------------------------------------------------------------------------
  CODE
    Relative segment, address: 00000BC7 - 00000BCD (0x7 bytes), align: 0
    Segment part 9.              Intra module refs:    No_Clobber_Axes
                                                       ST7579_Write
              LOCAL                    ADDRESS
              =====                    =======
              ?Subroutine1             00000BC7
    ---------------------------------------------------------------------------
  CODE
    Relative segment, address: 00000BCE - 0000115C (0x58f bytes), align: 0
    Segment part 10.             Intra module refs:    Segment part 43
                                                       Segment part 44
              ENTRY                    ADDRESS               REF BY
              =====                    =======               ======
              ST7579_Write             00000BCE              GlyphLCDOpen (glyph_register)
                  calls direct and indirect
```

Figure 6.5 Map file example for module ST7579_LCD.

If a program uses too much memory, first the compiler's options should be set to optimize for size. If the resulting program is still too large, the next step is to examine the contents of the map file to determine which modules use the most space. We will get the biggest payoff if we start optimizing the largest functions.

For example, Figure 6.5 shows a portion of the map file for the program YRKDRL78G13_Theremin_Demo, and specifically for the module ST7579_LCD. We see that the function ST7579 has a code segment starting at 0x0808 and ending at 0x087F. Its length is 0x78 bytes (120 bytes). By examining the map file (preferably by processing it with an automated tool) we can determine which modules require the most memory.

6.3.6   C Run-Time Start-Up Module

When the processor is first turned on it will start executing the code at a fixed address defined by the reset vector. The code in your **main** function cannot run immediately, as the hardware and the C run-time environment need to be set up. The **start-up module** performs these initialization tasks and then calls the **main** function.

6.3.6.1   *Initialize Hardware*

The stack pointer is initialized to ensure that the processor is able to use the stack to call and return from subroutine and ISRs, and save and restore data. The stack space may also be initialized to a fixed pattern to simplify later debugging and stack size measurement. Some user-defined basic microcontroller configuration may also be performed with a customizable _low_level_init function. This function runs very early in system start-up.

6.3.6.2   *Initialize C or C++ Run-Time Environment*

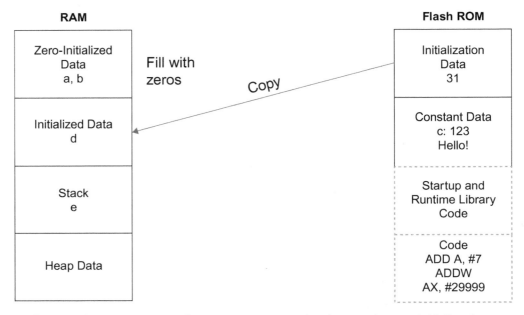

Figure 6.6   C start-up routine zeroes out or copies data sections to initialize them.

Consider the following global static variable declaration "int d = 31;". This variable will be allocated space in RAM. When the MCU comes out of reset, the RAM contents could be anything. The program expects variable d to be initialized to a value of 5, so something needs to make that happen. In addition, the standards for the C and C++ programming languages define that static variables without program-specified initial values (e.g., a, b, c) must be be initialized to zero. To ensure this, the start-up code needs to perform the following steps, as illustrated in Figure 6.6:

- Copy the initial values of initialized static variables from ROM into RAM.
- Write zeroes to uninitialized static variables.

There are other run-time initializations which may need to be performed. Heap memory must be initialized. If a C++ program is compiled, then static objects need to be constructed, so their constructors must be called. After these initializations are performed, the start-up routine calls the main function as a subroutine.

6.4   ACCESSING DATA

Let's take a look at some of the assembly code generated for the C code for accessing static and automatic variables and dereferencing pointers. We follow a variable naming convention for clarity; s and a indicate static or automatic, and i and p indicate integer or pointer.

```
 1. int siA;
 2.
 3. void static_auto_local() {
 4.     int aiB;
 5.     static int siC = 3;
 6.     int * apD;
 7.     int aiE = 4, aiF = 5, aiG = 6;
 8.
 9.     siA = 2;
10.     aiB = siC + siA;
11.     apD = &aiB;
12.     (*apD)++;
13.     apD = &siC;
14.     (*apD) += 9;
15.     apD = &siA;
16.     apD = &aiE;
17.     apD = &aiF;
18.     apD = &aiG;
```

```
19.     (*apD)++;
20.     aiE += 7;
21.     *apD = aiE + aiF;
22. }
```

6.4.1   Static Variables

Static variables have fixed addresses. The RL78 addressing modes which support this include direct addressing. There are different direct addressing modes (short, register, or extended) depending on how much of the address needs to be specified in the instruction. The compiler and linker try to place variables so that the resulting code will use the shortest and fastest addressing mode.

```
1. //   16   siA = 2;
2.            MOVW       AX, #0x2
3.            MOVW       N:siA, AX
4. //   17   aiB = siC + siA;
5.            MOVW       AX, N:??siC
6.            ADDW       AX, N:siA
```

In our example, variables siA and siC are static. We see that they are referenced with direct addressing in the assembly code by using their labels with some prefixes (N:??C_static_local, N:A_static). The assembler and linker convert these labels to numerical addresses. N: indicates that near data memory model is to be used.

6.4.2   Automatic Variables

Automatic variables may be located in registers or on the stack. If located on the stack, they can be accessed based on an offset from the stack pointer. As shown in Figure 6.7, the RL78 architecture has a based addressing mode which adds the SP with an unsigned byte offset to create the target address in the range F0000H to FFFFFFH. The maximum offset is 255, so this limits the stack frame size which can be accessed efficiently. Supporting a larger stack frame would require additional address calculation operations. Later in this chapter we discuss the other information which is also located in the stack frame. This information may also be accessed with this addressing mode.

```
1.            ; Auto size: 8
2.            SUBW       SP, #0x8
3. //   11   int aiB;
```

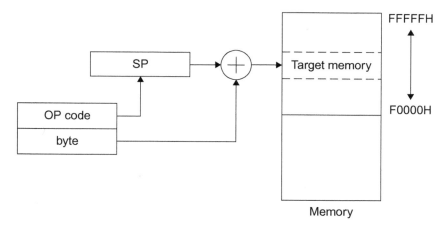

Figure 6.7   Automatic variables are located on the stack and accessed using the stack pointer register.

```
 4. //   12    static int siC = 3;
 5. //   13    int * apD;
 6. //   14    int aiE = 4, aiF = 5, aiG = 6;
 7.            MOVW      AX, #0x4
 8.            MOVW      [SP], AX
 9.            MOVW      AX, #0x5
10.            MOVW      [SP + 0x02], AX
11.            MOVW      AX, #0x6
12.            MOVW      [SP + 0x04], AX
    ...
13. //   17    aiB = siC + siA;
    ...
14.            MOVW      [SP + 0x06], AX
```

In our example, variables aiB, apD, aiE, aiF, and aiG are automatics. Eight bytes of space are allocated on the stack for them in line 2. The variables are allocated one word each: aiB at SP + 6, aiG at SP + 4, aiF at SP + 2, and aiE at SP. What happened to apD? Was it allocated any space on the stack? This is left as a homework problem.

6.4.3   Manipulating and Dereferencing Pointers

A pointer is simply a variable which holds the address of the data we wish to access. In our example, apD is a pointer to an integer.

```
1. //   18    apD = & aiB;
2.           MOVW      AX, SP
3.           ADDW      AX, #0x6
4.           MOVW      HL, AX
5. //   19    (*apD)++;
6.           MOVW      AX, [HL]
7.           INCW      AX
8.           MOVW      [HL], AX
9. //   20    apD = &siC;
10.          MOVW      HL, #??siC
11. //  21    (*apD) += 9;
12.          MOVW      AX, [HL]
13.          ADDW      AX, #0x9
14.          MOVW      [HL], AX
        . . .
```

- Addressing an automatic variable aiB in lines 2 through 4 involves adding an offset and the stack pointer to form the target address.
- Incrementing automatic variable aiB in lines 6 through 8 involves loading the AX register with the value from memory, incrementing it, and saving it back to memory. Why doesn't this use the form INCW [HL]? Is it due to a low setting for compiler optimizations, or is there a different reason? This is left as a homework question.
- Addressing a static variable siC in line 9 involves simply loading the address as an immediate operand.
- Adding nine to the variable involves loading the AX register with the value from memory, adding nine, and saving the result. Note that there is no instruction ADDW [HL], #9—all additions must use the AX register, as it is the accumulator.

6.4.4 Accessing Arrays

In order to understand how both one- and two-dimensional arrays are accessed, we examine the following C function:

```
1. void arrays(unsigned char n, unsigned char j) {
2.    volatile int i;
3.    i = buff2[0] + buff2[n];
4.    i += buff3[n][j];
5. }
```

6.4.4.1 1-Dimensional Arrays

ADDRESS	CONTENTS
buff2	buff2[0]
buff2 + 1	buff2[1]
buff2 + 2	buff2[2]

Figure 6.8 Memory layout of char buff2[3].

To access element number i of a one-dimensional array, we need to calculate the address of the element. This address is the sum of two parts:

- The start of the array, which can be referred to by the array name.
- The offset, which is calculated by multiplying the index i by the element size. In an array of chars, each element is one byte long. In an array of floats, each element is four bytes long.

```
    . . .
1.              MOV     C, A
    . . .
2. //    60     i = buff2[0] + buff2[n];
3.              MOV     A, (buff2 & 0xFFFF)[C]
4.              MOV     L, A
5.              MOV     A, N:buff2
6.              MOV     H, #0x0
7.              MOV     X, A
8.              CLRB    A
9.              ADDW    AX, HL
```

In this code we are adding two different elements of the array: buff2[0] and buff2[n].

- The second term (buff2[n]) is located at address buff2 + element_size*n. As this is an array of chars, each element is one byte, so we do not need to multiply n and the equation simplifies to buff2 + n. The function is passed the value of n as an argument through register A. Line 1 in the listing copies it to register C to save it. Line 3 computes the address of element n by using based addressing to add C to the start of the array (buff2 & 0xFFFF) to form the address. The byte at memory location C + (buff2 & 0xFFFF) is read and loaded into register A. Line 4 saves this byte in register L, since A will be used for other purposes. Note that the variable i, which is assigned the result of the addition, is an int (16 bits long). The type promotion rules of C state that we must promote each term from char to int before addition. So, line 6 loads register H with zero, so the register pair HL contains the 16-bit integer value promoted from buff2[n].

- The first term (buff2[0]) is always at address buff2. The offset is zero, since we are accessing element 0. Line 5 loads register A with the byte at memory location buff2 using near absolute addressing. Line 7 moves A's value to register X, which is the low byte of the AX register pair. Line 8 loads register A with 0, completing the promotion to a 16-bit integer.

- Now that AX holds the value of buff2[0] and HL holds the value of buff2[n] we can add them, using the ADDW instruction of line 9. The result is in register pair AX.

6.4.4.2 2-Dimensional Arrays

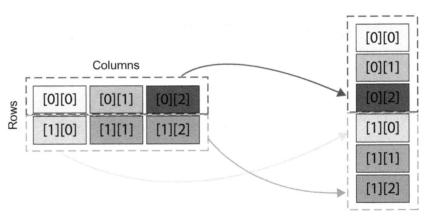

Figure 6.9 A generic 2-dimensional array as laid out in memory.

In C, two dimensional arrays are laid out in memory in a row-major form, which means that each row is stored contiguously, as shown in Figure 6.9. The first element is stored beginning at the smallest address. We can look at a specific example—the array declared by int buff3[5][7] is shown in Figure 6.10. Each element is 2 bytes long since the base type is int. There are five rows and seven columns, so a total of 2 * 5 * 7 = 70 bytes are needed to hold the array.

ADDRESS	CONTENTS
buff3	buff3[0][0]
buff3+1	
buff3+2	buff3[0][1]
buff3+3	
(etc.)	
buff3+10	buff3[0][5]
buff3+11	
buff3+12	buff3[0][6]
buff3+13	
buff3+14	buff3[1][0]
buff3+15	
buff3+16	buff3[1][1]
buff3+17	
buff3+18	buff3[1][2]
buff3+19	
(etc.)	
buff3+68	buff3[4][6]
buff3+69	

Figure 6.10 Memory layout for array int buff3[5][7].

Accessing an element of a two-dimensional array is similar to the one-dimensional case, but there are two offsets—one from the row index and another from the column index. The column offset calculation is the same as above. The row offset is calculated by multiplying the row index by the size of a row in bytes, which is the number of columns times the element size in bytes. Let's examine the code the compiler generates to access buff3, and let's assume $n = 1$ and $j = 4$.

```
1. //    61   i += buff3[n][j];
2.           MOV    D, #0x0
3.           MOVW   [SP], AX
4.           MOVW   AX, DE
```

```
 5.          ADDW       AX, AX
 6.          MOVW       DE, AX
 7.          MOV        A, C
 8.          MOV        X, A
 9.          CLRB       A
10.          MOVW       BC, #0xE
11.          ; * Stack frame (at entry) *
12.          ; Param size: 0
13.          ; Auto size: 2
14.          CALL       N:?I_MUL_L02
15.          ADDW       AX, #buff3
16.          ADDW       AX, DE
17.          MOVW       HL, AX
18.          MOVW       AX, [HL]
19.          MOVW       HL, AX
20.          MOVW       AX, [SP]
21.          ADDW       AX, HL
22.          MOVW       [SP], AX
```

The column offset is calculated as follows:

- Line 3 saves the result of the previous calculation (buff2[0]+buff2[n]) in temporary storage on stack.
- Lines 2 and 4 extend j (stored initially in register E) to 16 bits and puts the result in register AX.
- Line 5 calculates the byte offset for the column index. It adds AX to AX (multiplying it by two) since each element in this array is a 2-byte long integer.
- Line 6 saves this offset in register DE. If j is four, then the column offset will be $2 * 4 = 8$.

The row offset is calculated as follows:

- Lines 7 through 9 extend the row index n (stored initially in C) to a 16-bit value stored in AX.
- Line 14 calls a subroutine to multiply n by the row length in bytes (14, or 0x0E) to find the row offset in bytes. If n is 1, then the row offset will be $1 * 14 = 14$.

The addresses are now added together to find the address of buff3[n][j]:

- Line 15 adds the array's base address to the row offset.
- Line 16 adds in the column offset to create the complete address. The resulting address is buff3+14+8 = buff3+22.

- Lines 17 and 18 use register pair HL to access the array element and place it in AX.
- Line 19 moves the array element to HL, freeing up AX for use.
- Line 20 reloads AX with the result of the previous calculation (saved in line 3).
- Line 21 adds AX and HL, performing the $+=$ operation of the C source code.
- Line 22 saves the result on the stack.

6.5   FUNCTIONS

We have seen some of the code generated for the array-referencing function **arrays()**, but not all of it. The compiler generates the following RL78 assembly code **prologue** before (lines 1–8) and **epilogue** after (lines 9–13) the listings of the previous section:

```
1. //    53 void arrays(unsigned char n, unsigned char j) {
2.          arrays:
3.          PUSH      BC
4.          PUSH      DE
5.          MOV       C, A
6.          PUSH      AX
7.          MOV       A, B
8.          MOV       E, A
   ... (body deleted)
9. //    62 }
10.         ADDW      SP, #0x2
11.         POP       DE
12.         POP       BC
13.         RET
```

This code handles other "housekeeping" activities which are needed to make the function operate correctly:

- Sharing general purpose registers
- Handling function arguments and return values
- Allocating temporary storage space on the stack
- Returning control to the calling function

6.5.1   Activation Records

Some of these housekeeping activities need space to store information while the function executes. The compiler generates code to create an **activation record** to hold information about each active function. It is created in part by both the calling function and the function's prologue.

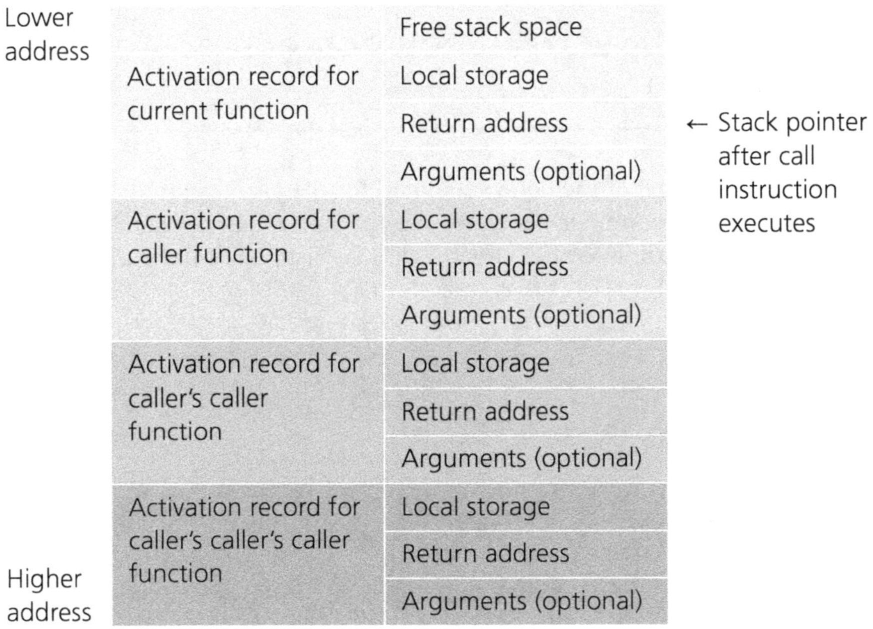

Figure 6.11 A function's activation record or stack frame.

Let's examine the prologue and epilogue to see how they create and delete the activation record for the function **arrays().** Lines 1 through 8 are the prologue, while lines 9 through 13 are the epilogue.

The function's activation record looks like the chart in Figure 6.12 as the prologue executes:

- Line 1 is a comment showing the original C source code.
- Line 2 is a label which marks the beginning of the code for the function.
- Lines 3 and 4 save register pairs BC and DE onto the stack (with PUSH instructions); they are restored by the corresponding POP instructions in lines 12 and 11, respectively.
- Lines 5 through 8 process the function arguments n and j. Register A holds argument n, while register B holds argument j. Line 6 saves register pair AX on the

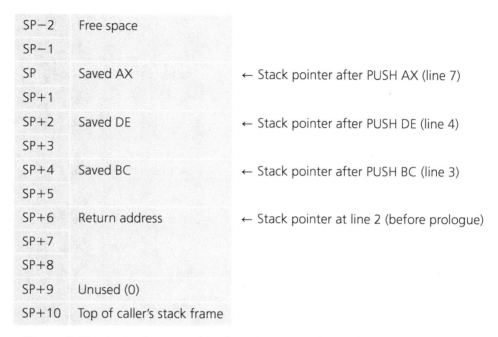

SP−2	Free space	
SP−1		
SP	Saved AX	← Stack pointer after PUSH AX (line 7)
SP+1		
SP+2	Saved DE	← Stack pointer after PUSH DE (line 4)
SP+3		
SP+4	Saved BC	← Stack pointer after PUSH BC (line 3)
SP+5		
SP+6	Return address	← Stack pointer at line 2 (before prologue)
SP+7		
SP+8		
SP+9	Unused (0)	
SP+10	Top of caller's stack frame	

Figure 6.12   Activation record for function "arrays" while executing prologue.

stack because register A will be used later in multiple places and modified (for indexing buff2 and buff3). Lines 5, 7, and 8 move the arguments to other registers for temporary storage.

Note that the byte at SP + 9 is not used. This is because the stack is only word-addressable, so the CALL instruction must use 32 bits to save the 20-bit program counter value.

Now let's look at the epilogue, which needs to restore the stack pointer to its original value so that the RET instruction pops the correct information off the stack to return to the calling function.

The function's activation record looks like the chart in Figure 6.13 as the epilogue executes:

- Line 10 adds 2 to the stack pointer, deallocating the space used to save AX since the function does not need it anymore.
- Lines 11 and 12 pop values off the stack to restore the DE and BC registers.
- Finally, line 13 is a return from subroutine address which pops the program counter from the stack to resume execution in the calling function.

SP−2	Free space	
SP−1		
SP	Saved AX	← Stack pointer before line 10
SP+1		
SP+2	Saved DE	← Stack pointer after ADDW SP, #02 (line 10)
SP+3		
SP+4	Saved BC	← Stack pointer after POP DE (line 11)
SP+5		
SP+6	Return address	← Stack pointer after POP BC (line 12)
SP+7		
SP+8		
SP+9	Unused (0)	
SP+10	Top of caller's stack frame	

Figure 6.13 Activation record for function "arrays" while executing epilogue.

6.5.2 Register Use Conventions

Notice that various registers were saved and restored in this code. There are certain rules which the compiler follows in order to create its code which is modular, isolated, and easily composed into a program without requiring excessive analysis. One such set of rules deals with how general-purpose and segment registers are used (A, B, C, D, E, H, L, X, CS, ES).

- Can a called function modify a register without restoring its value? If so, then the calling function must save that register (typically on the stack) before calling the function.
- Must a called function save and restore any register it uses? If so, then the calling function does not need to save any registers.

Typically some registers are specified in each category. For the IAR EW C compiler, a function can use **scratch** registers without saving them beforehand (AX, HL, CS, ES). A function must save and restore the **preserved** registers: BC, DE.

6.5.3 Calling Subroutines

In order to call a subroutine, the calling subroutine must specify the function arguments (if any) and then execute the CALL instruction (which saves the return address, which indicates the instruction following the CALL instruction).

How does a function pass arguments to subroutines—where should the arguments be placed? There are multiple possible solutions.

- Using fixed (i.e., static) memory locations per function argument prevents recursion.
- Using stack memory supports recursion but, memory accesses are slower than register access.
- Using registers is faster than memory, but recursion requires saving and restoring registers from the stack.

The compiler tries to use registers rather than the stack to pass arguments to subroutines, as this is faster. Some arguments are always passed on the stack: structures, unions and classes, except for those 1, 2, or 4 bytes long. Functions with unnamed arguments are also passed on the stack.

TABLE 6.1 Locations of Function Arguments.

ARGUMENT SIZE	REGISTERS USED FOR PASSING
8 bits	A, B, C, X, D, E
16 bits	AX, BC, DE
24 bits	Stack
32 bits	BC:AX
Larger	Stack

Registers are assigned by traversing the argument list from left to right. The stack pointer points to the first argument, and the remaining arguments at higher addresses. All objects on the stack are word-aligned (the address is a multiple of two), so single byte objects will take up two bytes. Arguments larger than 32 bits are passed on the stack.

After placing all arguments in registers or on the stack, the calling function will execute a CALL instruction, which pushes the return address (the address of the next instruction after the call) onto the stack.

6.5.4   Returning Results

Some functions return a result. How is this information passed back to the calling function? Again, registers are used if possible; otherwise the stack is used.

TABLE 6.2   Location of Function Return Value

RETURN VALUE SIZE	REGISTERS USED FOR PASSING
8 bits	A
16 bits	AX
24 bits	A:HL
32 bits	BC:AX
Larger	Stack

6.5.5   Example of Passing Arguments and Returning Results

Let's take a look at how arguments are passed to functions and results are returned.

```
1. int fun3(int arg3_1, int arg3_2, int arg3_3, int arg3_4) {
2.    return arg3_1*arg3_2*arg3_3*arg3_4;
3. }
4.
5. int fun2(int arg2_1, int arg2_2) {
6.    int i;
7.    arg2_2 += fun3(arg2_1, 4, 5, 6);
8.    return arg2_2;
9. }
```

The C code above shows fun2 calling fun3 with four arguments. The relevant RL78 assembly code appears below:

```
1. //    82    int fun2(int arg2_1, int arg2_2) {
2.          fun2:
3.          PUSH      AX
4.          PUSH      BC
5. ...
6. //    88    arg2_2 += fun3(arg2_1, 4, 5, 6);
7. ??fun1_8:
```

```
 8.            MOVW      AX, #0x6
 9.            PUSH      AX
10.            MOVW      DE, #0x5
11.            MOVW      BC, #0x4
12.            MOVW      AX, [SP + 0x04]
13.            CALL      fun3
14.            MOVW      HL, AX
15.            MOVW      AX, [SP]
16.            ADDW      AX, HL
17.            MOVW      [SP], AX
18. ...
```

SP	Return address	← Stack pointer before line 3	AX	arg2_1
SP+1			BC	arg2_2
SP+2			DE	
SP+3			HL	

Figure 6.14   Stack and registers on entry to fun2.

Figure 6.14 shows the stack and registers upon entry to fun2. Argument arg2_1 is in register AX and argument arg2_2 is in BC, and the return address is on the top of the stack.

SP	arg2_2	← Stack pointer before line 8		
SP+1				
SP+2	arg2_1			
SP+3				
SP+4	Return address		AX	arg2_1
SP+5			BC	arg2_2
SP+6			DE	
SP+7			HL	

Figure 6.15   Stack and registers after saving arg2_1 and arg2_2.

Figure 6.15 shows that lines 3 and 4 have pushed arguments arg2_1 (passed in AX) and arg2_2 (passed in BC) onto the stack so the registers can be used for other purposes, and to save the original values of the arguments.

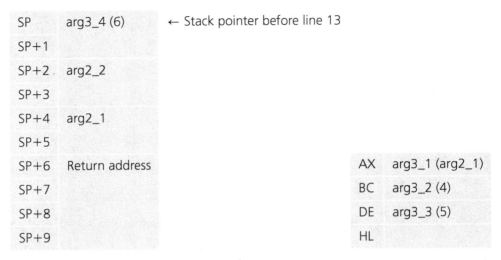

Figure 6.16   Stack and registers loaded with arguments to fun3, ready to execute CALL fun3.

Figure 6.16 shows the stack and registers as they have been prepared by lines 8 through 12 before calling subroutine fun3.

- Lines 8 and 9 create and push argument arg3_4 (with a value of 6) onto the stack.
- Line 10 loads argument arg3_3 (with a value of 5) into register DE.
- Line11 loads argument arg3_2 (with a value of 4) into register BC.
- Line 12 loads argument arg3_1 (which is arg2_1, which was saved on the stack in line 2) from the stack into register AX.
- Line 13 calls the subroutine fun3.

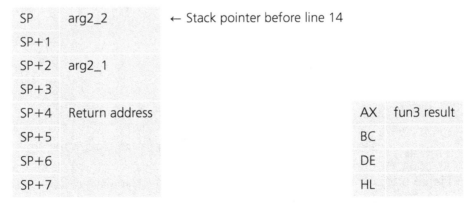

Figure 6.17   Stack and registers after return from subroutine fun3.

After subroutine fun3 returns, note that it has adjusted the stack pointer to remove argument arg3_4 from the stack. The stack pointer is now pointing to arg2_2 again, ready for line 15.

- Line 14 copies the result returned from fun3 from register AX into register HL.
- Line 15 copies the value of arg2_2 (which was saved onto the stack in line 4) to register AX.
- Line 16 adds arg2_2 and the result of fun3.
- Line 17 saves the sum on the stack in the location for arg2_2.
- Note that line 16 ensures that the return value for fun2 is located in register AX (the correct location for returning a 16-bit result).

6.6   CONTROL STRUCTURES

A program's **control flow** describes which instructions are executed. Normal control flow is sequential; the processor will step sequentially through the instructions in memory. Instructions such as jumps, branches, calls, and returns change the control flow. We have already examined subroutine calls and returns, so let's examine selection and iteration.

6.6.1   Selection

C provides two mechanisms for selecting one of multiple possible control flows: the if/else and the switch statements.

6.6.1.1   If/Else

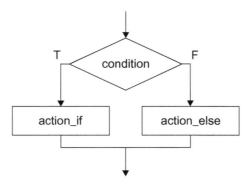

Figure 6.18   If/Else statement flowchart.

Here we see how a condition test is performed:

- Line 2 loads the value of variable *x* into register AX from the stack.
- Line 3 compares it with 0, setting the Z flag if it is equal.
- Line 4 prepares for the if and else cases. They both modify the value of variable y, so the compiler loads the value of Y from the stack into register AX. This load does not change the value of the condition codes.
- Line 5 is a conditional branch which will jump to label ??arrays_0 if the Z flag is set (if variable x is 0), or fall through to the next instruction otherwise.
- Lines 6 through 9 are comments.
- Line 10 is the "if" case. It adds one to AX by incrementing it.
- Line 11 branches over the "else" case to the label ??arrays_1.
- Line 14 is the "else" case. It subtracts one from AX by decrementing it.
- Line 14 is where the control flow merges again. Here the newly modified value of AX is saved back into variable y's location in the stack frame.

```
 1. //    18    if (x){
 2.               MOVW      AX, [SP + 0x02]
 3.               CMPW      AX, #0x0
 4.               MOVW      AX, [SP]
 5.               BZ        ??arrays_0
 6.               ; * Stack frame (at entry) *
 7.               ; Param size: 0
 8.               ; Auto size: 6
 9. //    19    y++;
10.               INCW      AX
11.               BR        S:??arrays_1
12. //    20    } else {
13. //    21    y--;
14. ??arrays_0:
15.               DECW      AX
16. ??arrays_1:
17.               MOVW      [SP], AX
18. //    22    }
```

6.6.1.2 Switch

The switch statement allows source code to be divided cleanly into separate cases. Here is an example code segment:

```
1. switch (x) {
2.    case 1:
```

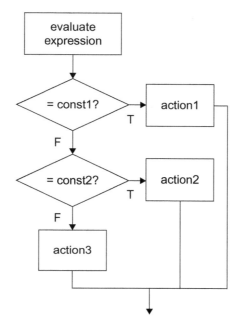

Figure 6.19   Switch statement flowchart.

```
 3.          y += 3;
 4.     break;
 5.     case 31:
 6.          y -= 5;
 7.     break;
 8.     default:
 9.          y-;
10.     break;
11. }
```

The corresponding assembly code is shown below and operates as follows:

- Lines 2 and 3 load variable x from the stack frame into register AX and subtract one from it.
- If x was 1, then the subtraction will result in zero, setting the Z flag, so the BZ instruction in line 4 (conditional branch if zero) will be taken and the code will jump to label arrays_2.
- Label arrays_2 starts the case for x ==1, implemented in lines 8 through 16. These lines load Y from the stack frame, add three, save it back to the stack frame, and then jump to arrays_5, which is the beginning of the next code segment.

▪ If x was not 1, then the BZ instruction in line 4 did not execute, so line 5 executes, subtracting 30 (0x1E) from AX.

▪ If x was 31 initially, then these two subtractions (1 and 30) will bring it to zero, so the Z flag will be set and the conditional branch (BZ) in line 6 will be taken so the code jumps to label arrays_3.

▪ Label arrays_3 starts the case for x == 31, implemented in lines 17 through 22. These lines load variable y and subtract five (by adding a negative 5), save it, and then jump to arrays_5, which is the beginning of the next code segment.

▪ If x was not 31 or 1 initially, then neither of the conditional branches (lines 4 and 6) was taken, so line 7 will execute. This is an unconditional branch to the default case at labels arrays_4, in lines 26 to 30. This default case decrements the variable y.

```
 1. //    25    switch (x) {
 2.              MOVW      AX, [SP]
 3.              SUBW      AX, #0x1
 4.              BZ        ??arrays_2
 5.              SUBW      AX, #0x1E
 6.              BZ        ??arrays_3
 7.              BR        S:??arrays_4
 8. //    26    case 1:
 9. //    27    y += 3;
10. ??arrays_2:
11.              MOVW      AX, [SP + 0x02]
12.              ADDW      AX, #0x3
13. ??control_structures_0:
14.              MOVW      [SP + 0x02], AX
15. //    28    break;
16.              BR        S:??arrays_5
17. //    29    case 31:
18. //    30    y -= 5;
19. ??arrays_3:
20.              MOVW      AX, [SP + 0x02]
21.              ADDW      AX, #0xFFFB
22.              BR        S:??control_structures_0
23. //    31    break;
24. //    32    default:
25. //    33    y--;
26. ??arrays_4:
27.              MOVW      AX, [SP + 0x02]
28.              DECW      AX
29.              BR        S:??control_structures_0
```

```
30. //    34    break;
31. //    35    }
32. ...
33. ??arrays_5:
```

6.6.2   Iteration

C provides three looping constructs to repeat the execution of code: **while, do/while,** and **for.**

6.6.2.1   While

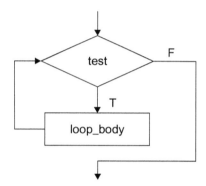

Figure 6.20   While loop flowchart.

The while loop is a top-test loop; if the test is false, then the loop body will not execute. Here is an example code segment:

```
1. while (x < 10) {
2.    x = x + 1;
3. }
```

The corresponding assembly code is shown below and operates as follows:

■   The first item to note is that the entry point for this code is line 8 (label arrays_5)! This is the target of the final branches in the precious code example. The code is laid out with the test at the bottom, but execution begins with the test. This is done to make the code run faster on average.

- Line 9 loads variable x from the stack into register AX and compares it with 10 (0x0A).
- Line 10 repeats the loop if AX is less than 10 by branching to line 3 (label control_structures_1).
- Lines 4 through 6 are the body of the loop, which loads x from stack memory, increments it and saves it.

```
1.  //    37    while (x < 10) {
2.  //    38    x = x + 1;
3.  ??control_structures_1:
4.             MOVW      AX, [SP]
5.             INCW      AX
6.             MOVW      [SP], AX
7.  //    39    }
8.  ??arrays_5:
9.             MOVW      AX, [SP]
10.            CMPW      AX, #0xA
11.            BC        ??control_structures_1
```

6.6.2.2   For

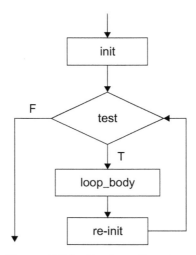

Figure 6.21   For loop flowchart

The for loop is the most complicated.

- Line 2 performs initialization of variable i (stored in register pair AX) to zero.
- Line 3 copies the value of i to register pair HL.
- Line 6 loads the variable x from memory (at [SP]).
- Line 7 adds variable i to variable x.
- Line 8 saves variable x back to memory. If we had not declared x as a volatile variable, the compiler would have optimized the code by keeping variable x in a register to eliminate all of the extra MOVW instructions.
- Lines 9 through 13 copy variable i to the accumulator register AX to increment it (i++), compare it against 10 (0x0A in hexadecimal) in the loop test (i < 10), and save it back to register HL.
- Line 15 is the loop-closing branch instruction which will jump to label control_structures_2 (line 5) if the tested condition (carry flag set) is true.

```
 1. //    41    for (i = 0; i < 10; i++){
 2.             CLRW      AX
 3.             MOVW      HL, AX
 4. //    42    x += i;
 5. ??control_structures_2:
 6.             MOVW      AX, [SP]
 7.             ADDW      AX, HL
 8.             MOVW      [SP], AX
 9. //    43    }
10.             MOVW      AX, HL
11.             INCW      AX
12.             CMPW      AX, #0xA
13.             MOVW      HL, AX
14.             BC        ??control_structures_2
```

6.6.2.3 Do/While

The do/while loop is a bottom-test loop.

- Lines 4 through 7 load variable x from the stack frame into register pair AX, add two (by incrementing twice), and save it back in the stack frame.
- Lines 9 and 10 load x from the stack frame into register pair AX, compare the result to see if the loop condition is still true (i.e., if x < 20, which is 0x14 in hexadecimal).
- Line 11 will branch to line 3 to repeat the loop if the condition is true.

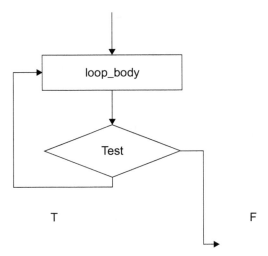

Figure 6.22   Do/while loop flowchart.

```
 1. //    45    do {
 2. //    46    x += 2;
 3. ??control_structures_3:
 4.            MOVW      AX, [SP]
 5.            INCW      AX
 6.            INCW      AX
 7.            MOVW      [SP], AX
 8. //    47    } while (x < 20);
 9.            MOVW      AX, [SP]
10.            CMPW      AX, #0x14
11.            BC        ??control_structures_3
```

6.7   RECAP

In this chapter we have seen how a C program is represented in assembly language. We have seen how different parts of the program require different types of memory, how different classes of variables are stored and accessed, how functions are called, and how program control-flow is implemented.

6.8   EXERCISES

1. Examine the map file from a program of your choosing. How much of each type of memory is used? Which functions or data variables dominate the size? How do size requirements change as you tell the compiler to optimize for size, speed, or not at all?

2. Compile a function which uses floating point division. How much space is required, and for which modules?

3. Was integer pointer apD from the example earlier in the chapter allocated any stack space, or was it allocated to a register? Compile the source code and find out. Can you affect this by changing the compiler's optimization settings?

4. Investigate and try to explain why the code in the pointer manipulation and dereferencing example does not use INCW [HL].

5. Compile a program to calculate a Fibonacci sequence. How are arguments passed to the subroutines? Draw a diagram showing each function's activation record. How large does the stack get?

6. Create the control flow graph using the assembly code of the Fibonacci sequence program.

Chapter Seven

Converting From the Analog to the Digital Domain

7.1 LEARNING OBJECTIVES

Embedded systems often measure physical parameters such as light intensity and temperature. These parameters are analog but the embedded system's microcontroller requires digital values to work on. An Analog to Digital Converter (ADC) is used to convert those parameters into a digital form.

In this chapter we will learn about:

- How an analog value is represented digitally
- How successive approximation converts from analog to digital
- How to configure the RL78 MCU's ADC peripheral
- How to architect the software when using the ADC and interrupts

7.2 BASIC CONCEPTS

A microcontroller represents information digitally: a voltage less than $V_{DD}/2$ represents a logical 0, while a voltage above $V_{DD}/2$ represents a logical 1. An analog signal can represent an infinite number of possible values. For example, consider an electronic thermometer with an output voltage which is proportional to the temperature in Celsius: V_{out} = Temperature * 0.05 V/°C. At 5°C, V_{out} = 0.25 V. At 40°C, V_{out} = 2.0 V. At 40.1°C, V_{out} = 2.005 V. If we connect this thermometer directly to a microcontroller's digital input we will not be able to measure temperatures very accurately. In fact, we can only determine if the voltage is above or below $V_{DD}/2$. Assuming a supply voltage of 3.3 V, we can only determine if the temperature is above or below (3.3 V/2)/(0.05 V/°C) = 33°C, throwing away all other temperature information. In order to preserve this information we need a more sophisticated conversion approach.

7.2.1 Quantization

An ADC measures an analog input voltage and determines a digital (binary) value which represents it best. This measurement process is called *quantization*. The conversion is based on reference voltages which define the high (V_{+Ref}) and low (V_{-Ref}) ends of the input voltage range. Often microcontrollers have V_{-Ref} connected to ground (0 V). An input voltage of V_{+Ref} or more will result in an output code which is all ones, while an input voltage of V_{-Ref} or less will result in an output code of all zeroes. An intermediate input voltage will result in the proportional binary code value. This is discussed in more detail below.

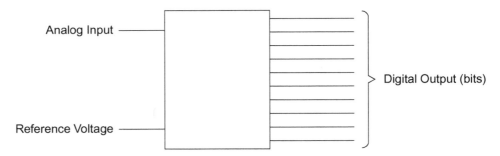

Figure 7.1   Simple analog to digital converter (ADC).

A block diagram for a simple ADC is shown in Figure 7.1. The number of bits in the digital output is called the *resolution* of the ADC. A 10-bit ADC produces an output with 10 bits, with 1024 (2^{10}) different binary outputs. Thus, in a 10-bit ADC, a range of input voltages (analog) will map to a unique binary output (0000000000 to 1111111111). A 12-bit ADC will have 4096 (2^{12}) unique binary outputs to represent 0 to 100 percent of an analog input.

7.2.1.1   Transfer Function

The digital approximation for a particular analog input value can be found mathematically. This can be useful as a guide to see if the ADC output obtained is correct.

If V_{in} is the sampled input voltage, V_{+ref} is the upper end of the input voltage range, V_{-ref} is the lower end of the input voltage range, and N is the number of bits of resolution in ADC, then the digital output n can be found using the following formula:

$$n = \text{int}\left(\frac{V_{in} - V_{-ref}}{V_{+ref} - V_{-ref}} * 2^N + 0.5\right)$$

We can simplify this equation if V_{-ref} is connected to ground (0 V):

$$n = \text{int}\left(\frac{V_{in}}{V_{+ref}} * 2^N + 0.5\right)$$

The RL78 ADC peripheral copies the result n (called the SAR value in the RL78) into the AD conversion result register (ADCR) when the conversion completes. It left-aligns the SAR value when storing it in ADCR.

$$ADCR = SAR * 64$$

The upper 8 bits of ADCR can be accessed as ADCRH, if an 8-bit conversion was performed.

We can also reverse the equation to determine what range of voltages corresponds to an ADCR value:

$$\left(\frac{ADCR}{64} - 0.5\right) \times \frac{AV_{REF}}{1024} \leq V_{AIN} < \left(\frac{ADCR}{64} + 0.5\right) \times \frac{AV_{REF}}{1024}$$

7.2.1.2   Quantization Error

Quantization usually introduces some error because each digital code (e.g., 0000101010) corresponds to a *range* of analog input voltages. The term *quantization error* describes how large the error can be, based on a codeword N bits long:

$$E_{Quantization} = \frac{1}{2 * 2^N} * 100\%$$

An ADC with higher resolution has more binary codes possible, which reduces the range of voltages corresponding to each code. This reduces the quantization error.

7.2.2   Successive Approximation

Analog to digital conversion (quantization) can be performed using various methods, such as flash conversion, dual slope integration, and successive approximation. The ADC method used in RL78 MCUs is successive approximation. This method gives good resolution and speed.

In successive approximation the ADC performs a binary search to measure the input voltage. The input voltage is repeatedly compared with a test voltage (generated by digital to analog converter), until the closest approximation is found. Successive approximation requires one comparison per output bits of the ADC; so a 10-bit ADC requires 10 comparisons to perform the A/D conversion.

This process can be understood better with an example. Let's consider a system with a reference voltage of 3.3 V. An input voltage of 2.5 V has to be converted to digital form and the ADC used is 10-bit.

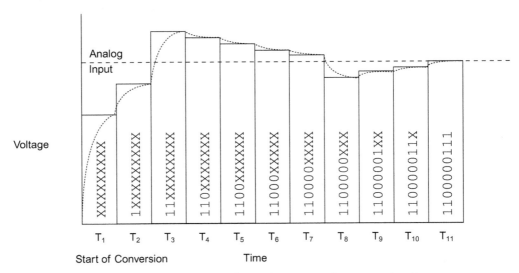

Figure 7.2   A/D Conversion using successive approximation.

TABLE 7.1   Analog to Digital Conversion Using Successive Approximation

CONVERSION CYCLE	POSSIBLE INPUT VOLTAGE RANGE	TEST VOLTAGE	INPUT > TEST VOLTAGE?	SUCCESSIVE APPROXIMATION REGISTER (SAR)
1	0 V–3.3 V	1.65 V	Yes	1xxxxxxxx
2	1.65 V–3.3 V	2.475 V	Yes	11xxxxxxx
3	2.475 V–3.3 V	2.888 V	No	110xxxxxx
4	2.475 V–2.888 V	2.682 V	No	1100xxxxx
5	2.475 V–2.682 V	2.579 V	No	11000xxxx
6	2.475 V–2.579 V	2.527 V	No	110000xxx
7	2.475 V–2.527 V	2.501 V	No	1100000xx
8	2.475 V–2.501 V	2.488 V	Yes	11000001xx
9	2.488 V–2.501 V	2.495 V	Yes	110000011x
10	2.495 V–2.501 V	2.498 V	Yes	1100000111

In the first conversion cycle, the ADC has no information about the possible value of the input voltage (the result register is xxxxxxxxxx), so it chooses a test voltage half-way between the upper (3.3 V) and lower (0 V) reference voltages. This test voltage of 1.65 V is generated by the DAC. The comparator then determines whether the test voltage (1.65 V) or the input voltage (2.5 V) is higher. The input voltage is higher, so the ADC determines that the first bit (MSB) of the conversion result is a 1, making the successive approximation register (SAR) 1xxxxxxxxx.

In the second conversion cycle, the ADC now knows that the voltage is in the range 1.65 V to 3.3 V, so will split that range in half by setting the test voltage at the middle (3.3 V + 1.65 V)/2 = 2.475 V. Since the input (2.5 V) is greater than the output from DAC (2.475 V), the next bit of the result register is set to 1, making the SAR 11xxxxxxxx.

In the third conversion cycle, the ADC now knows that the voltage is in the range 2.475 V to 3.3 V, so will split that range in half by setting the test voltage at the middle (3.3 V + 2.475 V)/2 = 2.888 V. Since the input (2.5 V) is less than the output from DAC (2.888 V), the next bit of the result register is set to 0, making the SAR 110xxxxxxx.

This process repeats until all result bits are found. The final result of this conversion is 1100000111.

7.2.3   Sampling Frequency Constraints

How often does the ADC *need to* sample a signal in order to accurately represent it? Sampling theory states that an input signal with no frequency components greater than or equal to one half of the sampling frequency (called the *Nyquist frequency*) will be completely and accurately represented by the samples. If the input signal has any frequency components above the Nyquist frequency, these will be *aliased* by the sampling and appear as noise in the signals (as lower frequency components).

Input signals may be bandwidth-limited with a low-pass filter before sampling and quantization. In addition, the system is typically designed so that the Nyquist frequency is well above the filter's corner frequency, allowing the use of less expensive, lower-order filters.

For example, we wish to create a device to record music. The audio spectrum ranges from 20 Hz to 20 kHz. To prevent aliasing, we need to sample at greater than 2 * 20 kHz = 40 kHz. As a practical matter, we will need to sample at a higher frequency in order to reduce the need for a high-order anti-aliasing filter on the input. When we play back the recorded signal, we will also need a low-pass filter to remove the high-frequency artifacts from sampling.

7.3 CONVERTING WITH THE RL78 ADC

We will now examine the RL78 MCU's ADC peripheral in order to configure, select, and scan input channels, select voltage references, set conversion speed, trigger conversions, and read results.

7.3.1 Enabling the ADC

The ADC needs a clock signal in order to be configured and operate. This is provided by setting the ADCEN bit in the PER0 register to 1. Clearing ADCEN to 0 removes the clock signal and keeps the ADC in reset state, reducing power consumption.

7.3.2 Enabling I/O Pins as Analog Inputs

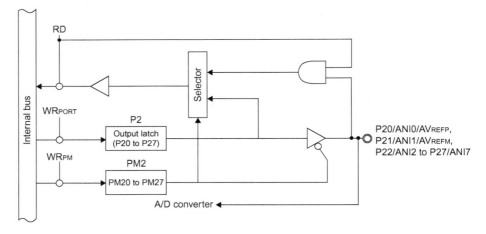

Figure 7.3 Block diagram of I/O port bit.

Figure 7.3 shows a block diagram of a typical port connected to an I/O pin (the double circle on the right). These components must be configured correctly to use the port as an analog input for the ADC.

Two port characteristics must be set: first, the digital output buffer (the triangle on the right) must be disabled; and second, analog rather than digital signals must be used.

Disabling the port's digital output buffer is straightforward and involves setting the appropriate port mode (PM) bit to 1. For example, to disable the digital output buffer for port 2 bit 0, set PM20 to 1.

Selecting the analog rather than digital signals is done in one of two different ways, depending on which analog input is used.

7.3.2.1 Analog Inputs ANI0 Through ANI14

A group of N inputs starting with ANI0 is specified; these inputs cannot be configured individually. The value $(N + 1)$ *modulo 16* must be stored in ADPC, as shown in Figure 7.4.

Address: F0076H After reset: 00H R/W

Symbol	7	6	5	4	3	2	1	0
ADPC	0	0	0	0	ADPC3	ADPC2	ADPC1	ADPC0

ADPC3	ADPC2	ADPC1	ADPC0	\multicolumn{15}{c}{ANALOG INPUT (A)/DIGITAL I/O (D) SWITCHING}

ADPC3	ADPC2	ADPC1	ADPC0	ANI14/P156	ANI13/P155	ANI12/P154	ANI11/P153	ANI10/P152	ANI9/P151	ANI8/P150	ANI7/P27	ANI6/P26	ANI5/P25	ANI4/P24	ANI3/P23	ANI2/P22	ANI1/P21	ANI0/P20
0	0	0	0	A	A	A	A	A	A	A	A	A	A	A	A	A	A	A
0	0	0	1	D	D	D	D	D	D	D	D	D	D	D	D	D	D	D
0	0	1	0	D	D	D	D	D	D	D	D	D	D	D	D	D	D	A
0	0	1	1	D	D	D	D	D	D	D	D	D	D	D	D	D	A	A
0	1	0	0	D	D	D	D	D	D	D	D	D	D	D	D	A	A	A
0	1	0	1	D	D	D	D	D	D	D	D	D	D	D	A	A	A	A
0	1	1	0	D	D	D	D	D	D	D	D	D	D	A	A	A	A	A
0	1	1	1	D	D	D	D	D	D	D	D	D	A	A	A	A	A	A
1	0	0	0	D	D	D	D	D	D	D	D	A	A	A	A	A	A	A
1	0	0	1	D	D	D	D	D	D	D	A	A	A	A	A	A	A	A
1	0	1	0	D	D	D	D	D	D	A	A	A	A	A	A	A	A	A
1	0	1	1	D	D	D	D	D	A	A	A	A	A	A	A	A	A	A
1	1	0	0	D	D	D	D	A	A	A	A	A	A	A	A	A	A	A
1	1	0	1	D	D	D	A	A	A	A	A	A	A	A	A	A	A	A
1	1	1	0	D	D	A	A	A	A	A	A	A	A	A	A	A	A	A
1	1	1	1	D	A	A	A	A	A	A	A	A	A	A	A	A	A	A
Other than above				Setting prohibited														

Figure 7.4 Using the ADPC register to enable analog inputs.

7.3.2.2 Analog Inputs ANI16 Through ANI19

These inputs can be configured individually. The PMC register controls whether the pin is used as an analog input or digital I/O. The bit for the signal of interest must be set to 1 to enable its use as an analog input. For example, signal ANI19 is located on port 12 bit 0, so bit PMC120 must be set.

7.3.3 Selecting Input Channels

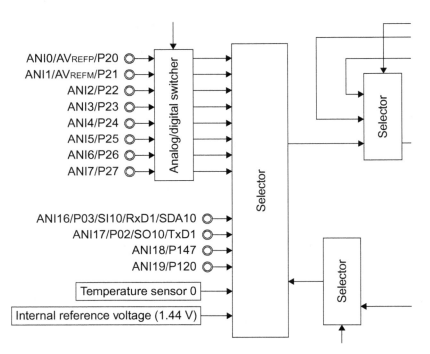

Figure 7.5 ADC input multiplexer.

An analog input multiplexer allows the ADC to convert different input channels without the need for rewiring the circuit or switching the signal externally. As shown in Figure 7.5, there are multiple analog voltage inputs (ANI0 through ANI7, ANI16 through ANI19) as well as internal signals such as a temperature sensor and an internal reference voltage (1.44 V).

The ADC can use the multiplexer in Select mode or Scan mode, determined by bit ADMD.

7.3.3.1   *Selecting a Single Input Channel*

Address: FFF31H After reset: 00H R/W

Symbol	7	6	5	4	3	2	1	0
ADS	ADISS	0	0	ADS4	ADS3	ADS2	ADS1	ADS0

○ Select mode (ADMD = 0)

ADISS	ADS4	ADS3	ADS2	ADS1	ADS0	ANALOG INPUT CHANNEL	INPUT SOURCE
0	0	0	0	0	0	ANI0	P20/ANI0/AV$_{REFP}$ pin
0	0	0	0	0	1	ANI1	P21/ANI1/AV$_{REFM}$ pin
0	0	0	0	1	0	ANI2	P22/ANI2 pin
0	0	0	0	1	1	ANI3	P23/ANI3 pin
0	0	0	1	0	0	ANI4	P24/ANI4 pin
0	0	0	1	0	1	ANI5	P25/ANI5 pin
0	0	0	1	1	0	ANI6	P26/ANI6 pin
0	0	0	1	1	1	ANI7	P27/ANI7 pin
0	1	0	0	0	0	ANI16	P03/ANI16 pin
0	1	0	0	0	1	ANI17	P02/ANI17 pin
0	1	0	0	1	0	ANI18	P147/ANI18 pin
0	1	0	0	1	1	ANI19	P120/ANI19 pin
1	0	0	0	0	0	—	Temperature sensor 0 output
1	0	0	0	0	1	—	Internal reference voltage output (1.44 V)
Other than the above							Setting prohibited

Figure 7.6   Identifying a single analog input channel in select mode.

In Select mode (ADMD = 0), a single channel is converted by the ADC. The analog input channel specification register (ADS) determines which input channel is to be converted, as shown in Figure 7.6. The ADISS bit selects whether an internal (1) or an external channel is selected. Bits ADS4 through ADS0 select the specific signal.

7.3.3.2 Scanning Multiple Input Channels

In Scan mode (ADMD = 1), four sequential channels are converted by the ADC in order. The starting channel is defined by the ADS register, as shown in Figure 7.7. Possible starting channels are ANI0, ANI1, ANI2, ANI3, and ANI4.

○ Scan mode (ADMD = 1)								
					ANALOG INPUT CHANNEL			
ADS4	**ADS3**	**ADS2**	**ADS1**	**ADS0**	**SCAN 0**	**SCAN 1**	**SCAN 2**	**SCAN 3**
0	0	0	0	0	ANI0	ANI1	ANI2	ANI3
0	0	0	0	1	ANI1	ANI2	ANI3	ANI4
0	0	0	1	0	ANI2	ANI3	ANI4	ANI5
0	0	0	1	1	ANI3	ANI4	ANI5	ANI6
0	0	1	0	0	ANI4	ANI5	ANI6	ANI7
Other than the above					Setting prohibited			

Figure 7.7 Identifying multiple analog input channels in scan mode.

7.3.4 Setting the Reference Voltages

The RL78 ADC allows software to select among multiple possible reference voltages, increasing the resolution of readings. The reference voltage selection circuits are shown in Figure 7.8.

V_{+ref} can be connected to three possible signals, based on the ADREFP1 and ADREFP0 bits in ADM2.

- 00: connect V_{+ref} to V_{DD} (the positive power supply voltage).
- 01: connect V_{+ref} to pin P20/AVREFP/ANI0.
- 10: connect V_{+ref} to the 1.44 V internal reference.

V_{-ref} can be connected to one of two possible signals, based on the ADREFM bit in ADM2.

- 0: connect V_{-ref} to V_{SS} (ground).
- 1: connect V_{-ref} to P21/AV$_{REFM}$/ANI1.

This enables the designer to create systems with very small quantization levels, potentially enabling systems which do not need input amplification or level shifting.

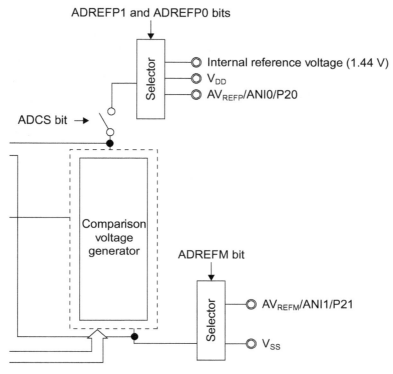

Figure 7.8 Reference voltage sources.

7.3.5   Conversion Modes

The ADSCM bit controls whether the ADC will repeatedly perform conversions (sequential conversion mode, ADSCM = 0) or only perform a single conversion (one-shot conversion mode, ADSCM = 1).

The ADC in the RL78 MCU can perform a 10-bit or 8-bit conversion, based on the ADTYP bit in the ADM1 control register (1 or 0, respectively).

7.3.6   Setting Converter Speed

We can control the speed of the ADC conversion by selecting the ADC conversion clock frequency (f_{AD}) which is divided down from f_{CLK}. As shown in Figure 7.9, the bits FR2, FR1, and F0 in the ADM0 register select the division ratio from possible values of 2, 4, 5, 6, 8, 16, 32, and 64. A conversion takes at least 17 f_{AD} cycles and possibly more if a wait mode or a lower operating voltage is used.

(2) 2.7 V ≤ V_{DD} < 3.6 V When there is no stabilization wait time (software trigger mode/hardware trigger no-wait mode)											
A/D CONVERTER MODE REGISTER 0 (ADM0)						CONVERSION TIME SELECTION					CONVERSION CLOCK (f_{AD})
FR2	FR1	FR0	LV1	LV0	MODE	f_{CLK} = 2 MHz	f_{CLK} = 4 MHz	f_{CLK} = 8 MHz	f_{CLK} = 16 MHz	f_{CLK} = 32 MHz	
0	0	0	0	0	Normal 1	Setting prohibited	Setting prohibited	Setting prohibited	Setting prohibited	38 μs	$f_{CLK}/64$
0	0	1							38 μs	19 μs	$f_{CLK}/32$
0	1	0						38 μs	19 μs	9.5 μs	$f_{CLK}/16$
0	1	1					38 μs	19 μs	9.5 μs	4.75 μs	$f_{CLK}/8$
1	0	0					28.5 μs	14.25 μs	7.125 μs	3.5625 μs	$f_{CLK}/6$
1	0	1					33.75 μs	11.875 μs	5.938 μs	2.9688 μs	$f_{CLK}/5$
1	1	0				38 μs	19 μs	9.5 μs	4.75 μs	Setting prohibited	$f_{CLK}/4$
1	1	1				19 μs	9.5 μs	4.75 μs	Setting prohibited		$f_{CLK}/2$

Figure 7.9 Example of A/D conversion time selection.

7.3.7 Triggering a Conversion

The ADC comparator must be enabled by setting the ADCE bit to 1, placing the ADC into conversion standby mode. The ADC must spend at least 1 μs in this state for the comparator to stabilize, at which point it is ready to be triggered.

The RL78 ADC peripheral provides three methods to start a conversion, determined by the ADTMD1 and ADTMD0 bits in the ADM1 register.

- In software trigger mode (00 or 01), the user program must set the start conversion bit (ADCS) to one.
- In no-wait hardware trigger mode (10), a hardware trigger starts the conversion.
- In hardware trigger with wait mode (11), the system remains in a low-power mode until a hardware trigger occurs. This wakes the system, waits for voltages to stabilize, and then starts the conversion.

The ADTRS1 and ADTRS0 bits select the hardware trigger:

- 01: When timer channel 1 reaches the end of its count, or its capture interrupt is triggered.
- 10: When the real-time clock generates an interrupt (INTRTC).
- 11: When the interval timer generates an interrupt (INTIT).

7.3.8 Conversion Speed

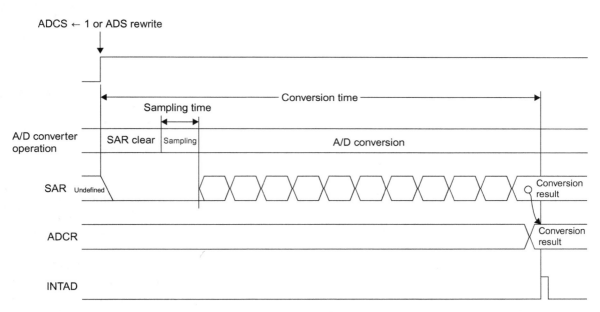

Figure 7.10 A/D sampling and conversion activities.

After triggering, the ADC performs a series of actions in order to perform a complete conversion, as shown in Figure 7.10. The actions are triggered by software setting the ADCS bit to 1, or by a hardware trigger activity.

- The SAR is cleared to all zeroes.
- The analog input is sampled.

■ Successive approximation determines the binary code representing the input voltage.
■ The SAR contents are copied to the result register (ADCR).
■ An interrupt (ADINT) may be generated.

7.3.9   INTAD Interrupt and Range Checking

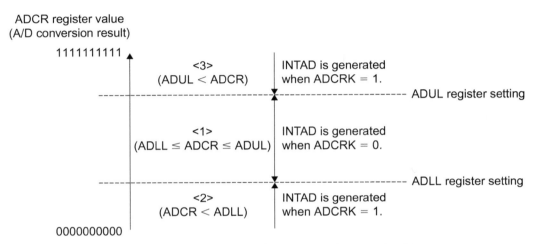

Figure 7.11   AD converter interrupt and range checking.

The AD converter can generate an INTAD interrupt when a conversion completes if the interrupt mask bit is zero. In addition, the RL78 AD converter offers range-checking hardware to inhibit the interrupt request if the conversion result does not match certain range criteria, as shown in Figure 7.11.

This feature can be helpful to prevent unneeded interrupts in order to save energy and time. For example, we can keep a device in sleep mode yet still monitor an input signal (e.g., temperature). We do this by configuring the interrupt to monitor the temperature and only generate an interrupt if the temperature is outside the range. Then we start the converter and put the processor to sleep. If the temperature exceeds the range we've defined, then the AD converter will generate an interrupt and wake up the rest of the processor to allow handling that condition.

The range checking hardware works as follows.

■ We use the ADUL and ADLL registers to define the upper and lower limits of a range of interest.
■ We use the ADCRK bit to define whether an interrupt should be generated when the conversion result is within the range of ADUL and ADLL (ADCRK = 0, region 1 in Figure 7.11) or beyond the range (ADCRK = 1, regions 2 and 3).

7.3.10   Reading Conversion Results

The AD converter loads ADCR register with the results of the conversion from the SAR upon completion. The ADCR register is 16 bits long, so the result is left-justified. For a ten bit conversion, bits 0 through 5 are read as zeroes, so your code may need to shift the result right by 6 bits. For an eight bit conversion, the upper eight bits of the ADCR register can be read as ADCRH and no shifting is needed.

7.4   EXAMPLES

We now examine how to use the RL78 AD converter in a series of examples.

7.4.1   Basic Voltage Monitor

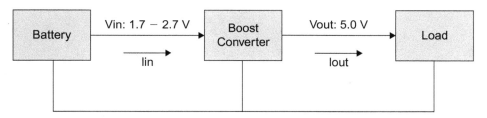

Figure 7.12   System block diagram.

We would like to use the ADC to determine how much longer our battery-operated device can operate before the battery dies. This system, shown in Figure 7.12, uses a battery consisting of two NiMH AA cells in series with a resulting voltage ranging from 1.7 V to 2.7 V. This voltage is supplied as V_{in} to a boost switch-mode power supply to drive the V_{DD} supply rail (marked V_{out}) at a regulated 5.0 V. The MCU and all other devices in the system (labeled as "load") run at 5.0 V.

We can write code to directly manipulate the control registers. The resulting program is shown below.

```
#define V_REF (5.0)

void  main(void)
{
    unsigned result;
    volatile float voltage;
```

```
// Enable the ADC:
ADCEN = 1;
// Disable the ADC interrupt
ADMK = 1;
// Input channel: We will use ANI2, which is on P2 bit 2.
ADPC = 5;
PM2_bit.no2 = 1;
ADS = 2;
// Channel select mode: Select one channel for conversion.
ADMD = 0;
// Reference voltages: Use supply voltage VDD as the pos.
// reference and ground as the negative reference.
ADREFP1 = 0;
ADREFP0 = 0;
ADREFM = 0;
// Single conversion: Perform only one conversion.
ADSCM = 1;
// Resolution: Use a 10 bit conversion.
ADTYP = 0;
// Conversion Speed: Fastest possible for 32 MHz fCLK.
FR2 = 1;
FR1 = 0;
FR0 = 1;
LV1 = 0;
LV0 = 0;
// Conversion Trigger: Select a software trigger.
ATDMD1 = 0;
ATDMD0 = 0;
// Finally we enable the ADC comparator.
ADCE = 1;

// Infinite loop for main operation
while (1) {
   // Start the conversion.
   ADCS = 1;
   while (ADCS)
       ;
   // Read the conversion result and convert to voltage
   result = ADCR;
   result >>= 6;
```

```
        voltage = result*V_REF;
        voltage /= 1024;
    }
}
```

7.4.2   Basic Voltage Monitor with Applilet

We can use Applilet to generate the code for our voltage monitor if we prefer. First, we need to make sure that port 2 bit 2 is not used as a digital I/O port, as we need to use it for analog input ANI2 instead, as shown in Figure 7.13.

Figure 7.13   Port 2 bit 2 must not be used for digital I/O to leave the pin free for ANI2.

As shown in Figure 7.14, we select the same A/D converter options as described in example 1a.
     We also disable the A/D interrupt, as shown in Figure 7.15.
     Now we select "Generate Code" and can examine the driver code generated for the A/D converter.

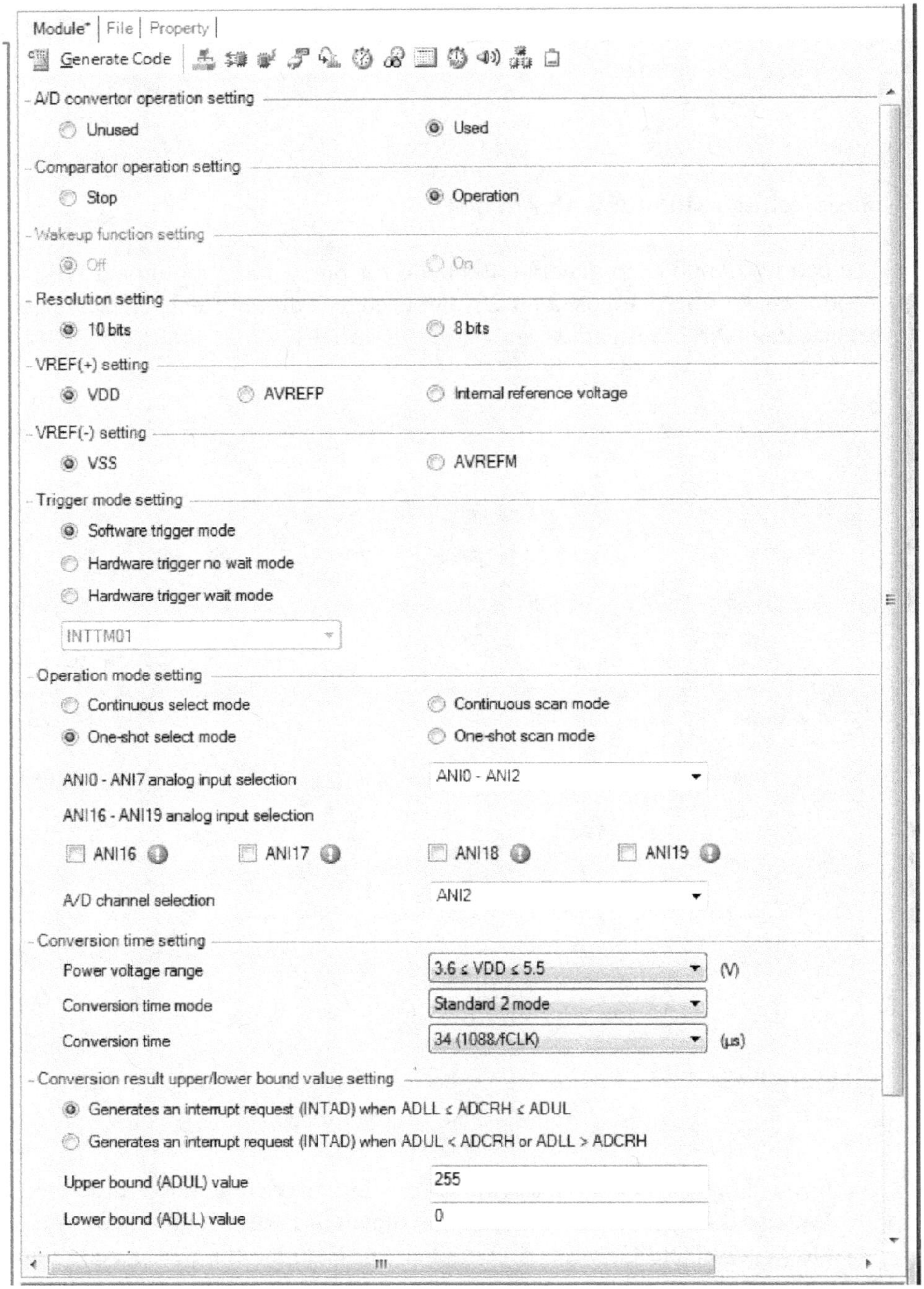

Figure 7.14   A/D Converter configuration options.

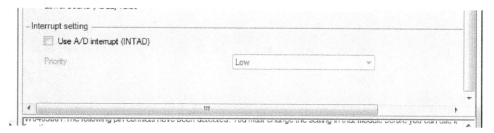

Figure 7.15   Disable A/D converter interrupt.

7.4.2.1   CG_ad.h

The file CG_ad.h is created with bit definitions for control registers, macro definitions, and function prototypes.

There are several functions created for our use in CG_ad.c:

- void AD_Init(void)—This function is called by systeminit() on startup and configures the A/D converter according to the initialization settings we specified in Applilet.
- void AD_Start(void), void AD_Stop(void)—These functions start and stop the A/D converter by controlling the ADCS bit.
- void AD_ComparatorOn(void), void AD_ComparatorOff(void)—These functions enable and disable the comparator using the ADCE bit.
- void AD_Read(USHORT *buffer)—This function places the result of the AD conversion in the location pointed to by buffer.
- MD_STATUS AD_SelectADChannel(enum ADChannel channel)—This function selects a new AD channel with the multiplexer.

7.4.2.2   CG_ad_user.c

The file CG_ad_user.c is created with space for user include files and global variables related to the A/D converter and user-defined functions such as interrupt service routines. In this example, we disabled the AD interrupt, so no code is generated for the ISR.

7.4.2.3   CG_userdefine.h

We place the definition #define V_REF (5.0) in CG_userdefine.h.

7.4.2.4   CGain.c

Next we examine the main function in CG_main.c.

```
void  main(void)
{
    /* Start user code. Do not edit comment generated here */
    while (1U)
        {
            ;
        }
    /* End user code. Do not edit comment generated here */
}

/* Start user code for adding. Do not edit comment generated here */
/* End user code. Do not edit comment generated here */
```

Now we are ready to add our code to the main function. We first need to turn on the comparator, and then we can get to the main loop body: starting the AD, waiting for it to finish, reading the result, and converting it to a voltage.

```
void  main(void)
{
    /* Start user code. Do not edit comment generated here */
    USHORT adc_result;
    float voltage;

    AD_ComparatorOn();   /* Enable ADC voltage comparator  */

    /* Endless control loop */
    while (1U) {
        AD_Start();       /* Start ADC (ADCS = 0n) */
        while (ADCS)
            ;
        // Read the conversion result and convert to voltage
        AD_Read(&adc_result);
        voltage = adc_result*V_REF;
        voltage /= 1024;
    }
    /* End user code. Do not edit comment generated here */
}
```

Note that this code has *busy waiting* (while (ADCS)) to wait for the converter to complete the conversion. This wastes processor time and reduces responsiveness.

7.4.3   Voltage Monitor with Continuous Select Conversion

One approach to reducing busy waiting is to have the ADC perform continuous conversions so we do not need to start and wait for the conversion to finish. In this case we would select continuous select rather than one-shot select mode. The main function will now look like this:

```
void  main(void)
{
   /* Start user code. Do not edit comment generated here */
   USHORT adc_result;
   float voltage;

   AD_ComparatorOn();    /* Enable ADC voltage comparator  */
   AD_Start();           /* Start ADC (ADCS = 0n) */
   while (ADCS)
      ;
   /* Endless control loop */
   while (1U) {
      // Read the conversion result and convert to voltage
      AD_Read(&adc_result);
      voltage = adc_result*V_REF;
      voltage /= 1024;
   }
   /* End user code. Do not edit comment generated here */
}
```

This approach will have the ADC dedicate all of its time to sampling one channel, and it will not work if we wish to sample from multiple channels.

7.4.4   Power Monitor with One-Shot Scan Conversion

We realize that we can measure the power used by our system if we can measure the current I_{in} drawn from the battery, shown in Figure 7.12. The power is then the voltage multiplied by the current. We can use a small series resistor or other device (e.g., Hall effect current sensor) to convert the current into a voltage which the ADC can read. In fact, we can also measure the efficiency of the power supply if we measure the power ($I_{out} * V_{out}$) used by the system excluding the power supply.

We need to make our system sample both the voltage and the current in two places. We only have one ADC, so we need to convert one channel and then the other. We will use

the scan mode (rather than select mode) as it will automatically scan through four channels sequentially for us. However, there is only one result register for the ADC, so we
need to read it before the next conversion completes. We will use the AD interrupt for this
data transfer operation, and it will place the results in four-element global array
ADC_value where they can be used by the main program. The resulting software architecture appears in Figure 7.16.

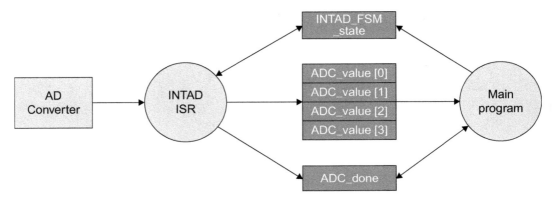

Figure 7.16   Software Architecture showing execution threads and shared data.

We will assign signals to channels and variables as shown in Table 7.2.

TABLE 7.2   Assignment of Signals to Input Channels and Variables

SIGNAL	INPUT CHANNEL	VARIABLE
Vin	ANI2	ADC_value[0]
Iin	ANI3	ADC_value[1]
Vout	ANI4	ADC_value[2]
Iout	ANI5	ADC_value[3]

We now load Applilet to change in the port and ADC configuration. We set port 2 bits
2 through 5 to "unused."
   Now we can modify the ADC configuration as follows, shown in Figure 7.17:

- Channels ANI0 through ANI5 are analog inputs
- One-shot scan mode is used
- An AD interrupt is generated with low priority

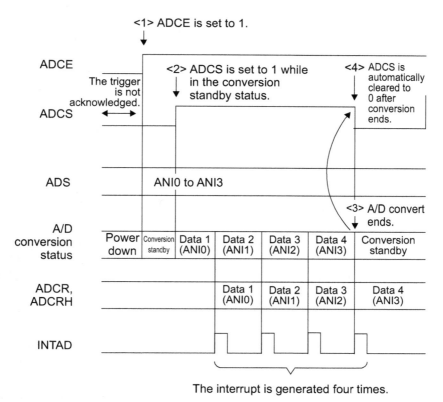

Figure 7.17   Configuring AD converter to scan channels ANI2 through ANI5.

<1> ADCE is set to 1.

ADCE

The trigger is not acknowledged.

<2> ADCS is set to 1 while in the conversion standby status.

<4> ADCS is automatically cleared to 0 after conversion ends.

ADCS

ADS   ANI0 to ANI3

<3> A/D convert ends.

A/D conversion status	Power down	Conversion standby	Data 1 (ANI0)	Data 2 (ANI1)	Data 3 (ANI2)	Data 4 (ANI3)	Conversion standby
ADCR, ADCRH			Data 1 (ANI0)	Data 2 (ANI1)	Data 3 (ANI2)	Data 4 (ANI3)	
INTAD							

The interrupt is generated four times.

Figure 7.18   AD converter operation and interrupts in one-shot scan mode.

We will change the software structure to take advantage of interrupts. We can configure the ADC to generate an interrupt request each time a conversion completes, as shown in Figure 7.18. The software will now consist of two separate threads of execution: one in an ISR and one in the main function. These two threads will interact with the hardware as shown in the sequence chart of Figure 7.19.

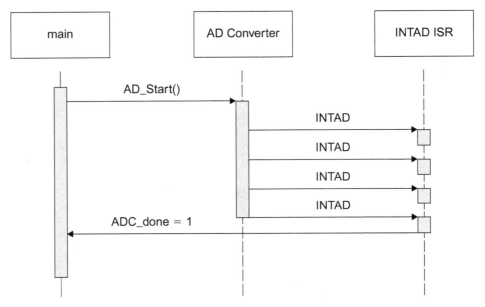

Figure 7.19   Sequence chart for AD converter, main function and ISR.

The ISR will set a flag ADC_done to allow the main program to determine when all conversions are complete. The program will follow these steps:

- The main program will initialize the INTAD state machine, clear ADC_done and then start the converter. It will then wait for the ISR to set ADC_done, indicating that all conversions have completed. Since ADC_done is shared between the main program and an ISR, it must be declared as volatile.
- The state machine in the ISR servicing INTAD will copy the ADC result into the appropriate temporary variable and advance to the next state.
- After four conversions, the ISR will signal that it is complete by setting the variable ADC_done to one. Note that if we are using a task scheduler we may be able to send a message or signal to communicate this information.
- The main program will determine that ADC_done has been set, at which point in time it can continue execution.

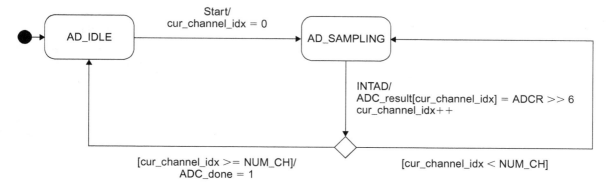

Figure 7.20 State machine for INTAD interrupt service routine.

The ISR will behave according to the state machine shown in Figure 7.20. A variable (cur_channel_idx) will keep track of how many channels have been converted.

Finally, we need to decide where to calculate the power. We have two options:

- We can calculate the power in the ISR. This will eliminate data race conditions but increase the amount of time the processor spends in the AD ISR, increasing possible response times for other processing.
- We can calculate the power in the main program. This eliminates the response time issue, but introduces a possible data race condition if the main program doesn't read a voltage or current from the temporary variable before it is updated. To deal with this we will not start a new set of conversions until we have completed converting the current set. In a system which requires faster conversions, we would use a queue to tolerate a greater delay before using the data, and we would add an interlock mechanism for preventing overflow.

Which option is better? It depends on other system factors.

- How long will it take to calculate power? This depends on how long it takes to multiply the voltage and current values together. If they are multiplied as integers, it will be relatively quick as the RL78 has an integer multiplier. If they are multiplied as floating point values, it will take a much longer time: the compiler will generate code to call the math library to perform integer-to-float conversions and then multiplication. Perhaps we can use fixed-point math to improve the performance. We will discuss this in a future chapter.
- How important is it to minimize response time for other processing activities? If there are other interrupts which must be serviced quickly for proper system operation, then this is may be a deciding factor. If there are no other time-critical operations, then perhaps making this ISR long does not have as much impact on the rest of the system.

We will look at this question in more detail in subsequent chapters on optimizing responsiveness and program speed. For this program we will compute power in the main program with floating-point calculations.

Our resulting program requires certain extensions to the Applilet-generated code.

7.4.4.1 CG_userdefine.h

In CG_userdefine.h we will define constants:

```
/*
**********
**   User define
**********
*/

/* Start user code for function. Do not edit comment generated here
*/
#define V_REF (5.0)

#define NUM_CHANNELS (4)
#define VIN_IDX (0)
#define IIN_IDX (1)
#define VOUT_IDX (2)
#define IOUT_IDX (3)

#define AD_SAMPLING (1)
#define AD_IDLE (0)

#define K_CONVERSION (0.123)
/* End user code. Do not edit comment generated here */
```

7.4.4.2 CG_main.c

We define global variables in CG_main.c to share data (voltage and current (or power), and conversion status) between the ISR and the main code.

```
/* Start user code for global. Do not edit comment generated here */
volatile UCHAR ADC_done = 0;        /* Flag: conversion complete */
volatile USHORT ADC_value[NUM_CHANNELS];
volatile UCHAR INTAD_FSM_state = AD_IDLE;
/* End user code. Do not edit comment generated here */
```

The main function is updated as follows:

```
void  main(void)
{
   /* Start user code. Do not edit comment generated here */
   float P_in, P_out, effic;

   /* Peripheral start function calls */
   AD_ComparatorOn();        /* Enable ADC voltage comparator */

   /* Endless control loop */
   while (1U)
      {
         INTAD_FSM_state = AD_SAMPLING;
         ADC_done = 0;
         AD_Start();                   /* Start ADC (ADCS = 0n) */
         while (!ADC_done)
            ;
         // Read the conversion results and calculate power
         P_in = K_CONVERSION*ADC_value[VIN_IDX]*ADC_value[IIN_IDX];
         P_out = K_CONVERSION*ADC_value[VOUT_IDX]
            *ADC_value[IOUT_IDX];
         effic = (P_in - P_out)/P_in;
      }
   /* End user code. Do not edit comment generated here */
}
```

7.4.4.3   CG_ad_user.c

We create references in CG_ad_user.c for the external variables which the INTAD ISR uses:

```
/*
******************
**   Global define
******************
*/
/* Start user code for global. Do not edit comment generated here */
extern volatile USHORT ADC_value[NUM_CHANNELS];
extern volatile UCHAR ADC_done;
extern volatile UCHAR INTAD_FSM_state;
/* End user code. Do not edit comment generated here */
```

Applilet has generated the skeleton ISR for INTAD (MD_INTAD) in CG_ad_user.c. We complete it with the state machine:

```
/*
** _ _ _ _ _ _ _ _ _ _ _ _ _ _ _ _ _ _ _ _ _ _ _ _ _ _ _ _ _
**
**   Abstract:
**   This function is INTAD interrupt service routine.
**
** _ _ _ _ _ _ _ _ _ _ _ _ _ _ _ _ _ _ _ _ _ _ _ _ _ _ _ _ */
#pragma vector = INTAD_vect
__interrupt void MD_INTAD(void)
{
    /* Start user code. Do not edit comment generated here */
    static UCHAR cur_channel_idx = 0;

    switch (INTAD_FSM_state) {
    case AD_SAMPLING:
        AD_Read(&(ADC_value[cur_channel_idx]));
        cur_channel_idx++;
        if (cur_channel_idx == NUM_CHANNELS) {
            INTAD_FSM_state = AD_IDLE;
            cur_channel_idx = 0;
            ADC_done = 1;
        }
        break;
    case AD_IDLE:
    default:
        INTAD_FSM_state = AD_IDLE;
        break;
    }
    /* End user code. Do not edit comment generated here */
}
```

7.4.5   Forward Reference: Energy Monitor

Monitoring power is good, but we might also like to monitor energy, which is power integrated over time. To do this we need accurate timing information. How can we use a timer to generate a periodic interrupt to trigger the ADC scan conversion? And how fast can we make the code run (can we use fixed point math)? A faster conversion rate will increase the accuracy of the measurement. We will revisit this example when discussing timers and code optimization.

7.5   RECAP

This chapter has presented the basic concepts behind analog to digital conversion and the specifics of the RL78 family's AD converter. We have seen how the details of how to use software to control and use the AD converter. We have also seen how to improve the software architecture to leverage the AD interrupt capability.

7.6   EXERCISES

1. What is the output code (in decimal) of a 10-bit ADC with V_{in} = 1.47 V? Assume that V_{+ref} = 5 V and V_{-ref} = 1.0 V.
2. What is the output code (in decimal) of an 8-bit ADC with V_{in} = 2.7 V? V_{+ref} = 3.3 V and V_{-ref} = 0 V?
3. Given the following information of a particular analog to digital converter, determine the value of the digitally represented voltage and the step size of the converter:
    a. The device is 10-bit ADC with V_{+ref} = 3.3 V and V_{-ref} = 0 volts.
    b. The digital representation is: 0110100010.
4. What is the maximum quantization error for a 10-bit ADC with V_{+ref} = 3.3 V, and V_{-ref} = 0 V?
5. What is the maximum quantization error for an 8-bit ADC with V_{+ref} = 2.5 V, and V_{-ref} = 0.7 V?
6. Write a simple subroutine to configure the AD converter as follows: select analog input channel ANI7, sequential conversion mode, ADREFP = internal 1.44 V reference, ADREFM = ANI1, conversion time as close to 10 μs as possible, software trigger, no interrupt.
7. Write a program to display the percentage of light intensity given a light sensor circuit. Record the values for 'darkness' (cover the sensor to make it dark) and 'brightness' (shine a bright LED or other light on the sensor). Identify the correct calibration such that the average room light lies between these values.
8. Modify the program from the Basic Voltage Monitor example to support a system *without* any voltage regulation. Assume that the battery voltage ranges from 2.6 V to 1.7 V. Hint: Use the internal voltage reference and a resistive voltage divider.

Chapter Eight

Serial Communications

8.1   LEARNING OBJECTIVES

In embedded systems applications, communication between the microcontroller and other outer peripherals is often required. Although some of the communicated signals are analog, others are digital. In this chapter we outline and explain the idea of digital communication between a microcontroller and various peripherals. We explore several different protocols in place and learn how they are used. We will see the advantages and disadvantages of using different types of serial communications and explore various applications of different protocols with different devices.

8.2   BASIC CONCEPTS

Let's consider an embedded system with an MCU and several external peripherals ICs or modules with digital information (e.g., byte-size data). The MCU needs to communicate with each device in order to operate.

Here we focus on how to move data between digital logic components. We do not address what the data means. Peripheral devices have their own protocols for how to communicate with them. For example, many peripherals require the master to first send a control byte of data indicating whether it intends to either read from a register or write to a register or perform some other function. In some cases, an initial control byte may indicate that several registers will be written or read sequentially on the peripheral device.

8.2.1   Connections

How can the devices be connected? One obvious approach, shown in Figure 8.1, is to use a **dedicated point-to-point** connection between the MCU and each device. We will need a separate connection for each device. We make each connection **parallel**—we use a discrete

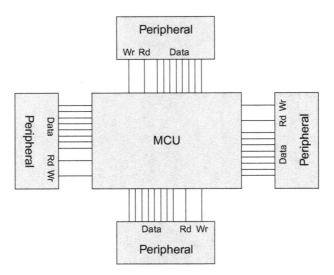

Figure 8.1 Digital communications using dedicated point-to-point connections.

signal for each data bit in the byte. We also provide control lines such as **read** and **write** to each device to indicate what it should do. This may be fast but it requires many signals, raising IC package sizes (due to pin counts) and PCB sizes (due to the number of traces).

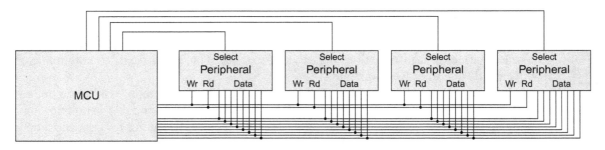

Figure 8.2 Digital communications using shared data and control buses and individual select lines.

Figure 8.2 shows some improvements. One simplification is to allow all devices to share the same set of data lines, forming a **data bus.** In this case we have a **parallel bus** which uses a signal for each of the eight data bits. Another simplification is to reduce the number of control signals. We can create a **control signal bus** which specifies read or write operations and connect it to all of the devices. We need to change each device slightly so that it only responds to the control signals if it has been selected with its device **select signal.**

If we have many devices, or we wish to address many locations within each device, we may wish to **encode** N select signals into an **address bus** which is ceiling ($\log_2 N$) bits wide. This is the approach used for external memory ICs.

8.2.2   Synchronous Serial Communication

Another major simplification is to replace the **parallel** data bus with a **serial** data bus, as shown in Figure 8.3. In this case we will need to convert data from parallel form to serial at the transmitter, and from serial to parallel at the receiver.

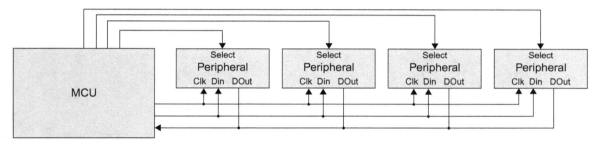

Figure 8.3   Digital communications using a clock and two shared buses: Serial data in and serial data out.

This is performed with **shift registers** as shown in Figure 8.4 and Figure 8.5. The parallel-in-serial-out shift register is first **loaded** with input data by using the multiplexers to select the parallel input data and clocking that data into the D flip-flops. The multiplexer control lines are then flipped so that the input data for each flip-flop is the output from the flip-flop to the left. Each subsequent clock pulse will cause the data to shift one bit to the right. The figures show four-bit shift registers, but in practice the shift register is large enough to hold an entire data word and potentially additional information.

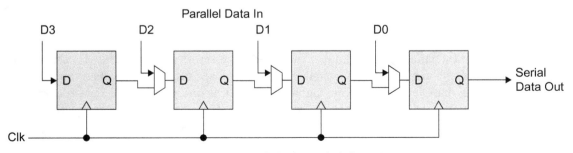

Figure 8.4   Parallel-to-serial shift register.

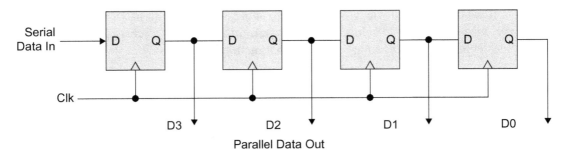

Figure 8.5 Serial-to-parallel shift register.

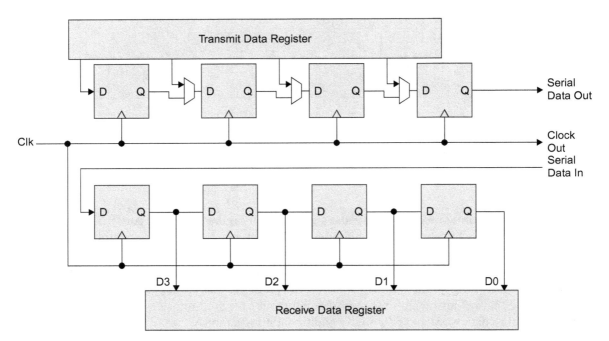

Figure 8.6 Example of internal shift registers in master device.

Each peripheral and MCU has internal shift registers to perform the conversion back and forth between parallel and serial formats. Figure 8.6 shows an example of a master device, which creates the clock signal. This is the approach used for CSI and SPI communications.

Notice that we have separate signal lines for transmit and receive data (data out and data in). This is called *full duplex mode*[1] and allows for simultaneous transmission and re-

---

[1] Full duplex mode—communication is allowed in two directions at the same time.

ception by any given device. If the receive and transmit information are sent on the same signal line then only *half duplex mode*[2] communications are possible.

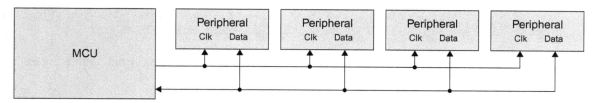

Figure 8.7 Digital communications using a clock and one shared signal: Serial data.

In Figure 8.7 we further reduce the number of signals needed for communication. First, we use only one signal line for data, allowing only half-duplex communication. Second, we send the address or device select information on the same bus as the data. Our data communication now uses a packet with both data and addressing information. Protocols such as I^2C use this approach because of the low pin count requirement.

8.2.3 Asynchronous Serial Communication

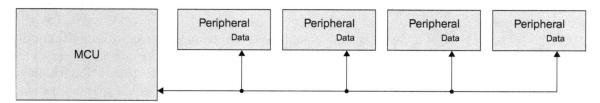

Figure 8.8 Digital communications using a shared serial data line without explicit clocking.

One further simplification is possible, as shown in Figure 8.8. We can eliminate the explicit clock line and rely on each peripheral to perform **asynchronous** communication. This is the communication approach which a UART and embedded protocols such as CAN use.

Asynchronous means that there is no clock signal transmitted along with the data to indicate when to sample it. Instead, the receiver has a clock running at the same frequency to determine **how frequently** to sample the signal line to capture each data bit, indicated by the triangles in the figure. The timing reference of **when to start sampling** is provided by a start bit as shown in Figure 8.9.

---

[2] Half duplex mode—communication is allowed in only one direction at a time.

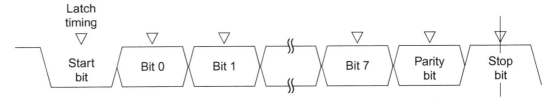

Figure 8.9 Example of asynchronous clocked serial communications timing references.

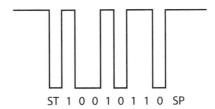

ST 1 0 0 1 0 1 1 0 SP

Figure 8.10 Waveform of byte 0x69 transmitted asynchronously.

Figure 8.10 shows an example of data being transmitted with a UART, a 0-start-bit and a 1-stop-bit. Depending on whether the LSB or MSB is sent first, this can be interpreted as 0x96 or 0x69.

The transmitter of a UART is quite simple. It simply needs to clock the data bits (and a few extras, like the start and stop bits and perhaps a parity bit) out of the transmit shift register every T_{bit} seconds.

The receiver of a UART is more complicated. It monitors the receive data line for the leading edge of the start bit. When it detects that edge, it starts its internal clock source which will generate signals to shift data into the receive data shift register at the middle of each bit time. To be specific, sampling the receive data line at $0.5* T_{bit}$ provides the start bit, the sample at $1.5* T_{bit}$ provides the first data bit, the sample at $2.5* T_{bit}$ provides the second data bit, and so forth, on up to the final bit (a stop bit). There is hardware which verifies frame has been received correctly: the start bit must be valid (e.g., 0), the stop bit must be valid (e.g., 1), and if parity is used it must be correct.

8.2.3.1 *Error Prevention and Detection*

There are two approaches used to improve the reliability of serial communications. The first is to make the transmitted signals more electrically robust, while the second is to send additional information to verify data integrity.

- The RS-232 standard represents ones and zeros with large voltages such as -10 V and $+10$ V, as shown in Figure 8.11. RS-232 drivers have low output impedances, allowing them to drive long, capacitive cables at high speeds.

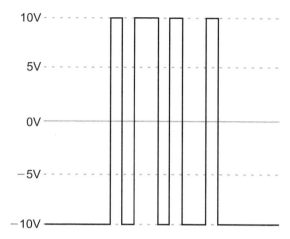

Figure 8.11 Waveform of byte transmitted asynchronously using RS-232 voltage levels.

■ Differential communications add another signal line with the opposite value of the signal. The receiver merely needs to determine which signal line has a larger voltage to determine whether a one or a zero was transmitted. This makes the resulting communication system immune to common-mode noise, in which the same noise voltage is induced in both signal wires.

Data integrity checks allow the receiver to verify that the received data is correct and has not been corrupted.

■ A **parity bit** may be sent with a byte of data in order to count the number of one-bits in the byte. The parity bit is set to a value such that the total number of one bits (in parity plus data) is either even or odd. In even parity, if the number of one-bits is even, this bit is zero, and one if it is odd. In odd parity, the bit is zero if there is an odd number of one-bits, and one otherwise. Adding parity is a simple way to perform error detection, because if a single bit is corrupted in transmission, then the UART hardware will be able to detect that the parity of the received byte is incorrect, and generate an interrupt indicating an error. Note that parity will not detect if an **even** number of bits are corrupted.

■ A parity bit is in fact a simple case of cyclic redundancy check code. A CRC appends multiple bits rather than just one and is typically able to detect multiple corrupted bits, making it a much more robust integrity-checking code. The CRC is calculated by performing a series of exclusive or operations and shifts on the data. Communication protocols such as CAN, USB, Ethernet, and Bluetooth use CRCs, as do storage devices such as Secure Digital cards.

8.2.4 Example Protocols

We now examine three separate protocols which are supported by the RL78 serial array unit peripheral.

8.2.4.1 CSI

One form of serial communications is the Clocked Serial Interface (CSI). CSI communications operate in full duplex mode, using one wire for transmission and one wire for reception. A third wire in CSI communications provides the clock for communication. CSI is therefore synchronous.

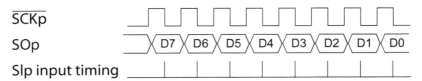

Figure 8.12 Example of clocked (synchronous) serial communications timing references.

Figure 8.12 is a timing diagram which shows the relationship between the clock signal (SCKp) and the output (SOp) and input (SIp) signals. In this example, a new output data bit is shifted out with the rising edge of the clock. The device receiving this data (the slave) uses the falling edge of the clock to shift SOp into its receiving shift register. In order for the slave to send data to the master, the slave uses the clock signal's rising edge to shift data out of its transmit shift register.

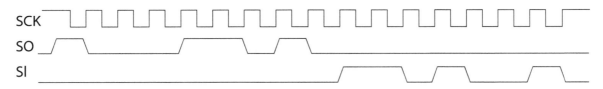

Figure 8.13 Example of data transmission with CSI.

Figure 8.13 shows an example of data transmission and reception. In this example, the rising edge of SCK clocks out data of transmit shift registers and the falling edge clocks data into receive shift registers. The signal on SO represents data 1 0 0 0 1 1 0 1 0 0 0 0 0 0 0 0 and the signal on SI represents data 0 0 0 0 0 0 0 0 1 1 0 1 0 0 1.

The master must provide the clock in order to enable communication. Typically, the microcontroller is the master and a peripheral device is the slave. A slave device only communicates when requested by the master.

Using CSI, communication (including transmission and reception) is often referred to in both directions as transferring. This is because the clock is dictated by the master, so in order for the slave to communicate back to the master, the master must transmit a byte of data to activate the clock. As the master transmits to the slave, the slave simultaneously transmits to the master, thus transferring a byte. If the master only intends to receive data from the slave, it will still need to transmit dummy bytes solely for the purpose of activating the clock to receive the data from the slave.

CSI communication is very similar to SPI (Serial Peripheral Interface) communication, which is typically a four wire interface. SPI tends to be used to have multiple slaves on a single channel, and uses the fourth wire as a chip select line to designate communication with a single slave at a time. If GPIO ports are available, the RL78 can share several slaves on one bus and use several GPIO port signals to select individual chips.

8.2.4.2 UART

Another form of serial communications is the Universal Asynchronous Receiver/Transmitter, or UART.

UARTs typically provide both a transmit line and a receive line, allowing full duplex communication. A UART may operate in *half duplex mode*[3] if the receive and transmit lines share a bus.

A UART most often transmits data in 8-bit (one byte) characters at a time, but normally can be configured to do more or less. In the digital domain, a transmitter keeps its output line high until the beginning of data communication. Once data communication begins, a start bit[4] is first sent, immediately followed by all eight bits of the byte, with the least significant bit first, and then normally one stop bit[5]. The next byte's start bit can be sent immediately. Depending on the specific settings, the most significant byte may be sent first, one or two stop bits may be used, and to verify the integrity of sent data, parity may also be added.

Because start and stop bits, and sometimes a parity bit, must be added to the communication of data, data speeds in serial communications are normally measured in symbols per second rather than bits per second. A symbol is any bit in communication that may represent start or stop of transmission, as well as any bit that is part of the transmitted data.

---

[3] Half duplex mode—communication is allowed in only one direction at a time.

[4] Start bit—a single bit where the data line transitions from high to low. This lets the hardware receiving the character know a character is about to be sent.

[5] Stop bit—a single bit that transitions the data line from low to high, or keeps it high if already high, in preparation for the data line to remain high while idle.

The term *baud rate*[6] refers to symbols per second, and in order for UART communication to successfully take place, the baud rates of both devices communicating must be equal. It is therefore important when programming a microcontroller to know the baud rates of peripherals using UART communication so as to be able to configure the UART correctly. Likewise, it is also important to properly configure how many data bits are sent in each frame (7, 8, or 9), how many stop bits are used (either 1 or 2), whether or not there will be even parity, odd parity, or no parity, etc. Having all of these aspects of UART communication pre-established allows for simple communication to occur over two wires.

8.2.4.3 I^2C

A third popular form of communications is called the Inter-Integrated Circuit (I^2C) protocol. Unlike the two former protocols, I^2C operates only in half duplex mode, and uses only two wires. For this reason, I^2C is also commonly referred to as a two-wire interface. I^2C is used most frequently for local communication with peripherals within one embedded system.

I^2C is synchronous like CSI—a clock signal is sent along with a data signal. Only one device can be a master at a time, as it will generate the clock signal. The second wire in I^2C provides data and addressing information, and is used for both reception and transmission (since I^2C provides half duplex mode operation). The I^2C communication protocol is intended to allow several devices to share a single bus. Among these devices, there may be one master node and multiple slave nodes, or even multiple master nodes and multiple slave nodes. The RL78 family of MCUs supports two forms of I^2C: simplified I^2C and advanced I^2C. Simplified I^2C communication can be performed by configuring part of the Serial Array Unit peripheral in IIC mode. This mode supports one master node (the RL78 microcontroller) and multiple slave nodes. The IICA is a separate peripheral from the SAU and it provides more complete I^2C protocol support, including multi-master support..

With I^2C all devices use open-drain drivers to control the SCL and SDA lines. This allows any device to pull down the data line or clock line; a resistor pulls up the line to a logic one if no node is trying to drive a zero. If multiple nodes attempt to simultaneously drive the line, the nodes attempting to drive it low will indeed drive it low. This can be detected by other nodes that simultaneously may be attempting to drive the line differently, letting those other nodes know that the line is active.

Since the data line is shared among several nodes, a protocol exists to define how the data line is to be used to communicate between master and slave. To illustrate the concepts, we will examine communication with an EEPROM memory device with an I^2C interface such as the R1EX24512ASAS0A. It supports multiple possible commands: write

---

[6] Typical baud rates include 4800 baud, 9600 baud, 57600 baud, 115200 baud, etc. where baud refers to symbols per second. Most devices that allow for configuration of baud rate will only allow selection of one of these predefined baud rates.

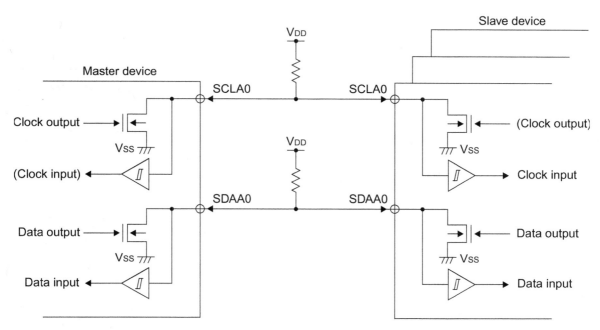

Figure 8.14   IC clock and data line connections.

data to address, write data with autoincrementing address, read data from an address, read from sequential addresses, and so forth. Other I²C devices have different communication formats.

Each slave node on an I²C bus has a unique, seven-bit address given to it (allowing $2^7 - 1$ or 127 possible slaves to exist on a single bus). The master includes this address in each data transaction to identify the targeted slave device. For our EEPROM device, this address consists of bits 10100 followed by two bits which are set by two dedicated pins on the IC package. This allows us to create a system with up to four of these devices on the same I²C bus while still allowing them to be addressed individually.

Note that the **I²C device bus address** is different from the device's internal **memory addresses.**

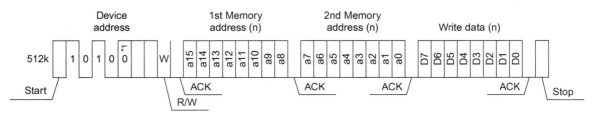

Figure 8.15   Example of writing data to EEPROM with I²C interface.

Let's examine how a byte of data is written to the EEPROM. The waveform of the data line (SDA) is shown in Figure 8.15.

- ▧ After verifying that the data line is not in use, the master first generates a start condition. This is followed by transmitting the slave node device bus address and write bit. The slave transmits an ACK bit back to acknowledge that its own device address matches the one transmitted by the master.
- ▧ The master sends the upper byte of the memory address (bits a15 through a8) and the slave device (memory) signals an acknowledgement.
- ▧ The master sends the lower byte of the memory address (bits a7 through a0) and the slave device an acknowledgement.
- ▧ The master sends the data byte to write and the slave device signals an acknowledgement.
- ▧ The master then generates a stop condition.

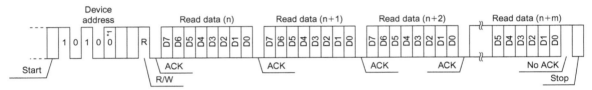

Figure 8.16 Example of sequential read from EEPROM with I²C interface.

Another example appears in Figure 8.16. Here we use the sequential read mode, which reads from the address after the previous read or write.

- ▧ After verifying that the data line is not in use, the master first generates a start condition. This is followed by transmitting the slave node address and a read. The slave transmits an ACK bit back to acknowledge that its own device address matches the one transmitted by the master.
- ▧ The slave sends the read data byte from address n and the master device signals an acknowledgement.
- ▧ The slave sends another read data byte (from address n+1) and the master signals an acknowledgement.
- ▧ The slave sends another read data byte (from address n+2) and the master signals an acknowledgement. This may repeat multiple times.
- ▧ The slave sends another read data byte (from address n+m) but the master **does not** signal an acknowledgement.
- ▧ The master then generates a stop condition.

8.3   SERIAL ARRAY UNIT CONCEPTS

UNIT	CHANNEL	CSI	UART	SIMPLIFIED I²C
			UNIT NAME BASED ON MODE	
0	0	CSI00	UART0	IIC00
	1	CSI01		IIC01
	2	CSI10	UART1	IIC10
	3	CSI11		IIC11
1	0	CSI20	UART2	IIC20
	1	CSI21		IIC21
	2	CSI30	UART3	IIC30
	3	CSI31		IIC31

Figure 8.17   Serial Array Unit channel names based on operating modes.

An RL78 MCU's Serial Array Unit, is shown in Figure 8.17. Serial Array Unit channel names based on operating modes has multiple channels which can be configured to operate in several modes: CSI, UART, and Simplified IIC. We begin by describing the aspects of the SAU behavior which are common across the modes, and then we examine each mode's operation and any mode-specific configuration options.

8.3.1   Common SAU Concepts

An SAU channel's operating mode is selected from CSI, UART and Simplified IIC using the MDmn2 and MDmn1 bits. Note that in these control register descriptions, m refers to the SAU number (0 or 1) and n refers to the channel with in the SAU.

8.3.1.1   Enabling a Channel

There are some basic configurations settings necessary.

- In order to use a SAU it must be provided with a clock signal by setting the SAUmEN bit in PER0 to 1.
- A channel can perform transmission, reception, or both simultaneously (depending on the operating mode). In order to enable transmission, bit TXEmn must be set to 1. In order to enable reception, bit RXEmn must be set to 1.

◼ Each channel has a read-only bit SEmn which enables communication when it is 1 and disables it otherwise. To set the bit, the corresponding serial channel start bit (SSmn) must be written with a 1. To clear SEmn, the corresponding serial channel stop bit (STmn) must be written with a 1.

8.3.1.2 Data Configuration

Transmit and receive data are sent through the lower bits of the SDRmn register. These bits have different names based on the operating mode and the data transfer size. The p, q, and r suffixes indicate which channel is used:

◼ The CSI mode refers to the lower eight bits as SIOp.
◼ The UART mode refers to the lower eight or nine bits as TXDq and RXDq.
◼ The Simplified IIC mode refers to the lower eight bits as SIOr.

Various aspects of data representation are configurable:

◼ Data length is set to seven, eight, or nine bits by the DLSmn bits.
◼ The "endianness" of data communication is controlled with bit DIRmn. Clearing it to 0 results in the most-significant bit being sent first (big-endian data), while setting it to 1 inverts the order to little-endian.
◼ The POMmn bit controls whether the output port signal is driven both high and low (push-pull) or just low (open-drain). Using the open-drain configuration enables us to safely connect multiple outputs to the same bus line, as shown in Figure 8.18.

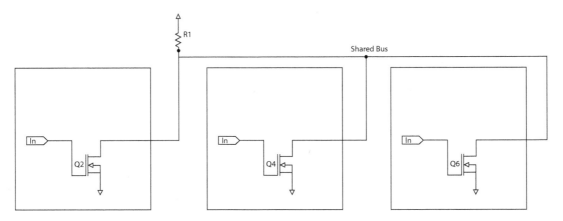

Figure 8.18 Open-drain outputs can drive a bus safely.

8.3.1.3 Software Control of Output Lines

There are several bits which allow software control (bit-banging) of the output data and clock lines when communication is stopped. These are used in I^2C to support creation of start and stop conditions.

- The SOEmn bit controls whether software can change the value of the serial output.
- The SOmn and CKOmn bits set the value serial output and clock output.

8.3.1.4 Status

The serial status register (SSRmn) holds flags indicating various status conditions:

- The BFFmn flag indicates the buffer register status. If the flag is one, then there is valid data in the SDRmn register. BFFmn is set when the program writes to SDRmn, and cleared when the program reads from SDRmn.
- The TSFmn flag indicates communication is in progress. It is set by hardware when transmission begins and cleared when transmission ends.
- The OVFmn flag indicates an overrun error has occurred. Either received data was not read from SDRmn before the next data was received, or the received data was not read from SDRmn before the next data to transmit was written.

8.3.1.5 Transfer Speed Control

The clock signals which control transfer speed are essential for both asynchronous and synchronous communications. Shown in Figure 8.19, the SAU clock generators are flexible and enable the generation of a wide range of frequencies based on an internal or an external source. Each SAU has two operation clock signals (CKm0 and CKm1, also called f_{MCK}); a channel can use either of these clocks. These operation clocks can be set to a frequency derived from f_{CLK} (divided by powers of two from 1 to 2^{15}). Alternatively, an external serial clock input can be used (e.g., in synchronous reception modes). Each channel then generates a transfer rate clock by dividing the selected clock signal down by a factor ranging from 2 to 256.

The clock speed is controlled by several registers.

- The PRSmn fields of the SPSm register control the division of f_{CLK} to generate the operation clocks CKm0 and CKm1.
- The CKSmn and CCSmn bits controls which prescaler output clock (CKm0 or CKm1) or the external clock is used.
- The upper seven bits of the SDRmn register control the division ratio of the operation clock. The resulting communication frequency is $f_{MCK}/(2(D+1))$, where D is the division factor stored in the SDRmn[15:9].

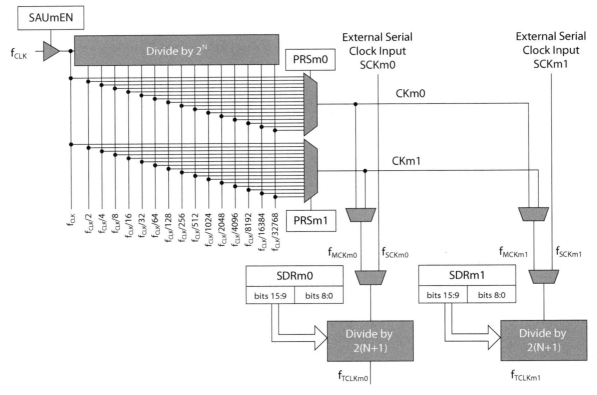

Figure 8.19 Clock generation system for serial communications.

8.3.1.6 *Interrupts*

Each channel can request several types of interrupt, based on the channel's operating mode.

- A transmitting SAU channel can request an interrupt either when a transfer ends (for single transfer mode) or when the transmit buffer is empty (for continuous transfer mode). This is controlled by the MDmn0 bit.
- A receiving SAU channel can request an interrupt when reception is completed. We will explore this in greater detail below.
- A receiving SAU channel can also request an interrupt if an error has occurred.

8.3.2   CSI Mode

8.3.2.1 *Basic Concepts*

There are six different types of communication possible based on whether the channel is configured as a master or slave, and whether a transfer operation is a transmission, a reception, or both simultaneously. In addition, there is a snooze mode function which allows the processor to save power and energy.

We will examine two communication modes, both of which involve both transmission and reception. The first uses the CSI mode's **single transfer** operation, while the second uses **continuous transfer** operation. In master modes, the channel generates the transfer clock signal.

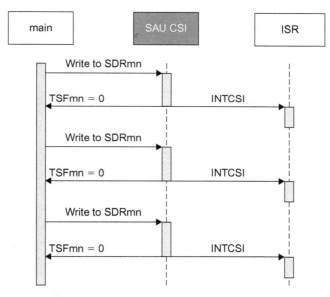

Figure 8.20   Interactions between main routine, SAU in CSI mode, and CSI ISR when operating in single transfer mode.

Figure 8.20 and Figure 8.21 present an overview of CSI master communication with simultaneous transmit/receive operation in single transfer mode. A CSI interrupt is generated after each transfer completes.

- The main routine writes transmit data item #1 into SDRmn.
- This write starts the transmission/reception process: the CSI controller cycles the clock line SCKp to shift transmit data out through SOp while shifting receive data in through SIp. During this activity the TSFmn bit is set, indicating that communication is in progress.
- When all seven or eight data bits have been transmitted and received, the INTCSIp interrupt is requested.

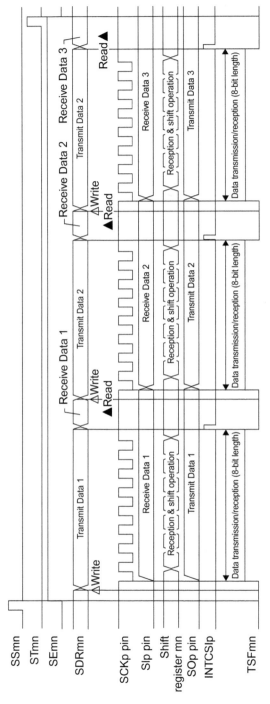

Figure 8.21 Timing diagram showing CSI master performing simultaneous transmission and reception in single transmission mode.

▓ The CSI ISR reads the received data item from SDRmn and stores in in a user-defined receive data buffer.

▓ The user program can repeat this process with each data item until all of the data has been sent and received.

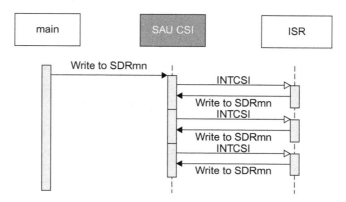

Figure 8.22   Interactions between main routine, SAU in CSI mode, and CSI ISR when operating in continuous transfer mode.

Figure 8.23 shows operation with continuous transfer mode. A sequence diagram appears in Figure 8.22.

The main difference from single transfer mode is that most of the data transfer processing occurs in the ISR rather than the main routine. The CSI interrupt is generated when data is copied from the SDRmn register to the shift register. Also, the SAU automatically copies data from SDRmn to the shift register when the current transmission completes. This mechanism allows us to implement a continuous operation within the ISR. We also have another interrupt to deal with at the beginning of the sequence, which changes the ISR slightly.

▓ The main routine writes data item #1 into the SDRmn.

▓ Unlike the single transfer mode, an INTCSIp interrupt is requested soon after the first data item is written into SDRmn. Because the SAU is idle (not currently transmitting), it automatically transfers the data from SDRmn into the transmit shift register. This transfer generates an interrupt.

▓ As above, the ISR needs to read received data from SDRmn. However, it has additional features:

   ☐ The ISR also needs to write transmit data to SDRmn.

   ☐ The ISR does not need to read the received data for the first interrupt.

   ☐ After loading the last data to transmit the ISR needs to disable further transfers by switching the interrupt source to end of transmission instead of buffer empty (by clearing MDmn0 to 0).

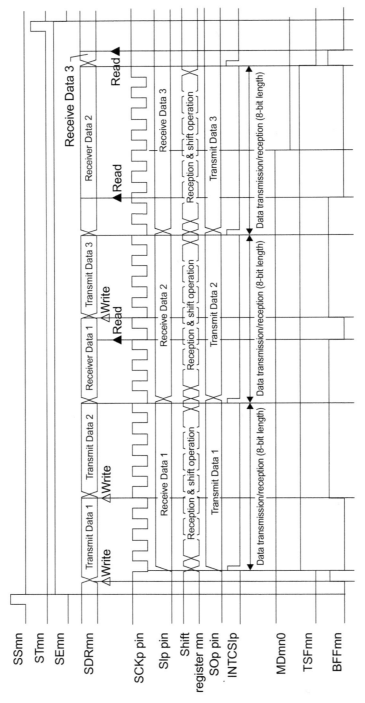

Figure 8.23 Timing diagram showing CSI master performing simultaneous transmission and reception in continuous transfer mode.

- The transmission/reception process again consists of the CSI controller cycling the clock line SCKp to shift transmit data out through SOp while shifting receive data in through SIp. During this activity the TSFmn bit is set, indicating that communication is in progress.
- When all seven or eight data bits have been transmitted and received, new transmit data is copied from SDRmn to the shift register and another INTCSIp interrupt is requested.
- The CSI ISR reads the received data from the SDRmn.

8.3.2.2 *CSI-Specific Configuration*

There are various additional configurable parameters for CSI mode.

- Data to be transmitted is written to the SIOp register, while received data is read from SIOp as well.
- Data phase and clock phase are controlled using the DAPmn and CKPmn bits. Data phase (DAP) determines whether data is valid after the starting edge of the clock or before. Clock phase determines whether the clock's rising or falling edge is used.

DAP mn	CKP mn	SELECTION OF DATA AND CLOCK PHASE IN CSI MODE	TYPE
0	0	SCKp / SOp (D7 D6 D5 D4 D3 D2 D1 D0) / SIp input timing	1
0	1	SCKp / SOp (D7 D6 D5 D4 D3 D2 D1 D0) / SIp input timing	2
1	0	SCKp / SOp (D7 D6 D5 D4 D3 D2 D1 D0) / SIp input timing	3
1	1	SCKp / SOp (D7 D6 D5 D4 D3 D2 D1 D0) / SIp input timing	4

8.3.3   UART Mode

8.3.3.1   Basic Concepts

The UART mode supports transmission and reception. Single and continuous transfers are possible when transmitting. In addition, there is a snooze mode function which allows the processor to save power and energy.

Figure 8.24 shows an example of a UART transmission using single transfer mode. After writing to SSmn to enable communications, the data to transmit is written to SDRmn. This data (with framing and optional parity) is then shifted out the TxDq pin. While the transmission occurs, the TSFmn bit is 1. When transmission completes, the TSFmn bit falls to 0 and an optional interrupt (INTSTq) request is generated. The program can use an ISR to load the next data to transmit into SDRmn. The program could instead use polling to wait until TSFmn falls to 0 but this is usually not the preferred solution for reasons of efficiency.

Figure 8.25 shows an example of UART reception. The program writes to SSmn to enable the receiver. After the first data item is received the UART can request an INTSRq interrupt which will trigger an ISR which reads the received data from SDRmn.

8.3.3.2   UART-Specific Configuration

There are additional configuration options for UART mode.

- One or two stop bits can be used.
- Parity can be set to none, even, or odd.
- The output data will be inverted if the SOLmn bit is set to 1.
- The input data will be inverted if the SISmn0 bit is set to 1.
- A noise filter for input data will be enabled if SNFENmn is set to 1.

8.3.3.3   Error Handling

There are two additional possible errors in UART mode.

- The FEFmn flag is set if a framing error occurred—the received stop bit was a 0 rather than the correct value of 1.
- The PEFmn flag is set if a parity error occurs—the received parity bit does not match the calculated parity value.

8.3.4   Simplified IIC Mode

The SAU supports a simplified version of I^2C communication which supports the most common features of I^2C: single master transmit and receive operations, 8-bit data length and

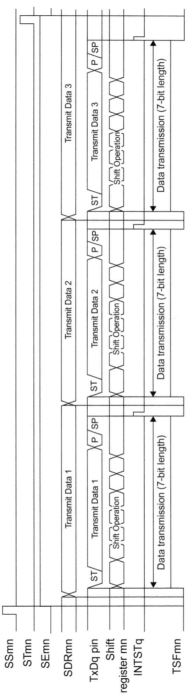

Figure 8.24 Timing diagram showing UART transmission in single transfer mode.

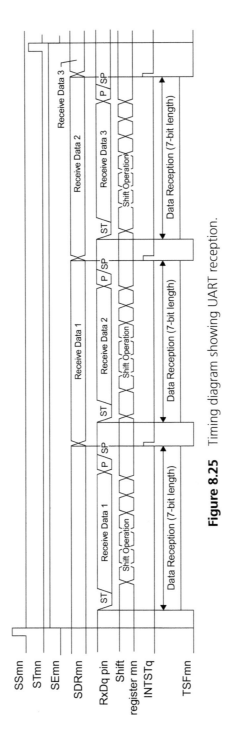

Figure 8.25   Timing diagram showing UART reception.

ACK generation and detection. More advanced features such as slave mode, arbitration support, and wait detection are not supported by SAU but instead by the IICA unit.

The simplified IIC communication mode works by operating on the individual sections within the I^{2}C packet: start condition, address and read/write command, send data, receive data, and stop condition.

8.3.4.1 Basic Concepts

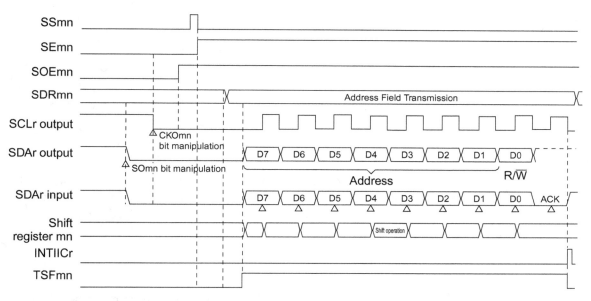

Figure 8.26 Timing diagram for start condition and device address transmission.

The start condition must be generated under software control as follows:

- Write 0 to SOmn to lower SDAr.
- Write 0 to CKOmn to lower SCLr.
- Write 1 to SOEmn to enable the serial communication output.
- Write 1 to SSmn to start transmission.

The address and the read/write bit must then be transmitted by writing them to the SIOr. The transfer end interrupt will be generated after all eight bits are transmitted. Note that the parity system is configured to expect a 0, which a slave device will send after it recognizes its address. The ACK field is read by examining the parity error flag PEFmn. If it is 1 then no ACK was sent by a slave. Otherwise a slave sent an ACK so communication can continue.

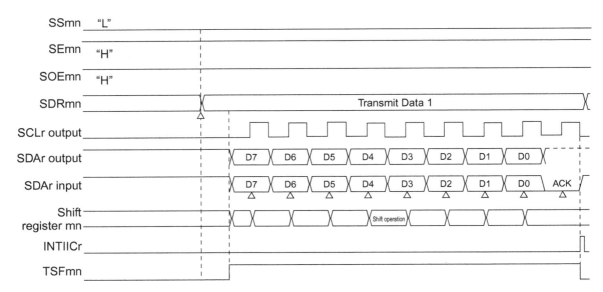

Figure 8.27 Timing diagram for data transmission.

Figure 8.27 shows the timing diagram for transmitting a byte of data. The master writes that data to SIOr and awaits the transfer end interrupt. If the PEFmn flag is one, then the data was not acknowledged by the slave. Otherwise it was acknowledged and communication can proceed.

Data reception proceeds as follows:

- Write 1 to STmn to stop communication temporarily and gain access to control registers.
- Write 0 to TXEmn to disable the transmitter and 1 to RXEmn to enable the receiver.
- Write 1 to SSmn to start communication.
- Write dummy data (hexadecimal FF) to SIOr.
- Wait for transfer end interrupt.
- Read receive data from SIOr.

Figure 8.28 shows the waveforms for the stop condition, which must be generated by software as follows:

- Stop transmission by writing a 1 to STmn.
- Write 0 to SOEmn to disable serial communication output.
- Write 0 to SOmn to lower the SDAr output.
- Write 1 to CKOmn to raise the SCLr output.

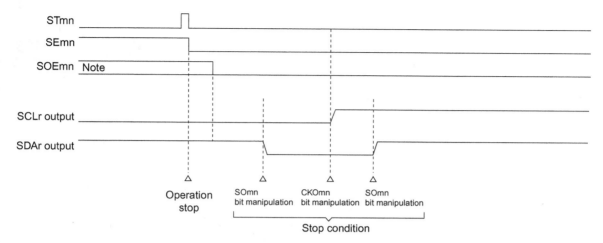

Figure 8.28 Timing diagram for stop condition

- Wait for a fixed time so that slave recognizes stop condition.
- Write 1 to SOmn to raise the SDAr output.

8.4   SERIAL COMMUNICATIONS DEVICE DRIVER CODE

Applilet allows for easy configuration and use of the Serial Array Unit, whether being used for UART, CSI, or I²C communication. When using Applilet to configure the Serial Array Unit, each different mode of communication has a predefined Application Programming Interface (API) with a set of functions and global variables used to control communication. Additionally, each API comes with several user-definable functions. For example, a user can define what happens when transmission or reception of data is complete. In this section we examine functions for both the SAU and the advanced IIC controller (IICA).

8.4.1   General Functions

8.4.1.1   SAU Functions

Table 8.1 shows a list of functions useful for every configuration of the Serial Array Unit (SAU).

8.4.1.2   SAU Function Definitions

void R_SAUn_Create(void): This is the function called to initialize Serial Array Unit n (e.g., SAU0 or SAU1). This function must be called before initializing or using any form of

TABLE 8.1 Functions Associated with Each Serial Array Unit (*n = 0,1 for SAU0 or SAU1)

FUNCTION NAME	FUNCTION DESCRIPTION
R_SAUn_Create()	Initializes Serial Array Unit n
R_SAUn_Set_SnoozeOn()	Enables start function from STOP state of chip
R_SAUn_Set_SnoozeOff()	Disables start function from STOP state of chip
R_SAUn_Set_PowerOff()	Stops supply of input clock and all special function registers are reset

serial communications. It is important to initialize the correct Serial Array Unit corresponding to the desired UART, CSI, or IIC.

Parameters: void
Returns: void

void R_SAUn_Set_SnoozeOn(void): If SNOOZE mode is available for the specified channel, this function enables SNOOZE mode. This allows for the channel to operate while the chip is in the STOP state, and makes possible data reception that does not require the CPU.

Parameters: void
Returns: void

void R_SAUn_SetSnoozeOff(void): If SNOOZE mode is available for the specified channel, this function disables SNOOZE mode.

Parameters: void
Returns: void

void R_SAUn_Set_PowerOff(void): This function stops supply of input clock and all Special Function Registers (SFR) are reset.

Parameters: void
Returns: void

8.4.2   CSI API

8.4.2.1   CSI Functions

Table 8.2 shows a list of functions and their brief descriptions. Note that all functions are associated with the CSI module to which they belong, so the "m" in the function name is

TABLE 8.2 Functions Associated with Each CSI.

FUNCTION NAME	FUNCTION DESCRIPTION	USER-DEFINED
R_CSIm_Create()	Initializes the CSIm module	
R_CSIm_Start()	Starts the CSIm module	
R_CSIm_Stop()	Stops the CSIm module	
R_CSIm_Receive()	Sets up buffer for data reception from CSIm module	
R_CSIm_Send()	Sends data from CSIm module	
R_CSIm_Send_Receive()	Simultaneously sends and receives data from CSIm module	
MD_INTCSIm()	Interrupt Service Routine called at the end of transmission/reception of each byte of CSIm module	
R_CSIm_Callback_ReceiveEnd ()[†]	Callback function after CSIm reception	
R_CSIm_Callback_Error ()[†]	Callback function after CSIm transmission/reception error	
R_CSIm_Callback_SendEnd ()[†]	Callback function after CSIm transmission	

replaced by 00, 01, 10, 11, 20, 21 for CSI00, CSI01, CSI10, CSI11, CSI20, or CSI21 respectively. Also, some functions are user-defined.

8.4.2.2 CSI Global Variables

The following table shows global variables used in the CSI API. These variables are associated with the buffers where data is transmitted and received. As above, m = 00, 01, 10, 11, 20, 21 for CSI00, CSI01, CSI10, CSI11, CSI20, or CSI21. Note that a separate set of variables is associated with each individual CSI module.

All of the variables are present for each instance of a CSI module, whether the CSI module is in transmit only mode, receive only mode, or transmit/receive mode. However, not all variables are used in every mode. Table 8.4 shows which variables are used in which mode.

Although these variables may be accessed globally, they need not be modified, as the functions controlling each CSI module do this automatically. It is fine to read their values, but it is also important to understand how each function modifies these values (see 8.4.2.3 CSI Function Definitions).

TABLE 8.3   Global Variables Associated with Each CSI Module.

GLOBAL VARIABLE NAME	DESCRIPTION
uint8_t *gp_CsimRxAddress	Address of uint8_t receive buffer for CSIm module
uint16_t g_CsimRxLen	Length of the CSIm module receive buffer
uint16_t g_CsimRxCnt	Number of bytes currently received so far by CSIm module
uint8_t *gp_CsimTxAddress	Address of uint8_t transmit buffer for CSIm module
uint16_t g_CsimTxLen	Length of the CSIm module transmit buffer
uint16_t g_CsimTxCnt	Number of bytes left to be transmitted from CSIm module

TABLE 8.4   Variables Used per Mode for Each CSI Module

TRANSMIT/RECEIVE MODE	GLOBAL VARIABLES USED
Receive Only Mode	gp_CsimRxAddress
	g_CsimRxLen
	g_CsimRxCnt
Transmit Only Mode	gp_CsimTxAddress
	g_CsimTxCnt
Transmit/Receive Mode	gp_CsimRxAddress
	gp_CsimTxAddress
	g_CsimTxCnt

8.4.2.3   CSI Function Definitions

void R_CSIm_Create(void): This is the function called to initialize CSI module m (e.g., CSI00, CSI01, CSI10, CSI11, CSI20, or CSI21). This function must be called prior to using any functions associated with the desired CSI module. However, this function is automatically called by the R_SAUn_Create() function, so it is only necessary to call the corresponding R_SAUn_Create() function.

Parameters: void
Returns: void

void R_CSIm_Start(void): This function begins the operation of CSIm module and enables communication. Once called, the interrupt associated with the CSIm module is also enabled. It is important to note that no communication with the CSIm module can be achieved until this function is called.

Parameters: void
Returns: void

void R_CSIm_Stop(void): When it is desired to stop communication with the CSIm module, the module can be ordered to stop. This function ends the operation of the CSIm module and disables communication on the module. Once called, the interrupt associated with the CSIm module is disabled as well. Communication will cease until R_CSIm_Start() is called again.

Parameters: void
Returns: void

MD_STATUS R_CSIm_Receive(uin t8_t *rxbuf, uint16_t rxnum): If the CSIm module is set up in receive only mode, this function may be called to receive data. This function activates the clock line (SCK) and writes dummy data to data out (SI) and reads rxnum bytes coming in on the data in line (SI) and stores it in the designated rxbuf. Because this function makes use of the CSIm hardware interrupt (see MD_INTCSIm()), this function only commences the data reception. The CSIm hardware interrupt will call the R_CSIm_Callback_ReceiveEnd() function when data reception is complete (when rxnum bytes have been recieved). This function is only available if the CSIm module is designated in Applilet to run in receive only mode.

Parameters: uint8_t * rxbuf—Pointer to the first element of the
                         receive buffer where the received data will be
                         placed
                         uint16_t rxnum—Number of bytes to receive and
                         place in the rxbuf buffer
Returns: MD_OK—Receive commenced successfully
                         MD_ARGERROR—Bad parameter
Global Variables Modified: g_CsimRxLen—Set to rxnum to indicate the length
                         of the receive buffer
                         g_CsimRxCnt—Set to zero to indicate zero bytes
                         received so far
                         gp_CsimRxAddress—Set to rxbuf to indicate the
                         head of the receive buffer

MD_STATUS R_CSIm_Send(uint8_t * txbuf, uint16_t txnum): If the CSIm module is set up in transmit only mode, this function may be called to transmit data. This function activates the clock line (SCK) and writes txnum bytes of the designated txbuf on the data out line (SO) and ignores any incoming data on the data in line (SI). Because this function makes use of the CSIm hardware interrupt (see MD_INTCSIm()), this function only commences the data transmission. The CSIm hardware interrupt will call the R_CSIm_Callback_SendEnd() function when data transmission is complete (when txnum bytes have been sent). This function is only available if the CSIm module is designated in Applilet to run in transmit only mode.

Parameters:	uint8_t * txbuf—Pointer to the first element of the transmit buffer where the designated string of data is
	uint16_t txnum—Number of bytes to send from the txbuf buffer
Returns:	MD_OK—Send commenced successfully
	MD_ARGERROR—Bad Parameter
Global Variables Modified:	g_CsimTxCnt—Set to txnum to indicate the number of bytes left to be sent, and decremented by one after the first byte is sent
	gp_CsimTxAddress—Set to txbuf to indicate the head of the transmit buffer, and then increased by one to point to the next spot in the buffer after the first byte is sent

MD_STATUS R_CSIm_Send_Receive(uint8_t * txbuf, uint16_t txnum, uint8_t * rxbuf): If the CSIm module is set up in transmit/receive mode, this function may be called to do a CSI transmit/receive data transfer. This function activates the clock line (SCK) for the duration of the transfer, and txnum bytes of the designated txbuf are sent on the data out line (SO) and simultaneously, txnum bytes are received on the data in line (SI) and stored in the designated rxbuf. Because this function makes use of the CSIm hardware interrupt (see MD_INTCSIm()), this function only commences transmission and reception. The CSIm hardware interrupt will call both the R_CSIm_Callback_SendEnd() and R_CSIm_Callback_ReceiveEnd() functions when the data transfer is complete (when all txnum bytes have been sent/received). This function is only available if the CSIm module is designated in Applilet to run in transmit/receive mode. It is important to make sure that txbuf and rxbuf both must be at least txnum bytes long to prevent out-of-bounds memory indexing.

Parameters:	uint8_t * txbuf—Pointer to the first element of the transmit buffer where the designated string of data is
	uint16_t txnum—Number of bytes to be transferred

	uint8_t * rxbuf—Pointer to the first element of the receive buffer where the received data will be placed
Returns:	MD_OK—Transfer commenced successfully
	MD_ARGERROR—Bad Parameter
Global Variables Modified:	g_CsimTxCnt—Set to txnum to indicate number of bytes to send, and decremented by one after the first byte is sent
	gp_CsimTxAddress—Set to txbuf to indicate the head of the transmit buffer, and then increased by one to point to the next spot in the buffer after the first byte is sent
	gp_CsimRxAddress—Set to rxbuf to indicate the head of the receive buffer

void MD_INTCSIm(void): This is the Interrupt Service Routine called by the hardware after transmission of each single byte of data from the CSIm module. This function behaves slightly differently depending on which transmit/receive mode the CSIm module is in.

If the CSIm module is in receive only mode, this interrupt is called after transmission of each dummy byte, and each time it is called, the next received byte is placed into the receive buffer designated by the R_CSIm_Receive() function. When the total number of bytes have been received (also designated by the call to the R_CSIm_Receive() function), the CSIm_Callback_ReceiveEnd () is called to indicate completion of reception.

If the CSIm module is in transmit only mode, this interrupt is called after transmission of each byte from the transmit buffer designated by the R_CSIm_Send() function. When transmission is complete, and the number of bytes designated to be sent by the R_CSIm_Send() function have been sent, the CSIm_Callback_SendEnd() function is called to indicate completion of transmission.

If the CSIm module is in transmit/receive mode, this interrupt is called after transmission of each byte from the transmit buffer designated by the R_CSIm_Send_Receive() function. Upon each call of this interrupt, the next received byte is placed into the receive buffer designated by the R_CSIm_Send_Receive() function, thus defining a single transfer of data. When the transfer is complete and the number of bytes designated to be sent by the R_CSIm_Send_Receive() function have been sent, both the CSIm_Callback_SendEnd() and the CSIm_Callback_ReceiveEnd() functions are called to indicate completion of transmission and reception.

Parameters:	void
Returns:	void

Global Variables Modified: In Receive Only Mode:

gp_CsimRxAddress—Pointer is increased
   by one to point to the next location in the
   designated receive buffer
   (see R_CSIm_Receive())

g_CsimRxCnt—Increased by one to indicate one
   more byte of data received

In Transmit Only Mode:

gp_CsimTxAddress—Pointer is increased by one
   to point to the next location in the designated
   transmit buffer (see R_CSIm_Send())

g_CsimTxCnt—Decreased by one to indicate one
   less byte of data to send

In Transmit/Receive Mode:

gp_CsimRxAddress—Pointer is increased by one
   to point to the next location in the designated
   receive buffer (see R_CSIm_Send_Receive())

gp_CsimTxAddress—Pointer is increased by one
   to point to the next location in the designated
   transmit buffer (see R_CSIm_Send_Receive())

g_Csim TxCnt—Decreased by one to indicate
   one less byte of data to be transferred

void   R_CSIm_Callback_ReceiveEnd(void): This   function   is   invoked   by   the
MD_INTCSIm() Interrupt Service Routine when data that was designated to be received
by either the R_CSIm_Receive() or the R_CSIm_Send_Receive() functions has finished
reception. This is one of the three user-definable functions of the CSI API, so the user can
designate what happens when the CSI data reception is complete.

Parameters: void
Returns: void

void R_CSIm_Callback_Error(uint8_t err_type): This function is invoked by the
MD_INTCSIm() Interrupt Service Routine when an error is indicated by the Serial Status
Register (SSR) in the ISR. This function takes the error type as a parameter, and is one of
the three user-definable functions of the CSI API, so the user can designate what happens
when bad data reception has occurred.

Parameters: uint8_t err_type—The type of error generated by error in
     the CSIm module data reception
Returns: void

void R_CSIm_Callback_SendEnd(void): This function is invoked by the MD_INTC-SIm() Interrupt Service Routine when data that was designated to be sent by either the R_CSIm_Send() or the R_CSIm_Send_Receive() functions has finished transmission. This is one of the three user-definable functions of the CSI API, so the user can designate what happens when CSI data transmission is complete.

Parameters: void
Returns: void

8.4.3 UART API

8.4.3.1 UART Functions

Table 8.5 shows a list of functions and their brief descriptions. Note that all functions are associated with which UART they belong to. Note that the "m" in the function name is replaced with 0, 1, 2 for UART0, UART1, or UART2, respectively. Certain functions are user-defined.

8.4.3.2 UART Global Variables

Table 8.6 shows global variables used in the UART API. These variables are associated with the buffers where data is transmitted and received. Note that the following set of variables are associated with each individual UART.

Although these variables may be accessed globally, they need not be modified, as the functions controlling the UART (see Table 8.5) do this automatically. It is fine to read their values, but it is also important to understand how each function modifies these values.

8.4.3.3 UART Function Definitions

void R_UARTm_Create(void): This is the function called to initialize UARTm (e.g., UART0, UART1, or UART2). This function must be called prior to using any functions associated with the desired UART. However, this function is automatically called by the R_ function, so it is only necessary to call the corresponding R_ function.

Parameters: void
Returns: void

void R_UARTm_Start(void): This function begins the operation of UARTm and enables communication with this UART. Once called, the interrupts associated with UARTm are

TABLE 8.5   Functions Associated with Each UART.

FUNCTION NAME	FUNCTION DESCRIPTION	USER-DEFINED
R_UARTm_Create()	Initializes UARTm	
R_UARTm_Start()	Starts reception/transmission of UARTm	
R_UARTm_Stop()	Stops reception/transmission of UARTm	
R_UARTm_Send()	Transmits a string of data from UARTm	
R_UARTm_Receive()	Designates receive buffer for data received by UARTm	
R_UARTm_Interrupt_Receive()	Interrupt Service Routine called at the end of UARTm reception	
R_UARTm_Interrupt_Error()	Interrupt Service Routine called upon error of UARTm reception	
R_UARTm_Interrupt_Send()	Interrupt Service Routine called at the end of UARTm transmission	
R_UARTm_Callback_ReceiveEnd()	Callback function when UARTm finishes reception	
R_UARTm_Callback_SendEnd()	Callback function when UARTm finishes transmission	
R_UARTm_Callback_Error()	Callback function when UARTm reception error occurs	
R_UARTm_Callback_SoftwareOverRun()	Callback function when UARTm receives overflow data	

TABLE 8.6   Global Variables Associated with Each UART; (m = 0, 1, 2 for UART0, UART1, or UART2)

GLOBAL VARIABLE NAME	DESCRIPTION
uint8_t *gp_UartmTxAddress	Address of uint8_t transmit buffer for UARTm
uint16_t g_UartmTxCnt	Number of bytes left to be transmitted from UARTm
uint8_t *gp_UartmRxAddress	Address of uint8_t receive buffer for UARTm
uint16_t g_UartmRxCnt	Number of bytes currently received so far by UARTm
uint16_t g_UartmRxLen	Length of UARTm receive buffer

also enabled. It is important to note that no communication with UARTm can be achieved until this function is called.

> *Parameters:*   void
> *Returns:*   void

void R_UARTm_Stop(void): When it is desired to stop communication with a specific UART, the UART can be ordered to stop. This function ends the operation of UARTm and disables communication with this UART. Once called, the interrupts associated with UARTm are disabled as well. This will prevent any further program interruption from outside communication to this UART, and all outside communication will be ignored until R_UARTm_Start() is called.

> *Parameters:*   void
> *Returns:*   void

MD_STATUS R_UARTm_Send (uint8_t * txbuf, uint16_t txnum): To send a string of data out through UARTm, this function may be called. The function takes a pointer to the beginning of the string of data and the length of the data string. This function invokes the UARTm transmit interrupt (R_UARTm_Interrupt_Send()), and although one byte of data is transmitted at a time, only one call of this function is required to send an entire string of data.

> *Parameters:*   uint8_t * txbuf—Pointer to the first element of the designated string of data
> uint16_t txnum—Number of bytes to transmit
> *Returns:*   MD_OK—Data transmission successfully started
> MD_ARGERROR—Bad parameter
> *Global Variables Modified:*   gp_UartmTxAddress—Set to txbuf pointer parameter to indicate the head of the string of data to transmit
> g_UartmTxCnt—Set to txnum parameter to indicate number of bytes of data to send

MD_STATUS R_UARTm_Receive(uint8_t * rxbuf, uint16_t rxnum): To set up the receive buffer for communications on UARTm, this function may be called. The function takes a pointer to the buffer and indicates the size of the buffer. By calling this function, all incoming UART data will automatically fill the designated buffer.

> *Parameters:*   uint8_t * rxbuf—Pointer to the first element of the designated receive buffer
> uint16_t rxnum—Length of the designated receive buffer

Returns:	MD_OK—Receive buffer assigned successfully
	MD_ARGERROR—Bad parameter
Global Variables Modified:	g_UartmRxCnt—Set to 0 to indicate buffer has not received any data
	g_UartmRxLen—Set to rxnum parameter to indicate how much space is available in the buffer before it is full
	gp_UartmRxAddress—Set to rxbuf pointer parameter to indicate the head of the receive buffer

void R_UARTm_Interrupt_Receive(void): This is the Interrupt Service Routine called by the hardware when each byte of data is received by UARTm. This function invokes the R_UARTm_Callback_ReceiveEnd() and R_UARTm_Callback_SoftwareOverRun () functions.

Parameters:	void
Returns:	void
Global Variables Modified:	gp_UartmRxAddress—The newest received byte of data is stored at the location this pointer points to, and the pointer is increased by one to point to the next element in the designated receive buffer (see R_UARTm_Receive()).
	g_UartmRxCnt—Increased by one to indicate that one more byte of data has been received.

void R_UARTm_Interrupt_Error(void): This is the Interrupt Service Routine called by the hardware upon error in reception of data for UARTm, such as incorrect parity. Every time this function is called, the R_UARTm_Callback_Error () function is invoked.

Parameters:	void
Returns:	void
Global Variables Modified:	gp_UartmRxAddress—The element that this pointer points to gets updated with the newest received byte of data, but unlike in R_UARTm_Interrupt_ Receive(), the pointer does not advance to the next element in the designated receive buffer (see R_UARTm_Receive()).

void R_UARTm_Interrupt_Send(void): This is the Interrupt Service Routine called by the hardware after successful transmission of each single byte of data from UARTm. This function invokes the R_UARTm_Callback_SendEnd() function at the end of transmission if R_UARTm_Send() was used to transmit the data.

Parameters:	void
Returns:	void
Global Variables Modified:	gp_UartmTxAddress—Pointer is increased by one to point to the next location in the designated send buffer (see R_UARTm_Send()).
	g_UartmTxCnt—Decreased by one to indicate one less byte of data to be sent.

void R_UARTm_Callback_ReceiveEnd(void): If the R_UARTm_Receive() function was used to designate a receive buffer for UARTm data reception, then this function is invoked by the R_UARTm_Interrupt_Receive() Interrupt Service Routine once the buffer becomes full. This function is one of the four user-definable functions of the UART API, so the user can designate what happens when the receive buffer becomes full.

Parameters:	void
Returns:	void

void R_UARTm_Callback_SendEnd(void): If the R_UARTm_Send() function was used to transmit a string of data from a buffer, then this function is invoked by the R_UARTm_Interrupt_Send() Interrupt Service Routine when the entire string has finished being transmitted. This function is one of the four user-definable functions of the UART API, so the user can designate what happens when a string has finished transmission.

Parameters:	void
Returns:	void

void R_UARTm_Callback_Error(void): This function is called every time R_UARTm_Interrupt_Error() Interrupt Service Routine is invoked by the hardware. This function takes the error type as a parameter, and is one of the four user-definable functions of the UART API, so the user can designate what happens when bad data reception has occurred.

Parameters:	err_type—The type of error generated by error in UARTm data reception (see Serial Status Register)
Returns:	void

void R_UARTm_Callback_SoftwareOverRun(uint8_t rxdata): If the R_UARTm_Receive() function was used to designate a receive buffer for UARTm data reception, then this function is invoked by the R_UARTm_Interrupt_Receive() Interrupt Service Routine when data has been received, but the buffer is completely full. When this function is called, the newest received byte of data will not have been put in the designated receive buffer, but instead passed as a parameter into this function. If the R_UARTm_Receive() function was not used to designate a receive buffer, then this function is invoked by the R_UARTm_ Interrupt_Receive() every time data is received. This function is one of the four user-definable functions of the UART API, so the user can designate what happens when data is received, but not able to be stored in the designated receive buffer.

> *Parameters:*   uint16_t rxdata—The newest received byte of data from UARTm
> *Returns:*   void

8.4.4 IIC API

Since the IIC modules in this API operate in simplified I^2C communication, all communication is based on the RL78 microcontroller acting in master mode on any given bus. To have an IIC module operate as a slave, use the IICA controller.

8.4.4.1 IIC Functions

Table 8.7 shows a list of functions and their brief descriptions. Note that all functions are associated with which IIC module they belong to. As before $m = 00, 01, 10, 11, 20, 21$ for IIC00, IIC01, IIC10, IIC11, IIC20, or IIC21. Certain functions are user-defined.

8.4.4.2 IIC Global Variables

The following table shows global variables used in the IIC API. These variables are associated with the buffers where data is transmitted and received. $m = 00, 01, 10, 11, 20, 21$ for IIC00, IIC01, IIC10, IIC11, IIC20, or IIC21. Note that a separate set of variables is associated with each individual IIC module.

Although these variables may be accessed globally, they need not be modified, as the functions controlling each IIC module (see Table 8.8) do this automatically. It is fine to read their values, but it is also important to understand how each function modifies these values.

8.4.4.3 IIC Function Definitions

void R_IICm_Create(void): This function is called to initialize IICm module (e.g., IIC00, IIC01, IIC10, IIC11, IIC20, or IIC21). This function must be called prior to using any functions associated with the desired IIC module. However, this function is automati-

TABLE 8.7 Functions Associated with Each IIC

FUNCTION NAME	FUNCTION DESCRIPTION	USER-DEFINED
R_IICm_Create()*	Initializes the IICm module	
R_IICm_Master_Send()	Sends data from the IICm module	
R_IICm_Master_Receive()	Receives data from the IICm module	
R_IICm_Stop()	Stops the IICm module	
R_IICm_StartCondition()	Generates a start condition on IICm module	
R_IICm_StopCondition()	Generates a stop condition on IICm module	
R_IICm_Interrupt()	Interrupt Service Routine called at the end of transmission/reception of each byte of IICm module	
R_IICm_Callback_Master_Error()	Callback function after IICm transmission/reception error	
R_IICm_Callback_Master_ReceiveEnd()	Callback function after IICm master mode reception	
R_IICm_Callback_Master_SendEnd()	Callback function after IICm master mode transmission	

cally called by the R_SAUn_Create() function, so it is only necessary to call the corresponding R_SAUn_Create() function.

Parameters: void
Returns: void

void R_IICm_Master_Send(uint8_t adr, uint8_t * txbuf, uint16_t txnum): To send data in master mode out of IICm module, this function may be called. Due to the nature of I^2C communication, the device address (adr) must be sent first. Then, this function initiates transmission of txnum bytes of the designated txbuf transmit buffer. Because this function makes use of the IICm hardware interrupt, this function only commences transmission. The IICm hardware interrupt will call the R_IICm_Callback_Master_SendEnd() function when transmission is complete (when txnum bytes have been sent). This function also invokes the R_IICm_StartCondition() function to generate a start condition to initiate the beginning of I^2C bus communication.

TABLE 8.8   Global Variables Associated with Each IIC Module.

GLOBAL VARIABLE NAME	DESCRIPTION
uint8_t g_IicmMasterStatusFlag	IICm module start flag for send address check by master mode
uint8_t * gp_IicmTxAddress	Address of uint8_t transmit buffer of IICm module
uint16_t g_IicmTxCnt	Number of bytes left to be transmitted from IICm module
uint8_t *gp_IicmRxAddress	Address of unit8_t receive buffer of IICm module
uint16_t g_CsimRxCnt	Number of bytes currently received so far by IICm module
uint16_t g_CsimRxLen	Length of the IICm module receive buffer

Parameters: uint8_t adr—The 7-bit device address (shifted left by one bit) of the desired device to communicate with on the I^2C bus

uint8_t * txbuf—Pointer to the first element of the transmit buffer where the designated string of data is

uint16_t txnum—Number of bytes to send from the txbuf buffer

Returns: void

Global Variables Modified: g_IicmMasterStatusFlag—Flag is cleared and set to SEND status

g_IicmTxCnt—Set to txnum to indicate the number of bytes left to be sent

gp_IicmTxAddress—Set to txbuf to indicate the head of the transmit buffer.

void R_IICm_Master_Receive(uint8_t adr, uint8_t * rxbuf, uint16_t rxnum): To receive data in master mode from the IICm module, this function may be called. Due to the nature of I^2C communication, the device address (adr) must be sent first. Then, this function initiates communication with the desired device on the bus, and rxnum bytes received from the device are placed in the designated rxbuf receive buffer. Because this function makes use of the IICm hardware interrupt, this function only commences reception. The IICm hardware interrupt will call the R_IICm_Callback_Master_ReceiveEnd() function when reception is complete (when rxnum bytes have been received). This function also invokes the R_IICm_StartCondition() function to generate a start condition to initiate the beginning of I^2C bus communication.

Parameters: uint8_t adr—The 7-bit device address (shifted left by one bit) of the desired device to communicate with on the I^2C bus uint8_t * rxbuf—Pointer to the first element of the receive buffer where the received data will be placed

uint16_t rxnum—Number of bytes to be received

Returns: void

Global Variables Modified: g_IicmMasterStatusFlag—Flag is cleared and set to RECEIVE status

g_IicmRxLen—Set to rxnum to indicate the length of the designated receive buffer

g_IicmRxCnt—Set to zero to indicate zero bytes received so far

gp_IicmRxAddress—Set to rxbuf to indicate the head of the receive buffer

void R_IICm_Stop(void): If at any point I^2C communication is needed to stop, whether or not communication is in progress, this function may be called to halt I^2C communication on the IICm module. Communication may begin again afterward with calls to the R_IICm_Master_Send() or the R_IICm_Master_Receive() functions (which both invoke the R_IICm_StartCondition() function).

Parameters: void
Returns: void

void R_IICm_StartCondition(void): This function creates a start condition on the I^2C bus. This must be done prior to I^2C bus communication, whether it is transmission or reception. However, if using the R_IICm_Master_Send() or R_IICm_Master_Receive() functions to communicate, this function is automatically invoked as to ensure proper communication.

Parameters: void
Returns: void

void R_IICm_StopCondition(void): This function creates a stop condition on the I^2C bus. This must be done to end I^2C bus communication, for both transmission and reception. However, if using the R_IICm_Master_Send() or R_IICm_Master_Receive() functions to communicate, this function is automatically invoked at the end of data communication by the IICm hardware interrupt service routine (see R_IICm_Interrupt()) as to ensure proper communication.

Parameters: void
Returns: void

void R_IICm_Interrupt(void): This is the Interrupt Service Routine called by the hardware after communication of each single byte on the I^2C bus, whether a byte was received by the master or sent from the master.

If communication was commenced with the R_IICm_Master_Send() function, this interrupt is called multiple times until transmission is complete (the designated number of bytes from the transmit buffer are sent). Communication is then terminated by invoking the R_IICm_StopCondition() function, and the R_IICm_Callback_Master_SendEnd() function is called.

If communication was commenced with the R_IICm_Master_Receive() function, this interrupt is called multiple times until reception is complete (the designated number of bytes have been received into the receive buffer). Communication is then terminated by invoking the R_IICm_StopCondition() function, and the R_IICm_Callback_Master_ReceiveEnd() function is called.

If at any point communication error occurs, communication commenced with either the R_IICm_Master_Send() or the R_IICm_Master_Receive() functions halts, and the interrupt calls the R_IICm_Callback_Master_Error() function. In this case, the R_IICm_StopCondition() function is not invoked.

Parameters:	void
Returns:	void
Global Variables Modified:	If communication was commenced with the R_IICm_Master_Send() function:
	gp_IicmTxAddress—Pointer is increased by one to point to the next location in the designated transmit buffer
	g_IicTxCnt—Decreased by one to indicate one less byte of data to be sent
	If communciation was commenced with the R_IICm_Master_Receive() function:
	g_IicmMasterStatusFlag—SENDED_ADDRESS bit in flag is set to indicate communication is in RECEIVE mode and is ready to receive to buffer
	gp_IicmRxAddress—Pointer is increased by one to point to the next location in the designated receive buffer
	g_IicmRxCnt—Increased by one to indicate one more byte of data received

void R_IICm_Callback_Master_Error(MD_STATUS flag): This function is invoked by the R_IICm_Interrupt() Interrupt Service Routine when an error is indicated by the Serial Status Register. The function takes the error status as a parameter, and is one of the three user-definable functions of the IIC API, so the user can designate what happens when bad data communication has occurred.

> *Parameters:*   MD_STATUS flag—error flag indicated by the IIC hardware interrupt. In the default set up of the IIC API, the only condition to generate this function call is receiving a NACK before expected. In this case, flag will be set to MD_NACK.
>
> *Returns:*   void

void R_IICm_Callback_Master_ReceiveEnd(void): This function is invoked by the R_IICm_Interrupt() Interrupt Service Routine when the data that was designated to be received by the R_IICm_Master_Receive() function has finished reception. This is one of the three user-definable functions of the IIC API, so the user can designate what happens when IIC data reception is complete.

> *Parameters:*   void
> *Returns:*   void

void R_IICm_Callback_Master_SendEnd(void): This function is invoked by the R_IICm_Interrupt() Interrupt Service Routine when data that was designated to be sent by the R_IIC_Master_Send() function has finished transmission. This is one of the three user-definable functions of the IIC API, so the user can designate what happens when IIC data transmission is complete.

> *Parameters:*   void
> *Returns:*   void

8.4.5   IICA API

Separate from both Serial Array Units, the RL78 provides an additional single IIC Advanced channel. Unlike the IIC modules associated with both Serial Array Units, the IICA module supports a multi-master I^2C bus, and is able to be set up as a slave node. The IICA module also supports features of simplified I^2C communication.

8.4.5.1   IICA Functions

Table 8.9 shows a list of functions and their brief descriptions. Since there is only one IICA channel, these functions are exclusively for that channel. Certain functions are only available when IICA0 is set up in Single Master mode, while others are only available in Slave mode. Finally, some functions are user-defined and are meant to be completed by the application developer.

8.4.5.2 IICA Global Variables

The following table shows global variables used in the IICA API. These variables are associated with the buffers where data is transmitted and received. There are also status flag variables that are read and written between different functions.

Although these variables may be accessed globablly, they need not be modified, as the functions controlling the IICA0 module (see Table 8.10) do this automatically. It is fine to read the values, but it is also important to understand how each function modifies these values (see Function Definitions).

8.4.5.3 IICA Function Definitions

void R_IICA0_Create(void): This function is called to initialize IICA0 module. This function must be called prior to using any functions associated with the IICA0.

Parameters:	void
Returns:	void

MD_STATUS R_IICm_Master_Send(uint8_t adr, uint8_t * txbuf, uint16_t txnum, uint8_t wait): If IICA0 module is setup in Single Master mode, this function may be called to transmit data. Due to the nature of I^2C communication, the device address (adr) must be sent first. Then, this function initiates transmission of txnum bytes of the designated txbuf transmit buffer. Because this function makes use of the IICA0 hardware interrupt, this function only commences transmission. The IICA0 hardware interrupt will call the R_IICA0_Callback_Master_SendEnd() function when transmission is complete (when txnum bytes have been sent). This function creates a start condition in hardware, and idles for *wait* cycles before transmitting the address.

Parameters: uint8_t adr—The 7-bit device address of the desired device to communicate with on the I^2C bus
uint8_t * txbuf—Pointer to the first element of the transmit buffer where the designated string of data is
uint16_t txnum—Number of bytes to send from the txbuf buffer
uint8_t wait—Number of processor cycles to wait before starting data transmission after the start condition is issued

TABLE 8.9 Functions Associated with the IICA0

FUNCTION NAME	FUNCTION DESCRIPTION	SINGLE MASTER ONLY	SLAVE ONLY	USER-DEFINED
R_IICA0_Create()	Initializes the IICA0 module			
R_IICA0_Master_Send()	Sends data as master from the IICA0 module			
R_IICA0_Master_Receive()	Receives data as master from the IICA0 module			
R_IICA0_Slave_Send()	Sends data as slave from the IICA0 module			
R_IICA0_Slave_Receive()	Receives data as slave from the IICA0 module			
R_IICA0_Stop()	Stops the IICA0 module			
R_IICA0_StopCondition()	Generates a stop condition on IICA0 module			
R_IICA0_Set_PowerOff()	Stops the clock supplied for IICA0			
R_IICA0_Create_UserInit()	Adds user-defined code after initializing IICA0 module			
R_IICA0_Interrupt()	Interrupt Service Routine called at the end of transmission/reception of each byte of IICA0 module			
R_IICA0_Callback_Master_SendEnd()	Callback function after IICA0 master mode transmission			
R_IICA0_Callback_Master_ReceiveEnd()	Callback function after IICA0 master mode reception			
R_IICA0_Callback_Slave_SendEnd()	Callback function after IICA0 slave mode transmission			
R_IICA0_Callback_Slave_ReceiveEnd()	Callback function after IICA0 slave mode reception			
R_IICA0_Callback_Master_Error()	Callback function after IICA0 master mode transmission/reception error			
R_IICA0_Callback_Slave_Error()	Callback function after IICA0 slave mode transmission/reception error			
R_IICA0_Callback_GetStopCondition()	Callback function after IICA0 slave mode stop condition			

TABLE 8.10 Global Variables Associated with the IICA0 Module.

GLOBAL VARIABLE NAME	DESCRIPTION
uint8_t g_IicmMasterStatusFlag	IICm module start flag for send address check by master mode
uint8_t * gp_IicmTxAddress	Address of uint8_t transmit buffer of IICm module
uint16_t g_IicmTxCnt	Number of bytes left to be transmitted from IICm module
uint8_t *gp_IicmRxAddress	Address of unit8_t receive buffer of IICm module
uint16_t g_CsimRxCnt	Number of bytes currently received so far by IICm module
uint16_t g_CsimRxLen	Length of the IICm module receive buffer

Returns:	MD_OK—Data transmission commenced successfully
	MD_ERROR1—I^{2}C bus is busy
	MD_ERROR2—Cannot trigger I^{2}C communication (start or stop condition is in progress)
Global Variables Modified:	g_Iica0MasterStatusFlag—Flag is cleared and set to SEND status
	g_Iica0TxCnt—Set to txnum to indicate the number of bytes left to be sent
	gp_Iica0TxAddress—Set to txbuf to indicate the head of the transmit buffer

8.5 RECAP

In this chapter we have learned basic concepts for serial communications and three types of communication protocols. We have examined the Serial Array Unit communication controller and how it is configured to support CSI, UART, and simplified IIC protocols. Finally, we have examined the serial communications API created by the Applilet code generator.

8.6 EXERCISES

1. Write the code to configure the SAU1 channels 2 and 3 in CSI master mode with clock phase reversed, data in phase with the serial clock, transfer rate of 1 MHz, data MSB first, and eight-bit data. Use single-transfer mode and generate an interrupt at the end of each transfer. Assume $f_{\text{CLK}} = 32$ MHz.

2. Draw the clock, data, and interrupt request waveforms for the three-byte data sequence 0x93, 0x11, 0x41 being transmitted by the CSI unit as configured in the previous exercise.
3. Write code to configure UART1 to operate at 12345 baud, one stop bit, eight data bits, odd parity, and the LSB first. Assume f_{CLK} = 32 MHz. What is the actual baud rate?
4. Write code to configure UART2 to operate at 4800 baud, two stop bits, eight data bits, odd parity, and the LSB first. Assume f_{CLK} = 32 MHz. What is the actual baud rate?
5. What are the lowest and highest baud rates possible for a UART with a f_{CLK} = 32 MHz?
6. Draw the waveform for the three-byte data sequence 0x93, 0x11, 0x41 being transmitted by UART at 60000 baud, MSB first, one stop bit, and even parity. Be sure to mark when each transition occurs.
7. What are the differences between the SAU's simplified I^{2}C operating mode and the IICA's full I^{2}C mode? Give an example of a system which could use the simplified I^{2}C, and another example of a system which would need to use the full I^{2}C. Be sure to explain your reasoning.
8. Why must the ACK bit in I^{2}C communications be a 0 rather than a 1?
9. Write the code to do the following, and draw a waveform showing I^{2}C signals and activity for parts b. and c. below.
   a. Configure the SAU0 channels 0 and 1 in simplified I^{2}C mode operating at 200 kbps.
   b. Write bytes 0x12, 0x34, 0x56 and 0x78 to address 0xA0.
   c. Generate the stop condition.

Chapter Nine

Timer Peripherals

9.1 LEARNING OBJECTIVES

In this chapter we show how timer peripherals work to measure elapsed time, count events, generate events at specified times, and perform other more advanced features. It is possible to cascade timers together when one timer does not provide the range needed. Using timers it is also possible to output a square wave with a controllable frequency and duty cycle. In this chapter we will cover the concepts behind these features and how to use them.

9.2 BASIC CONCEPTS

The core of a timer peripheral is a digital counter whose value changes by one each time it is clocked. The faster the clocking rate, the faster the device counts. If the timer's input clock frequency is 10 MHz, then its period is the inverse of 10 MHz: 1/10 MHz or 0.1 μs. Hence one count (increment or decrement) of the register represents 0.1 μs. We can measure how much time has passed since the counter was reset by reading the counter value and multiplying it by 0.1 μs. For example, if the counter value is 15821, and the count direction is up (incrementing), then we know that 1582.1 μs have passed since the counter was reset.

9.2.1 Support Circuitry

Timer peripherals are quite flexible. They are typically able to measure elapsed time, count events, generate events at fixed times, generate waveforms, or measure pulse widths and frequencies. The heart of the timer peripheral is a **counter.** This counter will count the number of rising edges on its inputs. This admittedly simple capability becomes quite valuable with additional support logic. This circuitry controls factors such as:

- what **signal source** it counts, if it counts a signal with a known frequency, then we can use it to measure elapsed time,

- when it starts and stop running,
- whether it counts rising or falling edges,
- which direction it counts,
- what happens when it overflows,
- how and if it is reloaded,
- whether its value is captured by another register or,
- whether it generates a signal or an interrupt.

9.2.2   Anemometer Example

We can use a timer peripheral in several ways to measure wind speed. We will use an anemometer to generate a signal whose frequency depends upon wind speed. There are two obvious methods:

- One way to measure wind speed is to measure the signal's **frequency**—how many cycles occur within a fixed amount of time. We can use the timer peripheral by setting it up in **event counter** mode. We clear the timer, start it running, wait for the fixed measurement time, and then read the count value. Dividing the count value by the measurement time gives the signal frequency, and this can be scaled to provide wind speed.
- Another way to measure the wind speed is to measure the signal's **period**—how long a period lasts. We can use the timer peripheral by setting it up in timer mode, so it counts at a given rate. We clear the timer and wait for a rising edge on the input signal, at which point we start the timer counting. We wait for the next rising edge on the input signal, at which point we stop the timer from counting. Dividing the count value by the count frequency gives the period of the signal. We invert the period and then scale it to determine wind speed.

The timer peripheral's additional support circuitry mentioned above can be used to simplify these measurement techniques to improve accuracy and reduce software processing and complexity. We will examine these techniques in a later section.

9.3   INTERVAL TIMER

9.3.1   Overview

We begin by examining the RL78 family's most basic timer peripheral—the **Interval Timer** (IT), as shown in Figure 9.1. This peripheral consists of a 12-bit counter and support circuitry: clock source selection, enable logic, comparison logic (ITMC), and control

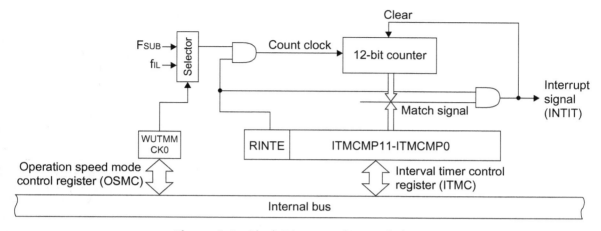

Figure 9.1   Block Diagram of Interval Timer.

logic. The IT generates an interrupt at a specified timer interval by counting an input clock source. When the counter matches a user-specified value in the interval timer control register (ITMC), a comparison circuit generates an interrupt (INTIT) and also clears the counter back to 0.

The IT can count one of two possible clock sources, based on the WUTMMCK0 bit in the **Operation Speed Mode Control Register** (OSMC):

- ▦ A 0 selects the subsystem clock f_{SUB}. This clock's frequency is typically 32.768 kHz, so the period is about 30.5176 μs.
- ▦ A 1 selects the internal low-speed oscillation clock f_{IL}. This clock's frequency is nominally 15 kHz but can vary by 15 percent.

The **Interval Timer Control Register** (ITMC) has several fields:

- ▦ RINTE enables counting when set to 1 and otherwise disables counting.
- ▦ Bits ITCMP11–0 form a 12-bit value which controls the interrupt rate $f_{interrupt} = f_{clock\ source}/(ITCMP + 1)$.

9.3.2   Operation

Let's examine the IT in operation, as shown in Figure 9.2. We configure the IT to use f_{SUB} so it will count at a frequency of 32.768 kHz. We load 0x0FF into ITCMP to set the compare value to 255 (0x0ff). We set RINTE to 1 to enable the IT. The counter will reach 255 after 255 count clock cycles, or 255*30.5176 μs = 7.782 ms. At that point it is reset

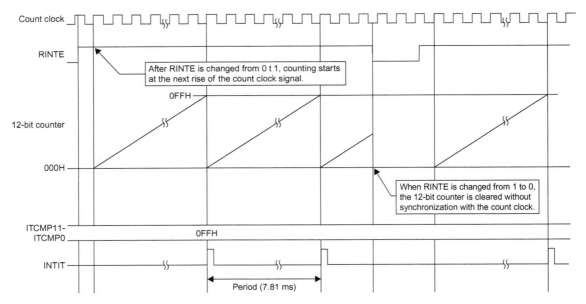

Figure 9.2 Interval Timer operation.

to 0 and an INTIT signal is generated. The period of the signal is $(255 + 1) * 30.5176\ \mu s = 7.78125$ ms, and its frequency is 32.768 kHz/(255 + 1) = 128 Hz.

The procedure to configure the interval timer to generate a target interrupt frequency is as follows.

1. Determine the desired frequency division ratio = $f_{\text{clock source}}/f_{\text{interrupt}}$.
2. Round the ratio to the nearest integer.
3. Subtract one and place the result in the compare register ITCMP.

9.3.3 Examples

- How should we configure the IT to generate an interrupt with a frequency of 1 kHz? We have two options, based on which count clock source we use.
  - □ If we use f_{SUB} then we will need to divide 32.768 kHz by 32.768 to reach 1 kHz. This is not possible as digital counters can only divide by integer values.[1] The best we can do is round the division factor to 33 and place $33 - 1 = 32$ in ITCMP. The resulting interrupt frequency will be 992.97 Hz

---

[1] Fractional dividers are outside the scope of this text. For extra credit, the interested student can present a solution which supports this feature!

□ If we use f_{IL} then we need to divide 15 kHz by precisely 15. Placing $15 - 1 = 14$ in ITCMP will result in an interrupt frequency of 1.0 kHz, assuming f_{IL} is in fact running at 15 kHz. Remember that there may be a timing error of up to 15 percent for this clock source, so we shouldn't use it for precision timing without compensating for the error.

▩ What is the **smallest** possible interval timer period?
We choose the faster of the available clock sources, which is f_{SUB}. We set ITCMP to the smallest possible value (0), so the resulting period is $(0 + 1)/32.768$ kHz = 30.52 μs.

▩ What is the **largest** possible interval timer period?
We choose the slower of the available clock sources, which is f_{IL}. We set ITCMP to the largest possible value (0x0fff, or 4191), so the resulting period is $(4191 + 1)/15$ kHz = 279 ms.

9.4   TIMER ARRAY UNIT

9.4.1   Overview

Figure 9.3 shows a single channel from an RL78 Timer Array Unit. In this figure, the counter is marked as **Timer counter register 0n (TCR0n).** Everything else in the diagram is a support system for the TCR.

Note that the TAU0EN bit in the PER0 register needs to be set to one to use TAU0. If the bit is zero, then the TAU is disabled to save power.

RL78-family microcontrollers may contain one or more timer array units (TAUs). Each TAU contains eight 16-bit timers and a prescaler to generate clock signals for these timers. RL78 MCUs in packages smaller than 80 pins only have one Timer Array Unit: TAU0. RL78 MCUs in packages 80 pins and larger have two: TAU0 and TAU1. Some but not all timer channels are connected to I/O pins. As shown in Figure 9.4, the package size determines which timers exist, and which have an I/O pin connected.

9.4.2   Prescaler and Clock Sources

Sometimes we don't want to count at the same frequency as the input clock. Dividing the input clock frequency down is called **prescaling.** This makes it possible to configure a timer to suit the application needs better.

Consider the previous example of a 16-bit counter with a 10 MHz clock source. We wish to use it to measure elapsed time. We reset it to zero and then it begins counting, incrementing once every 0.1 μs.

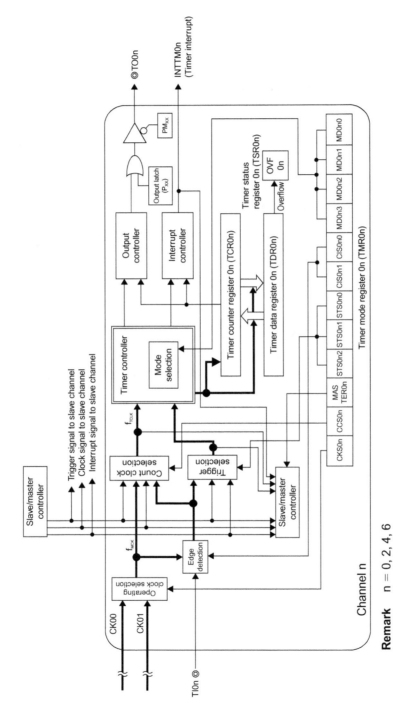

Figure 9.3 Block diagram of Timer Array Unit channel.

Remark n = 0, 2, 4, 6

TIMER ARRAY UNIT CHANNELS	I/O PINS OF EACH PRODUCT									
	128-pin	100-pin	80-pin	64-pin	52-pin	44, 48-pin	40-pin	30, 32, 36-pin	24, 25-pin	20-pin
Unit 0 — Channel 0	P00/TI00, P01/TO00									
Channel 1	P16/TI01/TO01									
Channel 2	P17/TI02/TO02									
Channel 3	P31/TI03/TO03									—
Channel 4	P42/TI04/TO04			—	—	—	—	—	—	—
Channel 5	P46/TI05/TO05	P05/TI05/TO05		—	—	—	—	—	—	—
Channel 6	P102/TI06/TO06	P06/TI06/TO06		—	—	—	—	—	—	—
Channel 7	P145/TI07/TO07	P41/TI07/TO07			—	—	—	—	—	—
Unit 1 — Channel 0	P64/TI10/TO10			×	×	×	×	×	×	×
Channel 1	P65/TI11/TO11			×	×	×	×	×	×	×
Channel 2	P66/TI12/TO12			×	×	×	×	×	×	×
Channel 3	P67/TI13/TO13			×	×	×	×	×	×	×
Channel 4	P103/TI14/TO14	×	×	×	×	×	×	×	×	×
Channel 5	P104/TI15/TO15	×	×	×	×	×	×	×	×	×
Channel 6	P105/TI16/TO16	×	×	×	×	×	×	×	×	×
Channel 7	P106/TI17/TO17		×	×	×	×	×	×	×	×

Remarks
1. When timer input and timer output are shared by the same pin, either only timer input or only timer output can be used.
2. —: There is no timer I/O pin, but the channel is available. (However, the channel can only be used as an interval timer.)
3. ×: The channel is not available.

Figure 9.4 Timer channels and I/O pins.

Eventually the counter will overflow because it has a limited count range. A 16-bit counter can hold a maximum value of 0xffff = 65535. Incrementing it from this value it will make it overflow ("roll over") to 0x0000 = 0. If we read the counter value after this has happened, our time reading will be too small by 65536 * 0.1 μs. So our counter only has a useful time measurement range of 0 to 6553.5 μs. One way to be able to measure longer time durations is by using a slower clock source. For example, if we reduce the clock frequency from 10 MHz to 5 MHz, then the counter will increment every 0.2 μs, and it will overflow after 65535 * 0.2 μs = 13107.0 μs. We can now measure a time period twice as long, and each count represents twice as much time as before.

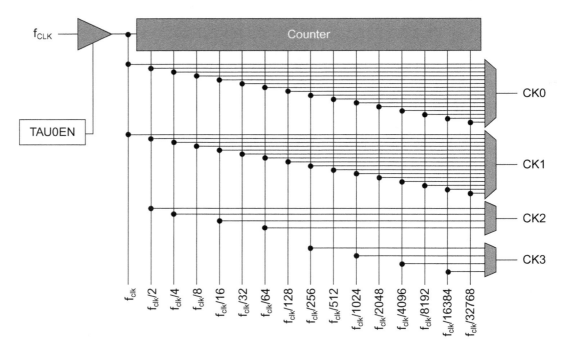

Figure 9.5 Count source prescaler and selection.

The TAU includes four prescalers which generate divide the input signal f_{CLK} to create signals CK0, CK1, CK2, and CK3. Each channel in the TAU can select use CK0 or CK1. CK2 and CK3 are available to channels 1 and 3 in certain modes to enable different prescaling factors.

The Timer Clock Select register **TPS0** sets the division factors for the four prescalers.

- The bits PRS003 to PRS000 and PRS013 to PRS010 are grouped as two four-bit values which control CK0 and CK1, respectively. Given a bit value of x in a field, the output frequency is equal to the input frequency divided by 2^x. This means that division ratios from $2^0 = 1$ to $2^{15} = 32768$ are possible.
- The bits PRS021 to PRS020 are used to control CK2. Possible division ratios are 2, 4, 16, and 64.
- The bits PRS031 to PRS030 are used to control CK3. Possible division ratios are 256, 1024, 4096, and 16384.

9.4.3   Basic Timer Circuitry

Each timer channel has the following components, as shown in Figure 9.3.

- The **Timer Counter Register** (TCR0n) is the actual counter. A valid clock signal makes it count. Certain events will cause it to be cleared to 0x0000 and others will set it to 0xffff.
- The **Timer Data Register** (TDR0n) is a register which can be used in multiple ways. It can hold a **reload** value to copy into the TDR0n when a certain event occurs (e.g., overflow or underflow). It can hold a value which is **compared** against the timer TCR value. It can **capture** the value in TCR0n when a certain event occurs.
- The timer can count different types of edges on the TI0n pin: falling edges, rising edges, or both falling and rising edges.
- The timer can use different operation clock sources: CK00 or CK01, and sometimes CK02 or CK03.
- Various events (software command, interrupt, or a signal on an input pin) can be used to trigger the start of counting or the capture of the counter value.
- The interrupt controller determines whether an interrupt (INTTM0n) is generated and its timing details.
- The output controller determines whether a pulse is generated on the output pin TO0 and its characteristics.

9.4.4   Independent Channel Operation Modes

The RL78 TAU timer channels can operate in several modes. In some of these modes, the channels work independently, while in others they are coordinated (simultaneous mode) to provide additional features.

9.4.4.1   Interval Timer and Square Wave Output

Two similar operation modes for a TAU channel are interval timer mode and square wave output. Both of these modes have the same basic internal behavior and are illustrated in Figure 9.6.

0 The data register TDR0n is loaded with one less than the desired count period.

1 When the channel is started, TDR0n's value is copied into TCR0n. TCR0n then proceeds to count down with each clock pulse until reaching 0.

2 At that point in time the counter underflows, triggering multiple actions. First, the value in TDR0n is copied into TCR0n to repeat the cycle. The second action depends on the operating mode. In interval timer mode, an interrupt INTM0n will be requested. In square wave output mode, the output pin TO0n will be toggled (inverted).

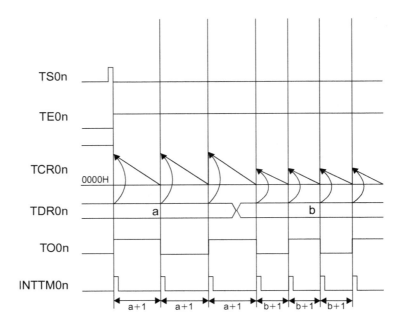

Remarks 1. n: Channel number (n = 0 to 7)
          2. TS0n: Bit n of timer channel start register 0 (TS0)
             TE0n: Bit n of timer channel enable status register 0 (TE0)
             TCR0n: Timer/counter register 0n (TCR0n)
             TDR0n: Timer data register 0n (TDR0n)
             TO0n: TO0n pin output signal

Figure 9.6 Interval timer and square wave output operation modes.

9.4.4.2 External Event Counter

This mode is used to count external events signaled by an input edge transition on the TI0n pin. The counter can generate an interrupt when a specified event count is reached.

1 The TDR0n register must be loaded with one less than the desired event count.
2 This value is loaded into the timer counter register TCR0n when a channel start trigger bit for the channel is set. The counter then counts down with each input event.
3 The counter generates an interrupt upon reaching zero, indicating that the specified number of events have occurred.

9.4.4.3 Divider Function

Channel 0 can operate as a frequency divider. As shown in Figure 9.7, an input signal is applied to pin TI00, routed to the timer for division, and the resulting signal is sent out pin

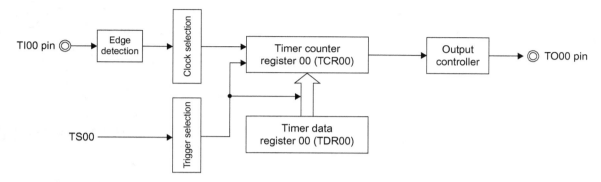

Figure 9.7   Frequency division of an external signal.

TO00. This function allows the input signal to be divided by a ratio of 1 to 131072. The output signal's frequency is:

- The input frequency divided by $TDR0n+1$, when both rising and falling edges are sensed by the edge detector.
- The input frequency divided by $2*(TDR0n+1)$, when only one type of edge is sensed by the edge detector.

9.4.4.4 Input Pulse Interval Measurement

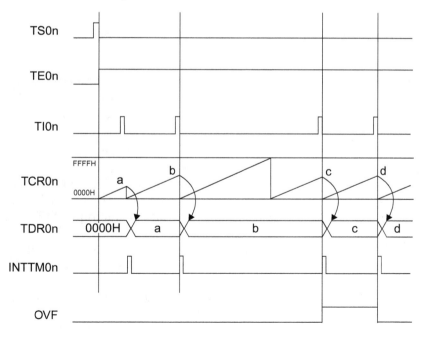

Figure 9.8   Input pulse interval measurement.

This useful mode measures an input pulse interval by automating several activities with hardware support. The counter counts up and is clocked by the operation clock.

1 Counting starts when the channel start trigger bit (TS0n) is set to 1.
2 When a valid edge occurs on the input pin TI0n, the value in counter register TCR0n is copied over to the data register TDR0n. TCR0n is then cleared to 0 and an interrupt signal INTTM0n is output.
3 An interrupt service routine is needed to read the value from TDR0n to determine the pulse interval, and also to determine if an overflow occurred.

9.4.4.5 Measurement of Input Signal Pulse Width

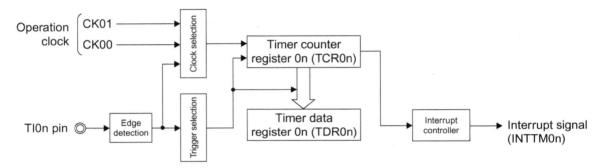

Figure 9.9 TAU channel configuration for pulse width measurement.

A timer channel can be used to measure how long an input signal is a one (or a zero). Consider the example in Figure 9.9 and Figure 9.10, in which we wish to measure how long the input signal (on pin TI0n) is a one.

1 The counter TCR0n is initially cleared to 0. It does not start counting until it is triggered by the rising edge of TI0n, at which point it starts counting up.
2 The falling edge of TI0n marks the end of the input pulse and will trigger three actions. First, the counter stops counting. Second, the counter value is copied from TCR0n to TDR0n for later reading by the program. Third, the interrupt INTTM0n is requested.
3 The rising edge of TI0n will reset the counter TCR0n to 0 and start it counting again, repeating the cycle.

We can then calculate the width of the input signal based on the input clock period, the capture value TDR0n, and whether an overflow occurred.

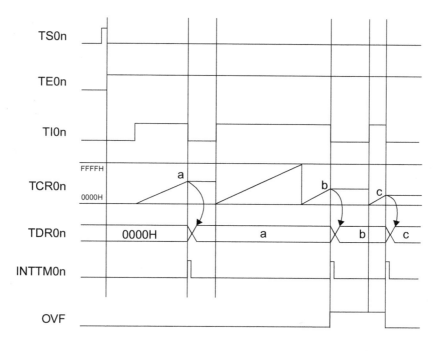

Remarks   1. n: Channel number (n = 0 to 7)
2. TS0n: Bit n of timer channel start register 0 (TS0)
TE0n: Bit n of timer channel enable status register 0 (TE0)
TI0n: TI0n pin input signal
TCR0n: Timer/counter register 0n (TCR0n)
TDR0n: Timer data register 0n (TDR0n)
OVF: Bit 0 of timer status register 0n (TSR0n)

Figure 9.10   Measuring input signal pulse width.

9.4.4.6 Delay Counter

A timer channel can be used to generate an interrupt a certain time after an event occurs, as shown in Figure 9.11.

1   We first load the TDR0n register with the desired delay value count. We connect the event signal to input pin TI0n.
2   When a valid event occurs on that input, the delay count value in TDR0n will be copied to TCR0n and down-counting will begin.
3   When TCR0n reaches 0, counting will stop and interrupt INTTM0n will be generated.

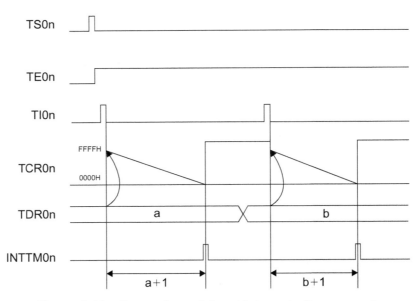

Figure 9.11 Generating a delayed interrupt after an event.

9.4.5 Simultaneous Channel Operation Modes

Multiple TAU channels can be connected together to provide more complex timing functions. In these modes, one channel operates as the master and one or more operate as slaves. Master channel registers are designated with an n suffix and slave channel registers with a p suffix in this section and in the hardware manual.

9.4.5.1 One-Shot Pulse

We can use the TAU to create a pulse of a specified width which occurs a specified delay time after an input event. In Figure 9.12 above the pulse is generated on signal TO0p. The *master* channel operates as a *delay counter* to generate an interrupt a specified time $(a + 2)$ after the input event occurs on pin TI0n. The *slave* channel defines the *pulse width* (b), by operating as another delay counter. The output pulse of a specified width is generated on pin TO0p.

1 The master channel data register TDR0n is loaded by the program with the count value a which will result in the desired delay. The slave channel data register TDR0p is loaded with the count value b for the desired pulse width.

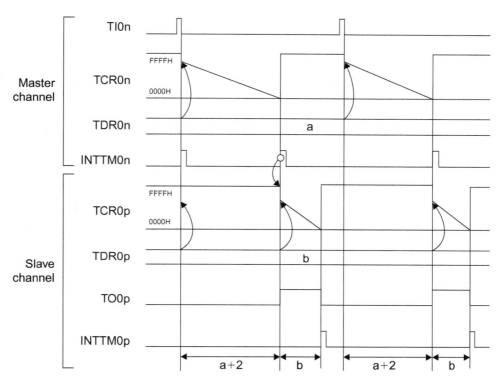

Figure 9.12   One-shot pulse output function.

2   A valid input event on pin TI0n causes the master channel to copy the value in TDR0n into the counter TCR0n and start it counting down, resulting in the desired time delay before the output pulse.

3   When TCR0n reaches zero it generates an interrupt INTTM0n, which is fed to the slave channel. The slave channel sets its output TO0p to a one, starting the output pulse. It copies the desired pulse width value from TDR0p to TCR0p and starts it counting down.

4   When TCR0p reaches zero it generates an interrupt INTTM0p and clears the output TO0p to a zero, ending the output pulse.

9.4.5.2   *Pulse Width Modulation*

We can use the TAU to create a pulse-width modulated (PWM) signal. In Figure 9.13, the PWM signal is the bottom waveform, labeled INTTMO0p. This mode is similar to the one-shot pulse mode listed above, but the master channel timer runs does not stop and then await an external trigger signal. Instead the master channel runs continuously.

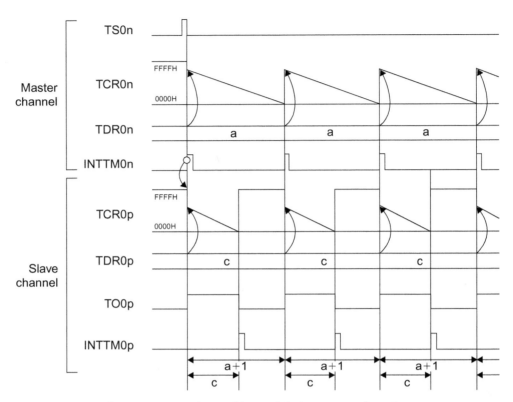

Figure 9.13 Pulse-width modulation output function.

The *master* channel defines the *frequency* of the PWM signal (defined with period $a + 1$), while the *slave* channel defines the *duty cycle*. The duration of the output pulse is set by parameter c. Hence we can calculate the duty cycle of the output signal as:

$$D = \left(\frac{c}{a + 1}\right) * 100\%$$

The frequency of the PWM signal is the count clock frequency divided by $a + 1$:

$$f = \frac{f_{CKn}}{(a + 1)}$$

The following sequence of operations shows how to configure the TAU channels, and describes how they operate in PWM mode.

1   The master channel data register TDR0n is loaded by the program with the count value which will result in the desired pulse frequency. The slave channel data register TDR0p is loaded with the count value for the desired pulse width.

2   When the master channel is started with by software setting the TS0n bit, two events occur:

2.1   The timer will copy the value in TDR0n into the counter TCR0n and start it counting down, measuring the time before the end of the period.

2.2   An overflow signal is asserted (which can trigger the INTTM0n interrupt). This overflow signal forces the slave channel to (a) set its output signal TO0p, (b) load its counter TCR0p from the data register TDR0p, and (c) start counter TCR0p counting down. Item (a) raises the PWM signal to start the high portion of the signal.

3   When the slave counter TCR0p finally reaches zero, it generates an overflow signal which clears the output signal TO0p, ending the high portion of the PWM signal. The overflow signal can generate be used to output signal INTTM0p.

4   At the end of the pulse period, TCR0n will reach zero it generates an interrupt INTTM0n, which is fed to the slave channel. The slave channel sets its output TO0p to a one, starting the output pulse. It copies the desired pulse width value from TDR0p to TCR0p and starts it counting down.

5   When TCR0p reaches zero it generates an interrupt INTTM0p and clears the output TO0p to a zero, ending the output pulse.

This example shows how to create a single PWM output signal using two channels. If we need to generate multiple PWM signals at the same frequency but independent duty cycles, we can use the same master channel to generate the base frequency, reducing the number of TAU channels required. Further details on this mode (called *multiple PWM output function*) are given in the hardware manual.

9.5   EXAMPLES

Let's see how to use the RL78 timers in a few different applications: an energy-measuring device, an anemometer, and a servo motor controller. We will use Applilet to generate the peripheral configuration and access code, which greatly simplifies our development process.

9.5.1   Energy Meter: Precision Timing for AD Conversions

In an example in the chapter on analog interfacing we discussed how to use the AD converter to measure a circuit's power use based on its voltage and current. We can compute energy by integrating power over time, but this requires an accurate timing reference.

In this example we will do this by using a timer peripheral to periodically trigger the AD converter.

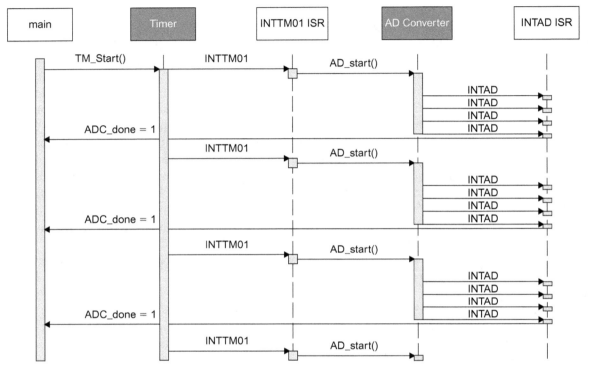

Figure 9.14 Sequence chart for energy meter using timer and AD converter.

Figure 9.14 presents an overview of how we will use both hardware and software to accomplish this. A timer will generate a periodic interrupt (INTTM01) each time the input signals are to be sampled. This interrupt will trigger an ISR which will then trigger the AD converter to perform a burst of four sequential conversions.[2] When each one of these conversions completes, the AD converter generates an INTAD interrupt which invokes the INTAD ISR. This ISR copies the results of the conversion from the AD conversion result register into temporary storage, at which point it is ready for power and energy calculations.

As shown in Figure 9.15, the main function will calculate the power and energy. The ISR will update the global array ADC_value, which is read by the main function.

---

[2] It is also possible to use INTTM01 to directly control the AD converter as a hardware trigger.

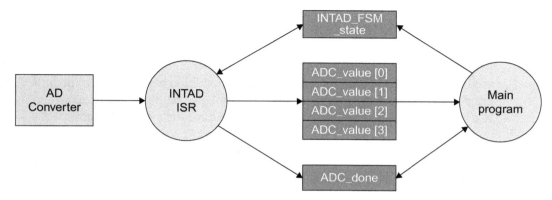

Figure 9.15   Software Architecture showing execution threads and shared data.

We now have a new problem. What happens if the main program does not read ADC_value fast enough, and the ISR updates the values? The resulting power and energy calculations will be wrong. This is a possible data race, which depends upon the timing of operations. We explore this problem and possible solutions in the chapter on task scheduling.

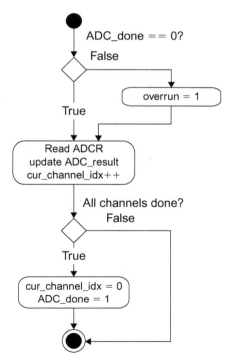

Figure 9.16   Activity chart for AD_SAMPLING state of INTAD ISR.

Our simple but limited solution is to have the FSM detect overruns, as shown in Figure 9.16. The FSM sets ADC_done to one after converting the last (fourth) channel. The main function clears ADC_done after reading the four conversion results. When the FSM converts the first channel, it checks to see if ADC_done is zero. If it is not, then main has not read the previous results of the conversion, and an overrun condition has occurred so the ISR will set the error flag overrun. Other possible approaches involve buffering the data or sending a signal to trigger a task to process the data. We will examine these in later chapters.

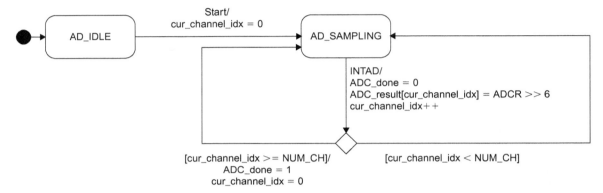

Figure 9.17 Revised state machine for INTAD ISR.

We also will need to change how the INTAD ISR FSM is controlled. In the power meter example, the main function directly controlled the state variable before triggering the AD converter. This will not work here because the timer will trigger the AD converter asynchronously with respect to the main function. To deal with this, we will have main initialize the FSM once (before starting the timer). We will also need to make the FSM step through the states on its own, as shown in Figure 9.17.

We will start with floating point calculation of power and energy, given our credos of 1) seeking correctness first, and performance second, and 2) premature optimization being the root of nearly all evil (Knuth). We will investigate optimizations in the later chapter on code optimizations.

We will use Applilet to configure the peripherals. First we need to set timer channel 1 to operate as an interval timer, as shown in Figure 9.18.

Figure 9.18 Configuring timer 0 channel 1 as an interval timer.

Next we set the period for the timer and interrupt characteristics, as shown in Figure 9.19. We choose 100 ms as the period; later we may be able to improve this sampling rate for better accuracy. We specify we would like the interrupt to be generated when counting first starts, and then at the end of each counting period.

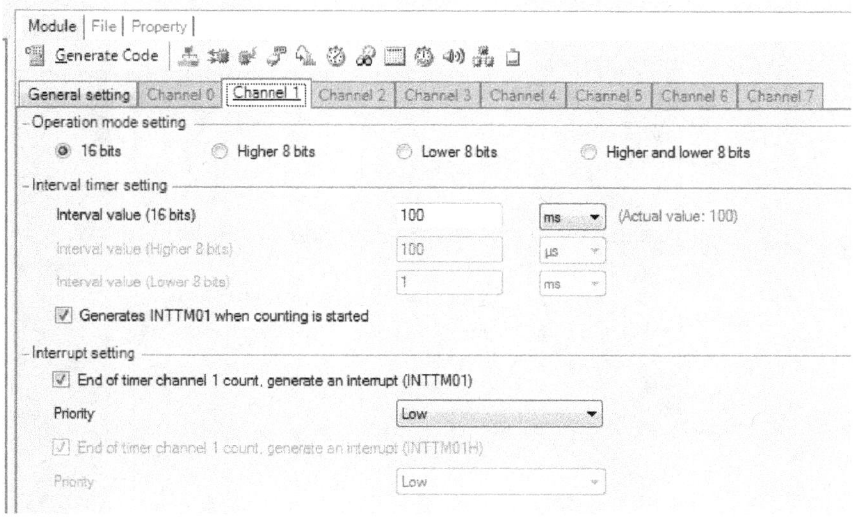

Figure 9.19   Defining timer 0 channel 1 interval and interrupt characteristics.

Now we are ready to modify our code to use the timer.

9.5.1.1   CG_timer_user.c

The timer ISR is filled in with a call to start the AD conversions.

```
#pragma vector = INTTM01_vect
_interrupt void MD_INTTM01(void)
{
   /* Start user code. Do not edit comment generated here */
   AD_Start();
   /* End user code. Do not edit comment generated here */
}
```

9.5.1.2   CG_ad_user.c

The state machine for the INTAD ISR is updated as follows to match the revised design of Figure 9.17.

```
#pragma vector = INTAD_vect
_interrupt void MD_INTAD(void)
{
   /* Start user code. Do not edit comment generated here */
   static UCHAR cur_channel_idx = 0;

   switch (INTAD_FSM_state) {
   case AD_SAMPLING:
      if (ADC_done != 0) {
         overrun = 1;
      }
      ADC_done = 0;
      AD_Read(&(ADC_value[cur_channel_idx]));
      cur_channel_idx++;
      if (cur_channel_idx >= NUM_CHANNELS) {
         cur_channel_idx = 0;
         ADC_done = 1;
      }
      break;
   case AD_IDLE:
   default:
      INTAD_FSM_state = AD_IDLE;
      break;
   }
   /* End user code. Do not edit comment generated here */
}
```

9.5.1.3   CG_main.c

Applilet generates a function TAU0_Init() to initialize timer array unit 0, and calls this function during systeminit() in __low_level_init(), which is called before main(). So this is taken care of already.

We need to start the timer counting, but do not need to trigger the AD converter in software anymore. However, we still need to enable the AD comparator, start the AD converter, and initialize related variables.

The body of the infinite loop changes slightly. First we wait for the ADC_done flag to be set, at which point we copy the data out of the array ADC_value. Note that there is a slim chance of a data race condition—the INTAD ISR executing during the middle of our copy. We could check ADC_done to ensure it is still set, which means our data was not overwritten.

Now we can calculate the input power, output power, efficiency and energy use. The energy use depends on time between samples, which is 100 ms in this example.

```
void  main(void)
{
   /* Start user code. Do not edit comment generated here */
   volatile float P_in, P_out, effic, energy = 0.0;
   unsigned Vin, Vout, Iin, Iout;

   /* Peripheral start function calls */
   ADC_done = 0;
   AD_ComparatorOn();       /* Enable ADC voltage comparator  */
   INTAD_FSM_state = AD_SAMPLING;
   TAU0_Channel1_Start();

   /* Endless control loop */
   while (1U)
      {
         while (!ADC_done)
            ;

         //Read the conversion results and calculate power in and out
         P_in = K_CONVERSION*ADC_value[VIN_IDX]*ADC_value[IIN_IDX];
         P_out = K_CONVERSION*ADC_value[VOUT_IDX]*ADC_value[IOUT_IDX];
         ADC_done = 0;
         effic = (P_in - P_out)/P_in;
         energy += P_in*SAMPLE_PERIOD;
      }

   /* End user code. Do not edit comment generated here */
}
```

9.5.2   Anemometer with Pulse Width Measurement

The rotational speed of an anemometer is proportional to the wind speed, neglecting the errors caused by inertia and friction. Let's consider how to use a TAU channel to measure wind speed using a cup anemometer, as shown in Figure 9.20.

Figure 9.20   A cup anemometer for measuring wind speed.

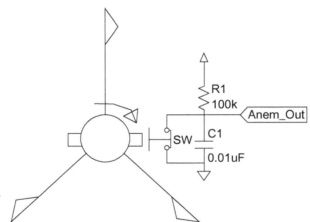

Figure 9.21   Schematic for cup anemometer circuit.

The anemometer has one or more magnets mounted on the rotating portion and a magnetic sensor (such as a reed switch) mounted on the fixed mast. The magnetic sensor generates a pulse each time a magnet passes by, so the frequency of the signal will be proportional to wind speed.

Consider an anemometer has a normally-closed reed switch and two magnets. The switch closes twice per rotation. By wiring it as shown in Figure 9.21, the output signal will be 0 V when the switch is closed, with a brief pulse to V_{CC} when the magnet passes by the switch SW.

We can calculate the frequency of the pulses by measuring the period $T_{\text{anemometer}}$ and then taking the inverse.

$$v_{\text{wind}} = \frac{K * f_{\text{clk}}}{T_{\text{anemometer}}}$$

We need to compensate for measuring just the low portion of the signal rather than the entire period. Examination with an oscilloscope reveals that the low part of the signal is about 90 percent of the total period. We will factor this into our calibration constant K above. We also factor in the fact that two pulses are generated per full anemometer rotation.

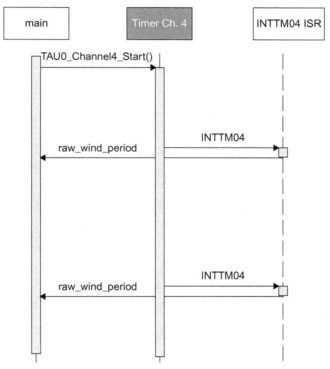

Figure 9.22   Sequence diagram for anemometer using pulse-width measurement.

The software for this approach is shown in Figure 9.22 and is quite simple, as the hardware takes care of the heavy lifting. The main thread configures and starts the timer. The timer generates an interrupt INTTM04 at the end of each input pulse. We modify the Applilet-generated ISR to determine if an overflow occurred. If so, then the wind speed is too low to measure, and we clear the global variable raw_wind_period to zero to indicate this error condition. Otherwise the ISR reads the pulse width count from the TDR04 register and place it in raw_wind_period.

```
/* Start user code for global. Do not edit comment generated here */
extern volatile unsigned raw_wind_period;
/* End user code. Do not edit comment generated here */

#pragma vector = INTTM04_vect
__interrupt void MD_INTTM04(void)
{
   /* Start user code. Do not edit comment generated here */
   if ((TSR04 & _0001_TAU_OVERFLOW_OCCURS) != 0U) {
      /* overflow occurs */
      raw_wind_period = 0;
   } else {
      raw_wind_period = TDR04;
   }
   /* End user code. Do not edit comment generated here */
}
```

At this point we have enough information to calculate wind speed. However, we will not do this calculation in the ISR unless truly necessary, as our initial implementation (with floating point math) will waste processor time, especially at high wind speeds. Instead, we will have the main function calculate the wind speed when needed as follows:[3] If raw_wind_period is equal to 0, we set wind_speed to 0, otherwise wind_speed = K_ANEMOMETER/raw_wind_period.

```
/* Start user code for global. Do not edit comment generated here */
volatile unsigned raw_wind_period=0;
/* End user code. Do not edit comment generated here */

void  main(void)
{
   /* Start user code. Do not edit comment generated here */
   float v_wind = 0.0, sum = 0.0;

   /* Peripheral start function calls */
```

---

[3] Note that there is a potential race condition here.

```
TAU0_Channel4_Start();

/* Endless control loop */
while (1U) {
    if (raw_wind_period > 0) {
        v_wind = K_ANEMOMETER/raw_wind_period;
    } else {
        v_wind = 0;
    }
    sum += v_wind;
}
/* End user code. Do not edit comment generated here */
}
```

We use Applilet to generate code to configure the port and timer peripherals, as shown in Figure 9.23, Figure 9.24, and Figure 9.25.

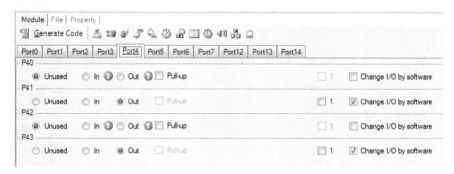

Figure 9.23   Configuring port 4 bit 2 for use as input to TAU0 channel 4.

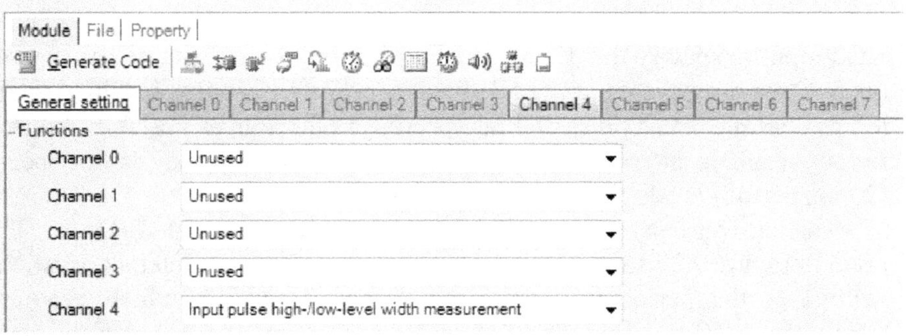

Figure 9.24   Selecting pulse width measurement mode for TAU0 channel 4.

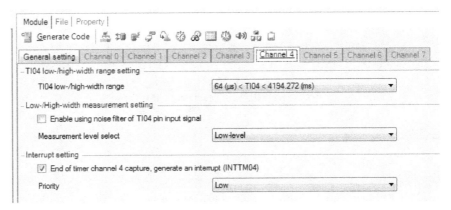

Figure 9.25 Configuring channel 4 for pulse width measurement particulars.

9.5.3 Using PWM Mode to Control a Servo Motor

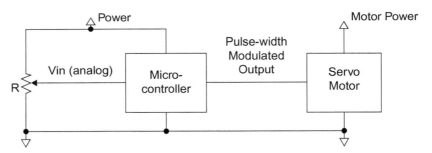

Figure 9.26 Schematic for servo motor circuit.

In this example we will use an analog input voltage (generated by a potentiometer) to control the angular position of a servo motor. Servo motors typically use a pulse-width modulated input to specify the desired output position. Specifications vary by motor, as per frequency and duty cycle required. For our servo, a 1 ms pulse specifies rotating as far to the left as possible, and a pulse of 2 ms specifies as far right as possible. Intermediate pulse durations result in intermediate positions. Usually a frequency is not specified, but 50 Hz (20 ms period) is adequate for smooth operation.

The hardware peripherals make the software quite simple to create. The sequence diagram in Figure 9.27 shows how the hardware and software interact. First, the main function configures the peripherals and starts timer channel 2, which generates an interrupt (INTM02) at 50 Hz. This interrupt provides a timing reference for the slave timer channel which generates the PWM signal. The interrupt also causes a timer interrupt service

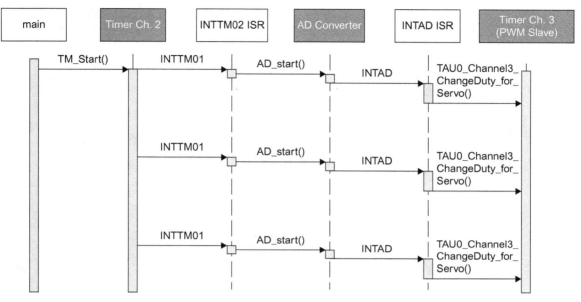

Figure 9.27   Sequence diagram for PWM servo motor controller.

routine to run, in which the AD converter samples the analog input. The AD converter generates an interrupt (ADINT) when the conversion completes. The ISR which services ADINT uses the AD conversion result to determine the appropriate pulse width and control the slave timer channel accordingly.

9.5.3.1 TAU Configuration

We configure the timer array unit as follows:

First the digital I/O port (P31) on the same pin as the PWM output must be left unused.

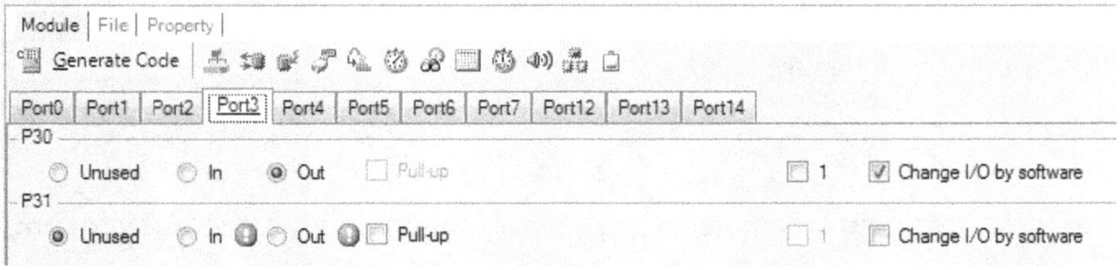

Figure 9.28   Leaving port 3 bit 1 unused by GPI/O circuitry.

Next we select PWM output mode for TAU 0 channel 2. This will prevent independent access to channel 3.

Figure 9.29   Selecting PWM mode for channels 2 and 3.

Next we configure channel 2 (the master channel) with the desired PWM period of 20 ms (1/50 Hz). We also specify that an interrupt INTTM02 will be generated at the end of each count sequence.

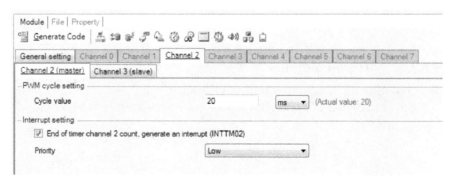

Figure 9.30   Setting channel 2 PWM period and interrupt.

Next we configure channel 3 (the slave channel) with the desired initial duty value of 7.5 percent, and indicate that we would like an interrupt to be generated. This is necessary for PWM operation.

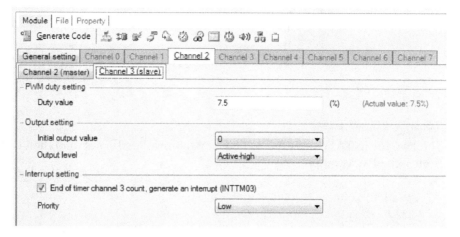

Figure 9.31   Setting channel 3 PWM characteristics.

9.5.3.2   CG_main.c

The main() function is trivial. After initialization of peripherals it has no further work to do.

```
void  main(void)
{
   /* Start user code. Do not edit comment generated here */
   /* Peripheral start function calls */
   AD_ComparatorOn();       /* Enable ADC voltage comparator */
   TAU0_Channel3_ChangeDuty_for_Servo(50);
   TAU0_Channel2_Start();

   /* Endless control loop */
   while (1U) {
   }
}
```

9.5.3.3   CG_timer_user.c

The ISR for INTTM01 simply triggers the AD converter.

```
#pragma vector = INTAD_vect
_interrupt void MD_INTAD(void)
{
   USHORT adcval;
   /* Start user code. Do not edit comment generated here */
```

```
AD_Read(&adcval);
TAU0_Channel3_ChangeDuty_for_Servo(adcval/10);
//scale result by 1/10
/* End user code. Do not edit comment generated here */
}
```

9.5.3.4 CG_ad_user.c
The ISR for INTAD reads the AD conversion result, scales it, and then calls a function to control the PWM output.

```
#pragma vector = INTTM02_vect
_interrupt void MD_INTTM02(void)
{
    /* Start user code. Do not edit comment generated here */
    AD_Start();                     /* Start ADC (ADCS = 0n) */
    /* End user code. Do not edit comment generated here */
}
```

9.5.3.5 CG_timer.c
The PWM control function TAU0_Channel3_ChangeDuty_for_Servo() is based on Applilet-generated function called TAU0_Channel3_ChangeDuty() in CG_timer.c. The calculations were broken out into separate lines to simplify debugging.

```
void TAU0_Channel3_ChangeDuty_for_Servo(UCHAR servo_ratio)
{
    ULONG w = 0U;
    ULONG period = 0;

    period = 0xffff & (TDR02 + 1);

    if (servo_ratio > 100U) {
        servo_ratio = 100U;
    }
    w = servo_ratio;   //use unsigned long math to avoid overflows
    w *= period;
    w /= 2000U;
    w += period/20U;   //add 5% for 0 position offset
    TDR03 = (USHORT)w;
}
```

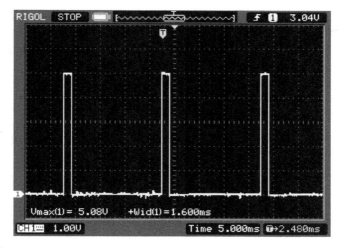

Figure 9.32 Example PWM output waveform for servo motor.

Figure 9.32 shows a sample waveform generated on the output pin P31 by this program. The pulse width is 1.6 ms.

9.6   RECAP

In this chapter we have learned about two different types of timer peripheral. The interval timer is a basic timer, while the timer array unit contains multiple powerful and highly configurable timers. We have seen how to use these timers to generate periodic interrupts and pulse-width modulated signals. We have also seen how to use them to measure the pulse width and frequency of digital input waveforms.

9.7   EXERCISES

1. Write the code to configure the interval timer to generate an interrupt with frequency of 440 Hz. What is the actual frequency generated?
2. The nominal frequency for f_{IL} is 15 kHz. Measure the actual frequency of this signal for your RL78-based system using software and an oscilloscope.
3. Write a program to configure the TAU to control a strobe light running at 120 Hz.
4. Write the code to generate a square wave with frequency as close to 31415.9265 Hz as possible, given a 32 MHz oscillator.
5. Explain the race condition mentioned in the anemometer example footnote.

6. Write a program to measure wind speed by counting anemometer rotations during a known time period. Configure a TAU channel to count external pulses. Use software to reset the counter every second and update a variable which represents the average wind speed for the previous second.

Chapter Ten

Peripherals for Robustness & Performance

10.1 LEARNING OBJECTIVES

In this chapter we examine two additional types of peripheral which improve system robustness or program execution speed. We first examine various peripherals which improve system robustness.

- A watchdog timer detects if a program runs out of control.
- The cyclic redundancy check unit and RAM parity error detection system help verify that data has not been corrupted.
- The invalid memory access detection unit helps detect illegal memory access operations that come from an out-of-control program.
- RAM and SFR guard functions protect certain RAM and SFR memory regions from being modified.
- A low voltage detector warns the program if the supply voltage is failing.

We then examine two peripherals which accelerate program performance (execution speed and responsiveness).

- The Direct Memory Access controller copies data between SFRs and RAM without requiring program intervention, improving speed, and responsiveness.
- The Multiplier/Divider/Accumulator performs complicated mathematical operations in hardware to reduce operation time.

10.2 PERIPHERALS FOR ROBUSTNESS

Embedded systems are expected to work correctly, but they may sometimes malfunction. Transient electrical noise from motors and other sources may lead to errors in program execution. Hardware devices may fail. Software may encounter unexpected (and therefore unsupported) events. It is very difficult and expensive to completely test a system in all possible environments. Microcontrollers often include peripherals to detect abnormal hardware or software behavior and reset the system in response.

10.2.1 Watchdog Timer

Many embedded systems are built to operate without an operator, so there should be a mechanism that monitors the system for unexpected errors due to some hardware fault, an unusual endless loop, or other fatal software bug. The watchdog timer serves the purpose of automatically monitoring and recovering the system from such situations.

The watchdog timer is an internal hardware timer peripheral in the CPU or an external device which resets the processor if it is not reset within a given period of time. The application software needs to periodically reset the watchdog timer. If the application software does not do this soon enough, the WDT overflows and the overflow signal is used to reset the system. So, the watchdog timer can only help the system recover from faults which prevent the timely refresh of the WDT.

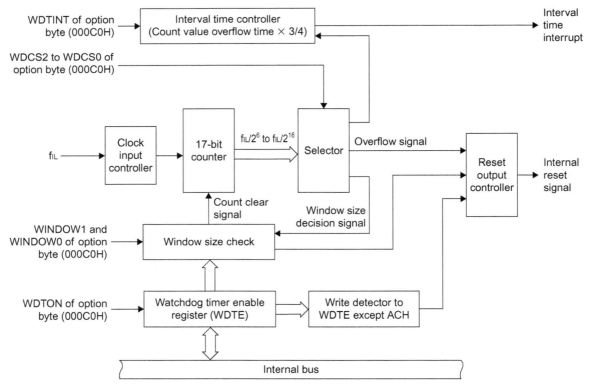

Figure 10.1　Block diagram of Watchdog Timer peripheral

10.2.1.1 Structure

The RL78 WDT peripheral is built around a 17-bit counter which generates a delay based on an on-chip low-speed oscillator running at f_{IL} (up to 17.25 kHz). If the WDT is not refreshed before the counter overflows, the overflow signal will reset the processor. In order to refresh the WDT, a specific byte (ACH) must be written to the WDTE register during a valid time window. This will clear the WDT counter and restart counting.

As there are several possible reset causes, which one is responsible can be determined by examining the RESF (Reset Control Flag) register. If the WDT caused the reset, then the WDTRF bit will be set.

Several aspects of the WDT peripheral can be configured and controlled using option byte 0 located at address 000C0H in flash memory. Because it is in flash memory, the option byte must be defined as an initialized static variable (at address 000C0H) and cannot be modified at run-time.

- The WDT can be enabled by setting the WDTON bit of the option byte 00C0H.
- The overflow time can be selected from a range of times from 3.7 ms to 3.8 s, using the WDCS2, WDCS1, and WDCS0 bits.
- The WDT can be configured to ignore refresh commands which occur outside of a valid time window. This provides greater reliability and fault detection coverage. The valid window can be the last 50%, 75%, or 100% of the watchdog timer period, using the WINDOW0 and WINDOW1 bits. The 100% setting essentially disables the window setting.
- The WDT can generate an interval interrupt (INTWDTI) when the counter reaches 75% of the overflow time. This is controlled with the WDTINT bit.

10.2.1.2 Using the WDT

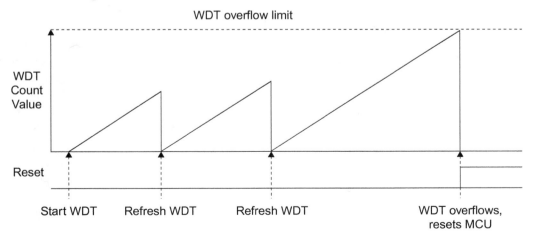

Figure 10.2 WDT refresh and overflow activity.

Figure 10.2 shows two examples of WDT activity. First, the WDT is operating with a 100% window, so any refresh before the WDT overflows will be valid. Our buggy program starts the WDT, refreshes it twice and then gets caught in a busy wait loop. In this loop the WDT is not refreshed, so the counter overflows and the WDT forces the processor to reset.

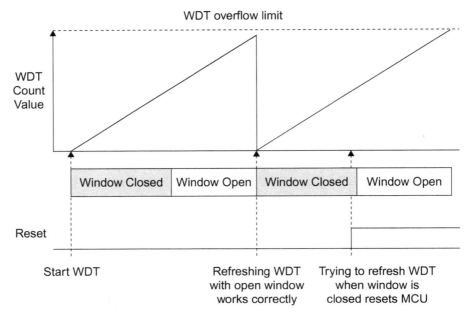

Figure 10.3   WDT refresh behavior with 50% window.

In Figure 10.3, we have limited the window to 50%. The first time the program tries to refresh the timer it occurs within the window, so the refresh is successful. This restarts the WDT and starts a new window cycle. Another bug in our program makes it try to reset the WDT too early (before the window opens). Even though the correct refresh code (ACH) is written to the WDTE register, it triggers a system reset because the window was closed. For some critical systems this window feature is needed to provide extra assurance that the program is operating correctly.

In a multitasking system, it is a best practice to have each task check in with a task which monitors system-wide task progress. This monitor task will only reset the WDT if **all tasks** are making adequate progress. One should never build a system in which the WDT is reset automatically by a task or ISR which operates autonomously of the rest of the system. This defeats the purpose of the WDT. For in-depth discussions of watchdog timer use, we refer the reader elsewhere (Koopman, 2010).

10.2.2 Cyclic Redundancy Check Unit

Often an embedded system needs to validate that data is correct and has not been corrupted. For example, a packet of data which is received from a network may have had some bits corrupted by noise. Similarly, the program memory should be validated upon system power-up to ensure that the system runs a valid program. One way of validating the data is to include a check code with the stored data. To validate the data, the program needs to recalculate the check code based on the stored data. If this calculated code value matches the stored code, then the data is correct.[1] If they differ, then some of the data has been corrupted and we cannot trust it.

One useful check code is a Cyclic Redundancy Check code. The CRC peripheral uses the CRC-16-CCITT generator polynomial and supports two different operating modes.

In the first operating mode, the user program writes each byte to include in the CRC calculation to the CRCIN register. The CRCD register holds the calculated CRC, and is used in subsequent CRC calculations After all input data has been written to CRCIN, the resulting CRC is available in the CRCD register.

In the second operating mode, dedicated hardware automatically scans an entire flash memory region and calculates its CRC. As this is performed in hardware, it is much faster than a software approach, such as the first operating mode. Checking 64 KB of flash ROM takes 512 μs with a 32 MHz system clock.

The CRC peripheral needs to be configured to specify amount of memory to check, beginning with address 0. The CRC check operation is triggered by the execution of the HALT instruction after the CRC0EN bit has been set. When the comparison has completed, the processor resumes executing the instruction following the HALT. It can then examine the result of the CRC operations, which is stored in the PGCRCL register. If the register does not match the stored value, then the program memory is corrupt and the processor should shut down.

10.2.3 RAM Parity Error Detection

Each byte of internal RAM in RL78 MCUs is protected with a parity bit. This parity bit is automatically calculated on writes and checked on reads. If a parity error is detected on a read, the parity error status flag RPEF will be set. In addition, if the RPERDIS bit is cleared, then the parity error will trigger an MCU Reset. The RPERF flag in the RESF register will be set if the processor was reset due to a RAM parity error.

---

[1] There is a slight chance that it is incorrect, in the case that the corrupted data and the original data have the same check code. However, the codes are designed to make this highly unlikely.

10.2.4 Invalid Memory Access Detection

CONTENTS	READ	WRITE	FETCH INSTRUCTIONS
SFRs		OK	Invalid
RAM			OK
Mirror	OK	Invalid	Invalid
Data Flash Memory			
Reserved		OK	OK
2nd set of SFRs			Invalid
Reserved			OK
Reserved	Invalid	Invalid	Invalid
Code Flash Memory	OK		OK

Figure 10.4 Invalid memory access detection regions. Region addresses are listed in the hardware manual memory map.

It is possible for the memory system to detect certain types of invalid memory accesses and respond by resetting the MCU. As shown in Figure 10.4, there are three types of memory access: read, write, and instruction fetch. Setting the IAWREN bit will cause detection of reads, writes, and fetches at invalid addresses. The IAWRF bit in RESF will be set if an illegal memory access caused the reset, simplifying diagnostics and debugging.

10.2.5 RAM & SFR Guard Functions

The RAM guard function prevents a portion of RAM from being written, though it can still be read. A write to a protected area of RAM has no effect. This is helpful for protecting critical operating parameters from corruption. The amount of RAM protected (0, 128, 256, or 512 bytes) is determined by bits GRAM1 and GRAM0.

The SFR guard function prevents certain critical special function registers from being written. The GPORT bit controls protection of GPIO port control registers. The GINT bit controls protection of interrupt control registers. The GCSC flag controls access to clock control, voltage detection, and RAM parity error detection registers.

10.2.6 Voltage Detector

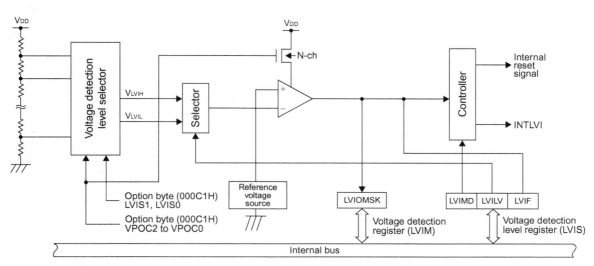

Figure 10.5 Block diagram of voltage detector peripheral.

A brownout condition in a microcontroller occurs when the supply voltage for the microcontroller temporarily drops enough that portions of the microcontroller may malfunction. The main purpose of automatically detecting the brownout condition is to prevent the processor from operating with a voltage below the guaranteed range. When a brownout occurs, the detector holds the processor in a reset state. It is also helpful to be warned early of an impending brownout condition with an interrupt. The processor can respond by shutting off output devices, saving critical data, and perhaps logging a fault code.

The RL78 Voltage Detector peripheral (shown in Figure 10.5) can compare the V_{DD} supply rail with two configurable voltage levels. The upper level (V_{LVIH}) determines at what voltage the low voltage interrupt is triggered. It also is used as the supply rail rises again to determine when the processor comes out of reset and starts running again. The lower level (V_{LVIL}) determines at what voltage the processor's reset signal is asserted.

As there are several possible reset causes, which one is responsible can be determined by examining the RESF register. If the LVD caused the reset, then the LVIRF bit will be set.

The reset and interrupt features can be used individually or together, based on the bits LVIMDS1 and LVIMDS0 in the option byte 00C1H. The output of the comparator can be read directly as LVIF. If the LVD is enabled and V_{DD} is below V_{LVI}, then the flag will be set.

■ When used as interrupt & reset mode

DETECTION VOLTAGE			OPTION BYTE SETTING VALUE						
V_{LVIH}		V_{LVIL}							
RISING EDGE	FALLING EDGE	FALLING EDGE	LVIMDS1	LVIMDS0	VPOC2	VPOC1	VPOC0	LVIS1	LVIS0
1.77 V	1.73 V	1.63 V	1	0	0	0	0	1	0
1.88 V	1.84 V							0	1
2.92 V	2.86 V							0	0
1.98 V	1.94 V	1.84 V			0	0	1	1	0
2.09 V	2.04 V							0	1
3.13 V	3.06 V							0	0
2.61 V	2.55 V	2.45 V			0	1	0	1	0
2.71 V	2.65 V							0	1
3.75 V	3.67 V							0	0
2.92 V	2.86 V	2.75 V			0	1	1	1	0
3.02 V	2.96 V							0	1
4.06 V	3.98 V							0	0
Other than above			Setting prohibited						

Figure 10.6   Configuring the LVD peripheral.

Let's take a look at using both features. Figure 10.6 shows various configuration options for the LVD when both interrupt and reset are enabled. The first issue to consider is what our MCU's normal supply voltage will be, as this affects which thresholds are useful to us. The MCU supports operation with V_{DD} ranging from 1.6 to 5.5 V; let's consider a nominal 1.8 V supply voltage. The LVD should not be triggered by this supply voltage, so we will need to select one of the first three rows in the figure, with VPOC2 = 0, VPOC1 = 0, and VPOC0 = 0. Let's configure the LVD as in the first row and see how the system behaves.

Figure 10.7 shows the circuit behavior.

■ V_{DD} is normally at 1.8 V but starts to fall.
■   An INTLVI interrupt will be generated when V_{DD} falls below V_{LVIH} = 1.73 V. The LVIF flag will be set, indicating a low supply voltage.

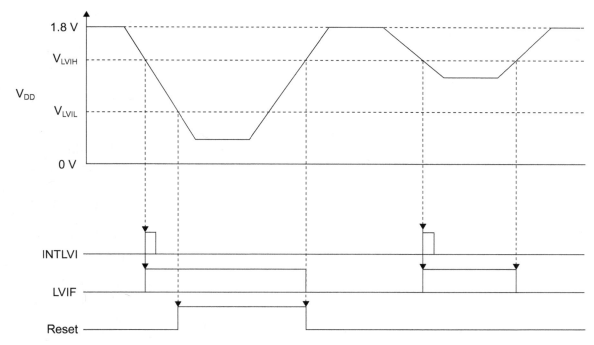

Figure 10.7 Low voltage detection circuit operation.

▪ If V_{DD} keeps falling, when it reaches $V_{LVIL} = 1.63$ V the MCU will be forced into reset. The MCU will not come out of reset until V_{DD} rises past 1.77 V.

▪ If instead V_{DD} doesn't fall to $V_{LVIL} = 1.63$ V then the processor will not be reset. When V_{DD} rises past $V_{LVIH} = 1.73$ V the LVIF flag will be cleared.

10.3   PERFORMANCE

There are various peripherals which are designed to speed up specific operations which are slower than desired when implemented in software. Here we examine the direct memory access controller and the hardware multiplier/divider/accumulator.

10.3.1 Direct Memory Access Controller

A Direct Memory Access (DMA) controller copies data in memory. It is much faster than a software move because no instructions need to be executed, and because dedicated hardware allows responsive triggering, again without involving software.

The RL78 family MCUs have two or four DMA controller channels. Each channel operates independently, and can transfer data between internal SRAM and SFR space. The DMA controllers are configured as follows, where n indicates the DMA controller channel number:

- The DENn bit enables the DMA controller.
- The DRSn bit defines the direction of the transfer: from RAM to SFR (1), or SFR to RAM (0).
- The DSn bit defines whether bytes (0) or words (1) will be transferred.
- The DRAn register specifies the low word of the SRAM address. The upper nibble is set to FH. This address is automatically incremented by 1 or 2 after each transfer based upon whether bytes or words are transferred.
- The DSAn register specifies the low byte of the SFR address. The upper portion is set to FFFH. This address is not incremented.
- The DBCn register specifies how many transfers to perform. Values from 1 to 1024 are possible.
- The STGn bit allows software to trigger a DMA transfer.
- The DSTn bit indicates that the DMA transfer is still ongoing (1) or completed (0).
- The DWAITn bit forces a DMA request to wait rather than be serviced immediately.
- The IFCn3 to IFCn0 bits specify the trigger condition for initiating the DMA transfer(s). Transfers can be triggered by software command or by a hardware interrupt signal from the ADC, serial communications interfaces, or timers.

After a DMA controller completes transferring all of its data it generates an INTDMAn interrupt request.

Let's consider how to use the DMA channel 1 controller in conjunction with the ADC. Figure 10.8 shows an overview of the behavior. We will set up a timer to generate a periodic interrupt which causes the ADC to scan and sample four channels. Each conversion results in an ADINT interrupt which is used to trigger a DMA transfer from the ADC result register (addresses FFF1EH and FFF1FH) to a buffer in RAM, starting at address FFCE0H. When all twelve words have been transferred, the DMA controller will generate a DMAINT interrupt to signal the completion. At this point we can notify the main code that its data is ready in RAM and disable the timer.

Note that the only software processing required after the peripherals have been configured and started is the ISR of the DMA controller. This allows very low run-time overhead, and quick, precise response.

10.3.2 Multiplier/Accumulator/Divider

Some RL78 family processors include a multiplier/accumulator/divider unit (called MD for brevity) to accelerate those mathematical operations. The MD unit supports several operations:

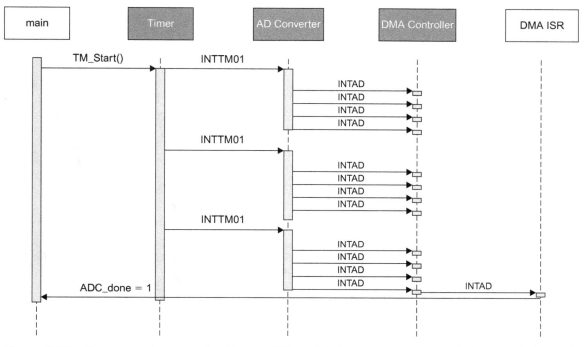

Figure 10.8 Sequence diagram using timer, ADC, and DMA controller to sample four ADC channels with minimal software intervention.

- Signed and unsigned multiplies: 16 bit × 16 bit = 32 bit
- Signed and unsigned multiply/accumulates: 16 bit × 16 bit + 32 bit = 32 bit
- Unsigned divide: 32 bits/32 bits = 32 bit integer quotient, 32 bit integer remainder

Rather than use the general purpose registers such as AX, BC, DE, and HL to hold operands, commands, and results, the MD unit uses its own special function registers. These consist of six 16-bit data registers (MDAH, MDAL, MDBH, MDBL, MDCH, and MDCL) and one 8-bit control register (MDUC). To use the MD unit the program configures MDUC to specify the desired operation, according to Table 10.1.

The program then loads the MD data registers with the input data as shown in Table 10.3. In multiply mode or multiply/accumulate mode, writing to MDAH and MDAL starts the multiplication. In division mode, the DIVST bit must also be set to 1 to start the division. After the operation completes, the results are available in the MD registers as shown in Table 10.4. The status flags shown in Table 10.2 can be examined if needed.

A multiply takes one clock cycle after the last operand is written, while a multiply accumulate takes two clock cycles. A division operation takes sixteen clock cycles after the DIVST flag is set. It is possible to configure MDUC so that the MD unit generates an INTMD interrupt when a division completes.

TABLE 10.1 Multiplier/Accumulator/Divider Operation Selection

DIVMODE	MACMODE	MDSM	OPERATION SELECTED
0	0	0	Multiply, unsigned
0	0	1	Multiply, signed
0	1	0	Multiply/accumulate, unsigned
0	1	1	Multiply/accumulate, signed
1	0	0	Divide, unsigned, generate interrupt when complete
1	1	0	Divide, unsigned, no interrupt generated

TABLE 10.2 Multiplier/Accumulator/Divider Flags

FLAG	DESCRIPTION
MACOF	Multiply/accumulate overflow
MACSF	Multiply/accumulate sign flag
DIVST	Division operation status. 1 = division in progress

TABLE 10.3 MD Operand Locations

OPERATION	MDAH	MDAL	MDBH	MDBL	MDCH	MDCL
Multiply	Multiplier	Multiplicand				
Multiply/ Accumulate	Multiplier	Multiplicand				
Divide	Dividend (high word)	Dividend (low word)	Divisor (high word)	Divisor (low word)		

TABLE 10.4 MD Result Locations

OPERATION	MDAH	MDAL	MDBH	MDBL	MDCH	MDCL
Multiply			Product (high word)	Product (low word)		
Multiply/ Accumulate			Product (high word)	Product (low word)	Accumulator (high word)	Accumulator (low word)
Divide	Quotient (high word)	Quotient (low word)			Remainder (high word)	Remainder (low word)

10.4   RECAP

In this chapter we have examined two types of peripherals.

The first improves robustness by detecting anomalous system behavior or operating conditions. The watchdog timer resets the processor if it is not refreshed at the right times. The CRC unit and RAM parity system detect corrupted data. Invalid memory accesses can be detected and trigger a reset. The RAM and SFR guard features prevent certain critical memory regions from being modified. The low voltage detector warns the processor of an impending power failure and can hold it in reset as appropriate.

The second improves program performance. The DMA controller accelerates data transfers by removing the need to execute instructions to perform them. The Multiplier/Divider/Accumulator performs those operations quickly.

10.5   REFERENCES

Koopman, P. J., *Better Embedded System Software.* Pittsburgh: Drumnadrochit Education, 2010.

10.6   EXERCISES

1. Write a function to configure the LVD to generate a low voltage interrupt when the supply voltage falls below 2.92 V.
2. Write a program which uses a timer and DMA to sample port P0 every 100 microseconds and store the results in RAM.
3. Write a two-dimensional matrix multiplication function which uses the MD unit. Assume 16-bit signed data and arbitrary matrix size.
4. Write a dot product function which uses the MD unit. Assume 16-bit signed data and arbitrary matrix size.

Chapter Eleven

Designing Responsive and Real-Time Systems

11.1   LEARNING OBJECTIVES

Most embedded systems have multiple independent tasks running at the same time. Which activity should the microprocessor perform first? This decision determines how responsive the system is, which then affects how fast a processor we must use, how much time we have for running intensive control algorithms, how much energy we can save, and many other factors. In this chapter we will discuss different ways for a microprocessor to schedule its tasks, and the implications for performance, program structure, and related issues.

11.2   MOTIVATION

Consider an embedded system which controls a doorbell in a house. When a person at the front door presses the switch, the bell should ring inside the house. The system's **responsiveness** describes how long it takes from pressing the switch to sounding the bell. It is easy to create a very responsive embedded system with only one task. The scheduling approach shown below is an obvious and simple approach:

```
1. void main (void){
2.    init_system();
3.    while(1){
4.       if(switch == PRESSED){
5.          Ring_The_Bell();
6.       }
7.    }
8. }
```

Our doorbell is very responsive. In fact, we like it so much that we decide to add in a smoke detector and a very loud beeper so we can be warned about a possible fire. We also add a burglar detector and another alarm bell. This results in the code shown on the next page.

```
1. void main (void){
2.    init_system();
3.    while(1){
4.        if(switch == PRESSED){
5.            Ring_The_Doorbell();
6.        }
7.        if(Burglar_Detected() == TRUE){
8.            Sound_The_Burglar_Alarm();
9.        }
10.       if(Smoke_Detected() == TRUE){
11.           Sound_The_Fire_Alarm();
12.       }
13.   }
14. }
```

Going from one task to three tasks has complicated the situation significantly.[1] How should we share the processor's time between these tasks?

■ How long of a delay are we willing to accept between smoke detection and the fire alarm sounding? And the delay between the switch being pressed and the doorbell sounding?

■ Should the system try to detect smoke or burglars while the doorbell is playing?

■ Should the doorbell work while the smoke alarm is being sounded? What about when the burglar alarm is sounding?

■ Which subsystem should the processor check first: the doorbell, the smoke detector, or the burglar detector? Or should it just alternate between them?

■ Should the doorbell switch be checked as often as the smoke and burglar detectors, or at a different rate?

■ What if the person at the door presses the switch again before the doorbell finishes sounding? Should that be detected?

Now that we have to share the processor, we have to worry about how long the bell rings and the alarms sound. If we use a doorbell ringtone which lasts for thirty seconds, then Ring_The_Bell will take at least thirty seconds to run. During this time, we won't know if our house is burning or being robbed. Similarly, what if the firemen come when the alarm is sounding? How quickly should the doorbell respond in that case?

---

[1] In fact, any number of tasks greater than one complicates the situation!

11.3   SCHEDULING FUNDAMENTALS

This example reveals the two fundamental issues in scheduling for responsive systems.

- If we have multiple tasks ready to run, which one do we run first? This decision defines the **ordering** of task execution.
- Do we allow one task to interrupt or **preempt** another task (or even itself)?
- Both of these decisions will determine the system's **responsiveness** (measured by response time):
    - □ How long will it take for the **most important** task to **start running?** To **finish running?** Does this depend on how long any other tasks take to run, and how often they run?
    - □ How long will it take for the **least important** task to **start running?** To **finish running?** We expect it will depend on how long all the other tasks take to run, and how often they run.
- If we allow tasks to preempt each other, then a task may start running very soon but finish much later, after multiple possible preemptions.

These response times in turn affect many performance-related issues, such as:

- How fast must the processor's clock rate be to ensure that nothing happens "late"?
- How much time do we have available for running compute-intensive algorithms?
- How much energy can we save by putting the processor to sleep?
- How much power can we save by slowing down the processor?

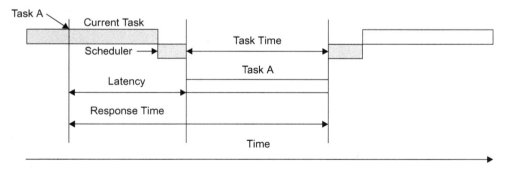

Figure 11.1   Diagram and definitions of scheduler concepts.

Figure 11.1 shows a visual representation of some arbitrary scheduling activity. Task *A* is released (becomes ready to run) at the first vertical bar. There is some **latency** between the release and when the task starts running, due to other processing in the system and scheduler overhead. Similarly, there is a **response time** which measures how long it takes task *A* to complete its processing. Some scheduling approaches allow a task to be preempted (delayed) after it has started running, which will increase the response time.

11.3.1 Task Ordering

The first factor affecting response time is the **order in which we run tasks.** We could always follow the same order by using a **static** schedule. The code shown for the Doorbell/Fire Alarm/Burglar Alarm uses a static schedule. Figure 11.2 shows an interesting case. If a burglar broke in and a fire broke out just after someone pressed the switch to ring the doorbell, we wouldn't find out about the burglar for almost thirty seconds and the fire for about sixty seconds. We probably do not want these large delays for such critical notifications.

We can change the order based on current conditions (e.g., if the house is on fire) using a **dynamic** schedule. An obvious way to do this is to reschedule after finishing each task. A dynamic schedule lets us improve the responsiveness of some tasks at the price of delaying other tasks. For example, let's prioritize fire detection over burglar detection over the doorbell.

```
 1. void main (void){
 2.     init_system();
 3.     while(1){
 4.         if(Smoke_Detected() == TRUE){
 5.             Sound_The_Fire_Alarm();
 6.         } else if (Burglar_Detected() == TRUE) {
 7.             Sound_The_Burglar_Alarm();
 8.         } else if (switch == PRESSED) {
 9.                 Ring_The_Doorbell();
10.         }
11.     }
12. }
```

Notice how this code is different—there are **else** clauses added, which change the schedule to a dynamic one. As long as smoke is detected, Sound_The_Fire_Alarm() will run repeatedly. The burglar alarm and doorbell will be ignored until no more smoke is detected. Similarly, burglar detection will disable the doorbell. This is shown in Figure 11.2.

This **strict prioritization** may or may not be appropriate for a given system. We may want to ensure some **fairness,** perhaps by limiting how often a task can run. Later in this chapter we present a periodic table-based approach which is much better than this hard-coded design.

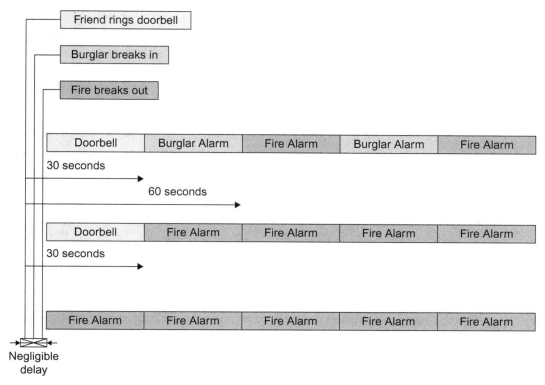

Figure 11.2   Doorbell/fire alarm/burglar alarm system behavior with different scheduling approaches.

11.3.2 Task Preemption

The second aspect to consider is whether one task can **preempt** another task. Consider our thirty-second doorbell ringtone—the task Ring_The_Doorbell will **run to completion** without stopping or yielding the processor.

What if a burglar breaks the window a split second after an accomplice rings the doorbell? In this worst-case scenario, we won't find out about the burglar (or a possible fire) for thirty seconds.[2] Let's say we'd like to find out within one second. We have several options:

- Limit the maximum duration for the doorbell ringtone to one second.
- Add another microprocessor which is dedicated to playing the doorbell ringtone. This will raise system costs.

---

[2] Imagine what Thomas Crown, James Bond, or Jason Bourne could do in that time!

- ■ Break the Ring_The_Doorbell function into thirty separate pieces (e.g., with a state machine or separate functions), each of which takes only one second to run. This code will be hard to maintain.
- ■ Allow the smoke and burglar detection code to preempt Ring_The_Doorbell. We will need to use a more sophisticated task scheduler which can (1) preempt and resume tasks, and (2) detect events which trigger switching and starting tasks. We will not need to break apart any source code. This will make code maintenance easier. However, we introduce the vulnerability to race conditions for shared data, and we also will need more memory (enough to hold each task's stack simultaneously).

Let's apply this preemption option to our system. We assign the highest priority to fire detection, then burglar detection, and then the doorbell. Now we have the response timeline shown in Figure 11.2. The system starts sounding the doorbell after the switch is pressed, but as soon as the fire is detected, the scheduler preempts the Ring_The_Doorbell and starts running Sound_The_Fire_Alarm. We find out about the fire essentially immediately, without having to wait for the doorbell to finish sounding.

As with the previous example, we have strict prioritization without control of how often tasks can run. As long as smoke is detected, Sound_The_Fire_Alarm() will run repeatedly. The burglar alarm and doorbell will be ignored until no more smoke is detected. Similarly, burglar detection will disable the doorbell.

11.3.3 Fairness and Prioritization

These examples all show one weakness of our system: prioritizing some tasks over others can lead to starvation of lower priority tasks (they may never get to run). For some systems this is acceptable, but for others it is not. Here are two ways of providing some kind of fairness:

- ■ We can allow multiple tasks to share the same priority level. If both tasks are ready to run, we alternate between executing each of them (whether by allowing each task to run to completion, or by preempting each periodically).
- ■ We can limit how often each task can run by defining the task frequency. This is the common approach used for designers of real-time systems. Note that we can still allow only one task per priority level.

11.3.4 Response Time

For the two non-preemptive examples in Figure 11.2, notice how the response time for the fire alarm and the burglar alarm depends on **how long the doorbell sounds.** However, for the preemptive approach those response times are **independent** of how long the doorbell sounds. This is the major benefit of a preemptive scheduling approach: it makes a task's response time essentially **independent** of all processing by lower priority tasks.[3] Instead, only **higher priority** tasks can delay that task.

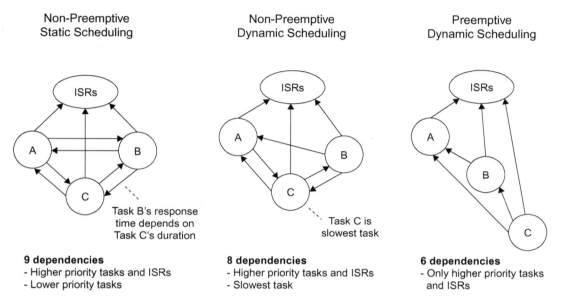

Non-Preemptive
Static Scheduling

Non-Preemptive
Dynamic Scheduling

Preemptive
Dynamic Scheduling

Task B's response
time depends on
Task C's duration

Task C is
slowest task

9 dependencies
- Higher priority tasks and ISRs
- Lower priority tasks

8 dependencies
- Higher priority tasks and ISRs
- Slowest task

6 dependencies
- Only higher priority tasks
  and ISRs

Figure 11.3   Timing dependences of different scheduling approaches.

In Figure 11.3 we present these relationships in a graph. Tasks and ISRs are nodes, while edges (or arcs) are timing dependences. For example, the edge from B to C indicates that task B's response time depends on task C's duration. We can now compare timing dependences for these three classes of scheduler.

- With the non-preemptive static scheduler, each task's response time depends on the duration of all other tasks and ISRs, so there are nine dependences.[4]
- With the non-preemptive dynamic scheduler, we assign priorities to tasks (A > B > C). In general, a task no longer depends on lower priority tasks, so we have more timing independence and isolation. This accounts for six dependences. The exception is the

---

[3] There are exceptions when tasks can communicate with each other with semaphores and other such mechanisms, but that is beyond the scope of this introductory text.

[4] Of course, if task code can disable interrupts, then there will be three more edges leading from the ISRs back to the tasks! That would be a total of twelve dependences, which is quite a few to handle.

slowest or longest duration task, which is C in this example. If task C has started running, it will delay any other task, regardless of priority. So the higher priority tasks A and B each have a dependence edge leading to task C in Figure 11.3, which results in a total of eight dependences.

▦ With the preemptive dynamic scheduler, we also prioritize the tasks (A > B > C). Because a task can preempt any lower priority task, the slowest task no longer matters. Each task can be preempted by an ISR, so there are three dependence edges to begin with. Task A cannot be preempted by B or C, so it adds no new edges. Task B can be preempted by task A, which adds one edge. Finally, task C can be preempted by task A or B, which adds two more edges. As a result we have only six dependences. Most importantly, these dependence edges **all point upwards.**[5] This means that in order to determine the response time for a task, we only need to consider **higher priority tasks.** This makes the analysis much easier.

The real-time system research and development communities have developed extensive precise mathematical methods for calculating worst-case response times, determining if deadlines can ever be missed, and other characteristics of a system. These methods consider semaphores, task interactions, scheduler overhead, and all sorts of other complexities of practical implementations. We provide an introduction to these concepts later in this chapter in Section 11.7.

11.3.5 Stack Memory Requirements

The non-preemptive scheduling approaches do not require as much data memory as the preemptive approaches. In particular, the non-preemptive approach requires only **one call stack,** while a preemptive approach typically requires **one call stack per task.**[6]

The function call stack holds a function's state information such as return address and limited lifetime variables (e.g., automatic variables, which only last for the duration of a function). Without task preemption, task execution does not overlap in time, so all tasks can share the same stack. Preemption allows tasks to preempt each other at essentially any point in time. Trying to reuse the same stack space for different tasks would lead to corruption of this information on the stack. For example, task B is running. Function B3 in task B calls function B4. The scheduler then preempts task B to run the higher priority task A, which was running function A2. Function A2 completes and it expects to return to function A1,

---

[5] This is called a DAG or directed acyclic graph.

[6] There are several ways to reduce the number of stacks needed for preemptive scheduling, but they are beyond the scope of this text.

which called A2. However, the call stack has function B3's information on the stack, so Task A will start executing function B3! And so the system fails to operate correctly.

As a result of these memory requirements for preemptive scheduling approaches, there are many cost-sensitive embedded systems which use a non-preemptive scheduler to minimize RAM sizes and therefore costs.

11.3.6 Interrupts

Interrupts are a special case of preemption with dedicated hardware and compiler support. They can be added to any of these scheduling approaches in order to provide faster, time-critical processing. In fact, for many systems **only** interrupt service routines are needed for the application's work. The main loop is simply an infinite loop which keeps putting the processor into a low-power idle mode.

When designing a system which splits between ISRs and task code, one must strike a balance. The more work which is placed in an ISR, the slower the response time for other processing (whether tasks or other ISRs[7]). The standard approach is to perform time-critical processing in the ISR (e.g., unloading a character from the UART received data buffer) and deferring remaining work for task code (pushing that character in a FIFO from which the task will eventually read). ISR execution duration affects the response time for other code, so it is included in the response time calculations described in Section 11.3.4 and in Figure 11.3.

11.4 TASK MANAGEMENT

11.4.1 Task States

A task will be in one of several possible states. The scheduler and the task code itself both affect which state is active. With a **non-preemptive dynamic scheduler,** a task can be in any one of the states[8] shown in Figure 11.4:

- Waiting for the scheduler to decide that this task is ready to run. For example, a task which asked the scheduler to delay it for 500 ms will be in this state for that amount of time.

---

[7] It is possible to make ISRs interruptable, but this introduces many new ways to build the system wrong. Hence it is discouraged.

[8] We consider preemption by an ISR as a separate state. However, since it operates automatically and saves and restores system context, we consider it as a separate enhancement to the RTC scheduler and leave it out of our diagrams. In fact, the scheduler relies on a tick ISR to track time and move tasks between certain states.

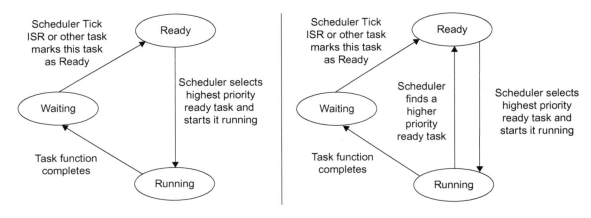

Non-preemptive Dynamic Scheduler   Preemptive Dynamic Scheduler

Figure 11.4 Task states and transitions for different schedulers.

- **Ready to start running** but not running yet. There may be a higher-priority task which is running. As this task has not started running, no automatic variables have been initialized, and there is no activation record.
- **Running** on the processor. The task **runs to the completion** of the task function, at which point the scheduler resumes execution and the task is moved to the waiting state. Automatic variables have been initialized, and there is at least one activation record on the stack frame for this task. A single processor system can have only one task in this state.

Consider a task which needs to write a block of data to flash memory. After issuing a write command to the flash memory controller, it may take some significant amount of time (e.g., 10 ms) to program the block. We have two options with a non-preemptive kernel:

- Our task can use a busy wait loop until the flash block programming is complete. The task remains in the **running** state while programming. This approach delays other processing and wastes processor cycles.
- We can break the task into a state machine so that task state one issues the write command, task state two checks to see if the programming is done, and task state three continues with the task's processing. The task executes task state two each time it is called as long as programming is not done. The task spends most of its time **waiting,** with occasional brief periods **running** when executing the code for task state two. This approach complicates program design but is practical for smaller systems. However, it grows unwieldy for complex systems.

Allowing tasks to **preempt** each other reduces response time and simplifies application design. With preemption, each task need not be built with a run-to-completion structure. Instead, the task can yield the processor to other tasks, or it can be preempted by a higher-priority task with more urgent processing. For example, our task can tell the scheduler "I don't have anything else to do for the next 10 ms, so you can run a different task." The scheduler then will save the state of this task, and swap in the state of the next highest priority task which is ready to run. This introduces another way to move from running to waiting, as well as a way to move from running to ready. We examine these in detail next.

11.4.2 Transitions between States

We now examine the ways in which a task can move between the various states. These rules govern how the system behaves, and therefore set some ground rules for how we should design our system.

- The transition from **ready to running:**
  - In a non-preemptive system, when the scheduler is ready to run a task, it selects the highest priority ready task and moves it to the running state, typically by calling it as a subroutine (as there is no context to restore).
  - In a preemptive system, when the kernel is ready to run a task, it selects the highest priority ready task and moves it to the running state by restoring its context to the processor.
- The transition from **running to waiting:**
  - In a non-preemptive system, the only way a task can move from running to waiting is if it **completes** (returns from the task function). At this point there is no more execution context for the task (return addresses, automatic variables), so there is no data to save or restore.
  - In a preemptive system, the task can yield the processor.[9] For example, it can request a delay ("Hey, RTOS! Wake me up in at least 10 ms!"), or it can wait or **pend** on an event ("Hey, RTOS! Wake me up when I get a message in my mailbox called foo!"). This makes application programming much easier, as mentioned before. At this point there still is execution context, so the kernel must save it for later restoration.
- The transition from **waiting to ready:**
  - In a non-preemptive system such as the RTC scheduler above, the timer tick ISR moves the task by setting the run flag. Alternatively, another task can set the run flag to request for this task to run.

---

[9] What happens if the task function finishes executing depends on the RTOS. The task could move to the waiting state, or to a terminated state.

□   In a preemptive system, the kernel is notified that some event has occurred. For example, time delay has expired or a task has sent a message to the mailbox called foo. The kernel knows which task is waiting for this event, so it moves that particular task from the waiting state to the ready state.

▪   The transition from **running to ready:**

□   In a non-preemptive system this transition does not exist, as a task cannot be preempted.

□   In a preemptive system, when the kernel determines a higher priority task is ready to run, it will save the context of the currently running task, and move that task to the ready state.

11.4.3   Context Switching for Preemptive Systems

In preemptive systems, some of these state transitions require the scheduler to save a task's execution context and restore another task's context to ensure programs execute correctly. This is called **context switching** and involves accessing the processor's general-purpose registers.

Figure 11.5 shows an example of the execution context for an RL78 family system as it is executing task A in a system with two tasks (A and B). The CPU uses the program counter PC to fetch the next instruction to execute, and the stack pointer to access the top of the task's stack. The CPU's general purpose registers are used to hold the program's data and intermediate computation results. The PSW holds status bits and control bits.

In order to perform a context switch from task A to task B correctly, we must first copy all of this task-specific processor register information to a storage location (e.g., task control block (TCB) A). This is shown in Figure 11.6.

Second, we must copy all of the data from TCB B into the CPU's registers. This operation is shown in Figure 11.7. Now the CPU will be able to resume execution of task B where it left off.

11.5   EXAMPLES OF SCHEDULERS _____

11.5.1   A Nonpreemptive Dynamic Scheduler

We will now examine a flexible nonpreemptive scheduler for periodic and aperiodic tasks. We call it the RTC (run-to-completion) scheduler. This simple tick-based scheduler is quite flexible and offers the various benefits:

▪   We can configure the system to run each task with a given period (e.g., every 40 ms) measured in time ticks. This simplifies the creation of multi-rate systems.

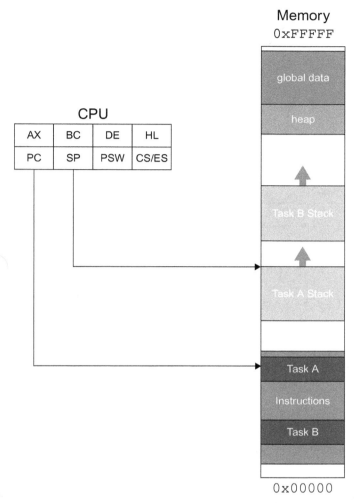

Figure 11.5   Example execution context when executing task A.

- We can define task priorities, allowing us to design the system's response (which tasks are executed earlier) when there are multiple tasks ready to run.
- We can selectively enable and disable tasks.

This scheduler has three fundamental parts.

- **Task Table:** This table holds information on each task, including:
  - ☐ The address of the task's root function.
  - ☐ The period with which the task should run (e.g., 10 ticks).

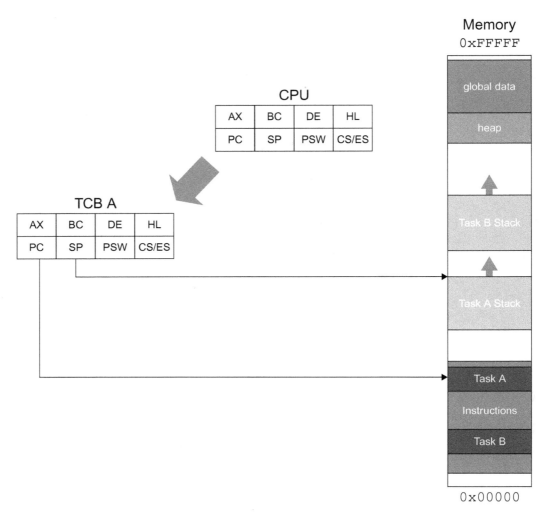

Figure 11.6   Saving task A's context from the CPU registers into task control block for task A.

      ❑   The time delay until the next time the task should run (measured in ticks).

      ❑   A flag indicating whether the task is ready to run.

▪ **Tick ISR:** Once per time tick (say each 1 millisecond) a hardware timer triggers an interrupt. The interrupt service routine decrements the time delay (**timer**) until the next run. If this reaches zero, then the task is ready to release, so the ISR sets its **run** flag.

▪ **Task Dispatcher:** The other part of the scheduler is what actually runs the tasks. It is simply an infinite loop which examines each task's run flag. If it finds a task with

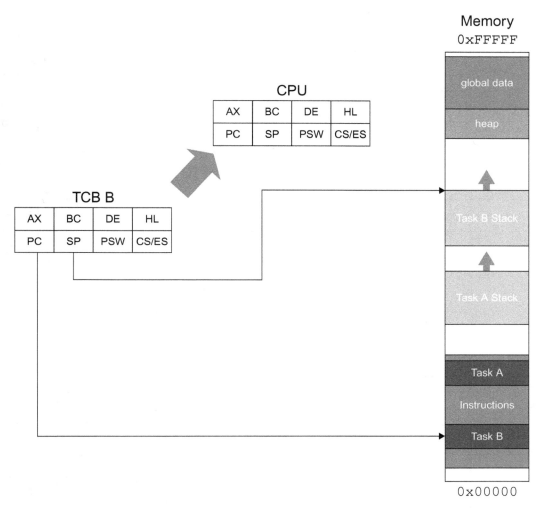

Figure 11.7   Restoring task B's context to the CPU.

the **run** flag set to 1, the scheduler will clear the **run** flag back to 0, execute the task, and then go back to examining the **run** flags (starting with the highest-priority task in the table).

Figure 11.8 shows a simple example of how this works with three tasks. Task 1 becomes active every twenty time intervals, and takes one time interval to complete. Task 2 is active every ten time intervals, and takes two time intervals to complete. Task 3 becomes active every five time intervals and takes one time interval to complete.

	Priority	Length	Frequency
Task 1	2	1	20
Task 2	1	2	10
Task 3	3	1	5

Elapsed time	0	1	2	3	4	5	6	7	8	9	10	11	12	13	14	15	16	17	18	19	20	21	22	23	24	25
Task executed						T3					T2		T3			T3					T2		T1	T3		T3
Time T1	20	19	18	17	16	15	14	13	12	11	10	9	8	7	6	5	4	3	2	1	20	19	18	17	16	15
Time T2	10	9	8	7	6	5	4	3	2	1	10	9	8	7	6	5	4	3	2	1	10	9	8	7	6	5
Time T3	5	4	3	2	1	5	4	3	2	1	5	4	3	2	1	5	4	3	2	1	5	4	3	2	1	5
Run T1																					W	W	R			
Run T2											R										R					
Run T3						R					W	W	R			R					W	W	W	R		R

R = Running on processor   W = Ready and waiting for processor

Figure 11.8   Simple Run-to-Completion Dynamic Scheduling.

	Priority	Length	Frequency
Task 1	2	1	20
Task 2	1	2	10
Task 3	3	1	5
Task 4	0	1	3

Elapsed time	0	1	2	3	4	5	6	7	8	9	10	11	12	13	14	15	16	17	18	19	20	21	22	23	24	25
Task executed				T4		T3	T4			T4	T2		T4	T3		T4	T3		T4		T2		T4	T1	T4	T3
Time T1	20	19	18	17	16	15	14	13	12	11	10	9	8	7	6	5	4	3	2	1	20	19	18	17	16	15
Time T2	10	9	8	7	6	5	4	3	2	1	10	9	8	7	6	5	4	3	2	1	10	9	8	7	6	5
Time T3	5	4	3	2	1	5	4	3	2	1	5	4	3	2	1	5	4	3	2	1	5	4	3	2	1	5
Time T4	3	2	1	3	2	1	3	2	1	3	2	1	3	2	1	3	2	1	3	2	1	3	2	1	3	2
Run T1																					W	W	W	R		
Run T2											R										R					
Run T3						R				W	W	W	R			W	R				W	W	W	W	W	R
Run T4				R		R				R			R			R			R			W	R		R	

R = Running on processor   W = Ready and waiting for processor

Figure 11.9   Complex Run-to-Completion Dynamic Scheduling.

If more than one task becomes ready simultaneously (as seen at elapsed time ten), the higher priority task is serviced first. When the higher priority task finishes, the next highest ready task is executed. This repeats until there are no ready tasks.

Another example of a run-to-completion dynamic scheduling with interrupts is shown in Figure 11.9. A new task, Task 4, is added, which becomes active every three time intervals and runs for one time interval. As shown in the figure, at time = 20, tasks T1, T2, T3 all become active and T2 is run based on priority. At time = 21, task T4 becomes active and is scheduled to run at time = 22. T1 runs at time = 23, but before T3 gets a chance to run, T4 becomes active again and gains the processor. At time = 25, T3 misses a turn since T3 becomes active again and the T3 is serviced as if it were active only once. This is an example of an overload situation which leads to one of the tasks missing its turn.[10]

Figure 11.10 shows a complex overloaded example where the scheduler fails to service every task that is ready.

	Priority	Length	Frequency
Task 1	2	1	20
Task 2	1	2	10
Task 3	3	1	5
Task 4	0	2	3

Elapsed time	0	1	2	3	4	5	6	7	8	9	10	11	12	13	14	15	16	17	18	19	20	21	22	23	24	25	26	27	28	29	30
Task executed				T4	T3	T4			T4		T2		T4		T4		T3	T4			T2		T4		T4		T1	T4		T3	T4
Time T1	20	19	18	17	16	15	14	13	12	11	10	9	8	7	6	5	4	3	2	1	20	19	18	17	16	15	14	13	12	11	10
Time T2	10	9	8	7	6	5	4	3	2	1	10	9	8	7	6	5	4	3	2	1	10	9	8	7	6	5	4	3	2	1	10
Time T3	5	4	3	2	1	5	4	3	2	1	5	4	3	2	1	5	4	3	2	1	5	4	3	2	1	5	4	3	2	1	5
Time T4	3	2	1	3	2	1	3	2	1	3	2	1	3	2	1	3	2	1	3	2	1	3	2	1	3	2	1	3	2	1	3
Run T1																					W	W	W	W	W	W	R				
Run T2							W	R													R										W
Run T3					R						W	W	W	W	W	W	W	R			W	W	W	W	W	W	W	W	W	R	W
Run T4				R		R		R		W	R		R			R			W	R			W	R		R			R		R

R = Running on processor   W = Ready and waiting for processor

Figure 11.10 Overload Example of Run-to-Completion Dynamic Scheduling

---

[10] We could use a counter rather than a flag for the run variable, to allow for processing backlogs. In this case the ISR would increment run rather than set it, and the scheduler function would decrement it rather than clear it. This could be useful in some situations, but it would complicate the analysis.

11.5.1.1 *Implementation*

11.5.1.1.1   Task Table: A scheduler uses a table to store information on each task. Each task has been assigned a timer value. A task becomes active at regular intervals based on this value. This timer value is decremented each tick by the timer tick ISR. Once the timer value reaches zero, the task becomes ready to run. To reset this value after it has reached zero, an initial Timer Value variable is used to store the time at which the task has to be active. Two variables, enabled and run, are used to signal when a task is enabled and when it is ready to run. Variables enabled and run are used to indicate to the scheduler if a task is enabled and if it is ready to run. The function pointer *task indicates to the scheduler which function to perform.

The task's priority is defined by its position within this array. Entry 0 has the highest priority; whenever the scheduler needs to find a task to run, it begins at entry 0 and then works its way through the table.

The scheduler's task table is defined as follows:

```
1. #define MAX_TASKS 10
2. #define NULL ((void *)0)
3. typedef struct {
4.     int initialTimerValue;
5.     int timer;
6.     int run;
7.     int enabled;
8.     void (* task)(void);
9. } task_t;
10. task_t GBL_task_table[MAX_TASKS];
```

Before running the scheduler, the application must initialize the task table as follows:

```
1. void init_Task_Timers(void){
2.     int i;
3.     /* Initialize all tasks */
4.     for(i = 0; i < MAX_TASKS; i++){
5.         GBL_task_table[i].initialTimerValue = 0;
6.         GBL_task_table[i].run = 0;
7.         GBL_task_table[i].timer = 0;
8.         GBL_task_table[i].enabled = 0;
9.         GBL_task_table[i].task = NULL;
10.     }
11. }
```

11.5.1.1.2   Managing Tasks: Once the initialization is completed, tasks must be added to the task structure. The new tasks can be added before starting the scheduler or during the scheduler's execution time. When adding a task, the following must be specified: the time interval in which the task has to be active, its priority, and the function on which the task has to operate. The following code shows how adding a task is added:

```
1. int Add_Task(void (*task)(void), int time, int priority){
2.     /* Check for valid priority */
3.     if(priority >= MAX_TASKS || priority < 0)
4.     return 0;
5.     /* Check to see if we are overwriting an already scheduled
           task */
6.     if(GBL_task_table[priority].task != NULL)
7.     return 0;
8.     /* Schedule the task */
9.     GBL_task_table[priority].task = task;
10.    GBL_task_table[priority].run = 0;
11.    GBL_task_table[priority].timer = time;
12.    GBL_task_table[priority].enabled = 1;
13.    GBL_task_table[priority].initialTimerValue = time;
14.    return 1;
15. }
```

We can remove an existing task:

```
1. void removeTask(void (* task)(void)){
2.     int i;
3.     for(i = 0; i < MAX_TASKS; i++){
4.         if(GBL_task_table[i].task == task){
5.             GBL_task_table[i].task = NULL;
6.             GBL_task_table[i].timer = 0;
7.             GBL_task_table[i].initialTimerValue = 0;
8.             GBL_task_table[i].run = enabled = 0;
9.             return;
10.        }
11.    }
12. }
```

We can also selectively enable or disable a task by changing its **enabled** flag:

```
1. void Enable_Task(int task_number){
2.     GBL_task_table[task_number].enabled = 1;
3. }
```

```
4. void Disable_Task(int task_number){
5.     GBL_task_table[task_number].enabled = 0;
6. }
```

Finally, we can change the period with which a task runs:

```
1. void Reschedule_Task(int task_number, int new_timer_val){
2.     GBL_task_table[task_number].initialTimerValue =
3.     new_timer_val;
4.     GBL_task_table[task_number].timer = new_timer_val;
5. }
```

11.5.1.1.3   Tick Timer Configuration and ISR: A run-to-completion dynamic scheduler uses a timer to help determine when tasks are ready to run (are released). A timer is set up to generate an interrupt at regular intervals, as explained in Chapter 9. Within the interrupt service routine the timer value for each task is decremented. When the timer value reaches zero, the task becomes ready to run.

```
 1. void RTC_Tick_ISR(void){
 2.     int i;
 3.     for(i = 0; i < MAX_TASKS; i++){
 4.         if(GBL_task_table[i].task != NULL) &&
 5.         (GBL_task_table[i].enabled == 1) &&
 6.         (GBL_task_table[i].timer > 0))
 7.         {
 8.             if(--GBL_task_table[i].timer == 0){
 9.                 GBL_task_table[i].run = 1;
10.                 GBL_task_table[i].timer =
11.                 GBL_task_table[i].initialTimerValue;
12.             }
13.         }
14.     }
15. }
```

11.5.1.1.4   Scheduler: The scheduler looks for ready tasks starting at the top of the table (highest priority task). It runs every ready task it finds, calling it as a function (in line 16).

```
1. void Run_RTC_Scheduler(void){
2.     int i;
3.     /* Loop forever */
4.     while(1){
```

```
5.          /* Check each task */
6.          for(i = 0; i < MAX_TASKS; i++){
7.              /* check if valid task */
8.              if(GBL_task_table[i].task != NULL){
9.                  /* check if enabled */
10.                 if(GBL_task_table[i].enabled == 1){
11.                     /* check if ready to run */
12.                     if(GBL_task_table[i].run == 1){
13.                         /* Reset the run flag */
14.                         GBL_task_table[i].run = 0;
15.                         /* Run the task */
16.                         GBL_task_table[i].task();
17.                         /* break out of loop to start at entry 0 */
18.                         break;
19.                     }
20.                 }
21.             }
22.         }
23.     }
24. }
```

11.5.1.2 *Example Application using RTC Scheduler*

Let's use the RTC scheduler to create a toy with red and green LEDs flashing at various frequencies. The Toggle_Green_LED task inverts a green LED every 0.33 seconds, and the Toggle_Red_LED task inverts a red LED every 0.25 seconds.

The tasks and the main program are shown below:

```
1. void Toggle_Green_LED(void){
2.    if(GREEN_LED == LED_ON)
3.    GREEN_LED = LED_OFF;
4.    else
5.    GREEN_LED = LED_ON;
6. }
7. void Toggle_Red_LED(void){
8.    if(RED_LED == LED_ON)
9.    RED_LED = LED_OFF;
10.    else
11.    RED_LED = LED_ON;
12. }
13. void main(void){
```

```
14.     ENABLE_LEDS;
15.     init_Task_Timers();
16.     Add_Task(Toggle_Green_LED,330,0);
17.     Add_Task(Toggle_Red_LED,250,1);
18.     Init_RTC_Scheduler();
19.     Run_RTC_Scheduler();
20. }
```

11.5.2 A Preemptive Dynamic Scheduler

At first glance, a preemptive scheduler may seem to be the same as a non-preemptive scheduler, but with a little extra support for saving, switching, and restoring contexts. This apparently small addition in fact has a **major impact** on how programs are structured and built. A task no longer needs to run to completion. Instead, it is allowed to block and wait for an event to occur. While that task blocks (waits), the scheduler is able to work on the next highest priority ready task. When the event occurs, the scheduler will move the task from the blocking state to the ready state, so it can run again (when it becomes the highest priority ready task). This opens the door to creating event-triggered multithreaded programs, which are much easier to develop, maintain, and enhance than the equivalent run-to-completion versions.

Since event support is so valuable to (and so tightly integrated with) preemptive schedulers, we refer to **real-time operating systems** which include the scheduler, event support, and additional features which build upon both. We will use examples from the RTOS μC/OS-II to illustrate the key concepts (Labrosse, 2002).

11.5.2.1 *Yielding the Processor to Eliminate Busy Waiting*

```
1. void Log_Data_To_Flash(void) {
2.     Compute_Data(data);
3.     Program_Flash(data);
4.     while (!Flash_Done()) {
5.         OSTimeDly(1);
6.         // try again later
7.     }
8.     if (flash_result == ERROR) {
9.         Handle_Flash_Error();
10.    }
11. }
```

An RTOS typically provides a way for a task to explicitly yield control to another task, potentially for a minimum time delay. For example, consider a task which writes data to flash memory, shown below. This operation could take a long time (3 ms for a page). Rather than spin in busy-wait loop (line 4) until the flash programming is done (indicated by Flash_Done() returning 1), we insert an OSTimeDly(1) call at line 5. This tells the RTOS that the task would like to yield control of the processor, and furthermore would like to be placed back into the ready queue after one scheduler tick has passed. At some point in the future, the scheduler will restore this task's context and resume its execution, at which point the task will once again check to see if Flash_Done() is true or not. Eventually it will be true and the task will then continue on with the code at line eight following the loop.

11.5.2.2 *Yielding the Processor to Run Code in a Task Periodically*

Often we wish to have a task run periodically. For example, let's flash an LED as shown in Figure 11.11.

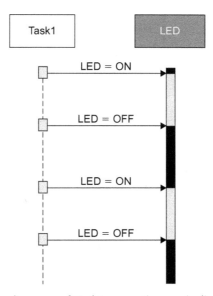

Figure 11.11 Sequence diagram of Task1 executing periodically and toggling an LED.

```
1. void Task1(void * data)
2. {
3.     char state = 0;
4.     for (;;)
5.     {
6.         RED_LED = state;
7.         state = 1-state;
```

```
8.          OSTimeDly(MSEC_TO_TICKS(TASK1_PERIOD_MSEC));
9.     }
10. }
```

In this function an infinite loop will run forever, toggling RED_LED at line 6. The function will stop once per iteration as it yields control of the processor with the OSTimeDly() call at line 8.

11.5.2.3 Signaling another Task to Run

We can generate scheduling events from more than just time delays. For example, we may want task A to be able to signal task B that it should resume running. One way to do this is with a semaphore, a common RTOS communication mechanism.

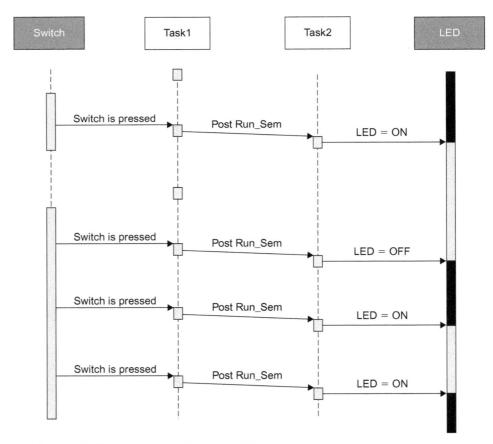

Figure 11.12 Sequence diagram of Task1 triggering Task2 with semaphore.

Figure 11.12 shows the desired system behavior. We would like Task1 to run periodically. Each time it runs it should check to see if switch S1 is pressed. If it is, it should signal Task2 by using the semaphore Run_Sem. Task2 will wait for the semaphore Run_Sem to be signaled. When it is, then Task2 can run, toggling the LED and waiting for the next semaphore signaling.

Details of the code are shown below. Note that the semaphore needs to be created and initialized by the RTOS, as shown in line 3. Lines 4 through 6 handle error conditions.

```
1.  OS_EVENT * Run_Sem;
2.
3.  void TaskStartup() {
4.  . . .
5.     Run_Sem = OSSemCreate(0);
6.     if (!Run_Sem) {
7.          // error handling
8.     }
9.  }
10. void Task1(void * data)
11. {
12.    char state = 0;
13.    for (;;)
14.    {
15.       if (!S1) {
16.          OSSemPost(Run_Sem);  // signal the event has happened
17.       }
18.       OSTimeDly(MSEC_TO_TICKS(TASK1_PERIOD_MSEC));
19.    }
20. }
21. void Task2(void*data)
22. {
23.    char state = 0;
24.    INT8U err = OS_NO_ERR;
25.    for (;;)
26.    {
27.       OSSemPend(Run_Sem, TIMEOUT_NEVER, &err); // await event
28.       if (err == OS_NO_ERR) {  // We got the semaphore
29.          YLW_LED = state;
30.          state = 1 - state;
31.       }
32.    }
33. }
```

Note that semaphores are also commonly used to protect shared resources by providing mutually exclusive access to them. We will investigate this in Section 11.6.4.3.

11.5.2.4 Sending Data to another Task

A task may need to send data (in addition to an event notification) to another task. RTOSs typically provide mailboxes and message queues to do this. A mailbox holds one item of data, while a queue can buffer multiple items of data.

The desired system behavior is almost the same as the previous example. We would like Task1 to run periodically. Each time it runs it should check to see if switch S1 is pressed. If it is, it should signal Task2 by sending a message SWITCH1_PRESSED to the Switch1_Mbox mailbox. Task2 will wait for the mailbox Switch1_Mbox to be signaled. When it is, then Task2 can run, toggling the LED and waiting for the next message in the mailbox.

Details of the code are shown below. Note that the mailbox needs to be created and initialized by the RTOS, as shown in line 5. Lines 6 through 8 handle error conditions.

```
1. OS_EVENT * Switch1_Mbox;
2. ...
3. void TaskStartup() {
4.     ...
5.     Switch1_Mbox = OSMboxCreate(NULL);
6.     if (!Switch1_Mbox) {
7.         // error handling
8.     }
9.     ...
10. }
11. void Task1(void * data)
12. {
13.    char state = 0;
14.    for (;;)
15.    {
16.       if (!S1) {        // if switch 1 is pressed, send a message
via mbox
17.          OSMboxPost(Switch1_Mbox, (void *) SWITCH1_PRESSED);
18.       }
19.       OSTimeDly(MSEC_TO_TICKS(TASK1_PERIOD_MSEC));
20.    }
21. }
22. void Task2(void * data)
23. {
```

```
24.     char state = 0;
25.     INT8U err = OS_NO_ERR;
26.     INT16U message;
27.
28.     YLW_LED = state;
29.     for (;;)
30.     {
31.        message = (INT16U) OSMboxPend(Switch1_Mbox, 0, &err);
32.        if (err == OS_NO_ERR) { // got a message
33.           if (message == SWITCH1_PRESSED) {
34.              YLW_LED = state;
35.              state = 1 - state;
36.           } else {
37.              // different message received
38.              // so do something else
39.           }
40.        } else {
41.           // handle the error ...
42.        }
43.     }
44. }
```

11.6   SHARING DATA SAFELY

Preemption among tasks introduces a vulnerability to data race conditions. Now a task can be considered to be as bug-prone and difficult to debug as an ISR! The system can fail in new ways when:

■ Multiple tasks or ISRs share data,[11] or
■ Multiple instances of a function can execute concurrently.

In order to prevent these failures we need to be careful when designing our system.

---

[11] Hardware registers which change outside of the program's control also introduce problems but we do not discuss them further here.

11.6.1   Data Shared Objects

If a data object is accessed by code which can be interrupted (is not *atomic*), then there is a risk of data corruption. *Atomic* code is the smallest part of a program that executes without interruption. Generally a single machine instruction is atomic,[12] but sequences of instructions are not atomic unless interrupts are disabled.

Consider an example where task A starts modifying object O. Task B preempts it before it finishes. At this point in time object O is corrupted, as it is only partially updated. If task B needs to read or write O, the computation results will be incorrect and the system will likely fail.

```
 1. unsigned time_minutes, time_seconds;
 2. void task1 (void){
 3.    time_seconds++;
 4.    if(time_seconds >= 60){
 5.       time_minutes++;
 6.       time_seconds = 0;
 7.    }
 8. }
 9. void task2 (void){
10.    unsigned elapsed_sec;
11.    elapsed_seconds = time_minutes * 60 + time_seconds;
12. }
```

Here is a more specific example. Our shared object is a pair of variables which measure the current time in minutes and seconds. Task1 runs once per second to increment the seconds, and possibly the minutes as well. Task2 calculates how many total seconds have elapsed since time zero. There are data races possible:

■ If task1 is preempted between lines 4 and 5 or lines 5 and 6, then when task2 runs it will only have a partially updated version of the current time, and elapsed seconds will be incorrect.

■ If task2 is preempted during line 11, then it is possible that time_minutes is read **before** task1 updates it and time_seconds is read **after** task1 updates it. Again, this leads to a corrupted elapsed_seconds value.

---

[12] Some instruction sets have long instructions (e.g. string copy, block move) which can be interrupted, in which case those instructions are **not** atomic.

11.6.2 Function Reentrancy

Another type of shared data problem comes with the use of non-reentrant functions. In this case, the problem arises from multiple instances of the **same function** accessing the same object. Consider the following example:

```
1. void task1 ( ){
2.      . . . . . . . . . . . . . .
3.      swap(&x, &y);
4.      . . . . . . . . . . . . . .
5. }
6. void task2 ( ){
7.      . . . . . . . . . . . . . .
8.      swap(&p, &q);
9.      . . . . . . . . . . . . .
10. }
11. int Temp;
12. void swap (*i, *j ){
13.     Temp = *j;
14.     *j = *i;
15.     *i = Temp;
16. }
```

Suppose task1 is running and calls the swap function. After line 13 is executed, task2 becomes ready. If task2 has a higher priority, task1 is suspended and task2 is serviced. Later, task1 resumes to line 14. Since Temp is a shared variable, it is not stored in the TASK subroutine shared data stack. When task1 line 15 is executed, variable *x* (of task1 pointed by variable pointer *i*) gets the wrong value. Such function executions should not be suspended in between or shared by more than one task. Such functions are called **non-reentrant.** The code which can have multiple simultaneous, interleaved, or nested invocations which will not interfere with each other is called reentrant code. These types of code are important for parallel processing, recursive functions or subroutines, and for interrupt handling. An example of a reentrant code is as follows:

```
1. void swap (*i, *j ){
2.     static int Temp;
3.     Temp = *j;
4.     *j = *i;
5.     *i = Temp;
6. }
```

Since the variable `Temp` is declared within the function, if any other task interrupts the execution of the `swap` function, the variable `Temp` will be stored in the corresponding task's stack and will be retrieved when the task resumes its function. In most cases, especially in a multi-processing environment, the non-reentrant functions should be eliminated. A function can be checked for its reentrancy based on these three rules:

1. A reentrant function may not use variables in a non-atomic way unless they are stored on the stack of the calling task or are the private variables of that task.
2. A reentrant function may not call other functions which are not reentrant.
3. A reentrant function may not use the hardware in a non-atomic way.

11.6.3 High-Level Languages and Atomicity

We can identify **some but not all** non-atomic operations by examining high-level source code. Since the processor executes machine code rather than a high-level language such as C or Java, we can't identify all possible non-atomic operations just by examining the C source code. Something may seem atomic in C but actually be implemented by multiple machine instructions. We need to examine the assembly code to know for sure. Let's examine the following function and determine whether it is atomic or not:

```
1. static int event_count;
2. void event_counter (void){
3.     ++event_count;
4. }
```

Example 1 in assembly language (not RL78):

```
1. MOV.L #0000100CH, R4
2. MOV.L [R4], R5
3. ADD #1H, R5
4. MOV.L R5, [R4]
5. RTS
```

Consider example 1, and then apply the first rule. Does it use shared variable `event_count` in an atomic way? The `++event_count` operation is not atomic, and that single line of C code is implemented with three lines of assembly code (lines two through four). The processor loads R4 with a pointer to event_count, copies the value of event_count into register R5, adds 1 to R5, and then stores it back into memory. Hence, example 1 **is not atomic and not reentrant.**

However, what if the processor instruction set supports in-place memory operations? In that case, the assembly code could look like this:

Example 1 in assembly language, compiled for a different processor architecture:

```
1. MOV.L #0000100CH, A0
2. ADD #1H, [A0]
3. RTS
```

This code **is atomic,** since there is only one instruction needed to update the value of the event count. Instruction 1 is only loading a pointer to the event count, so interrupting between 1 and 2 does not cause a problem. Hence it **is reentrant.**

The RL78 architecture supports modifications in memory, so the compiler can generate code which takes a single instruction to perform the increment. An example from a previous chapter is also **atomic:**

```
1. INCW        N:int_count
```

Now consider a slightly different example:

```
1. void add_sum (int *j){
2.     ++(*j);
3.     DisplayString(LCDLINE1, Int_to_ascii(*j));
4. }
```

Even though `line 2` in this example is not atomic, the `variable * j` is task's private variable, hence rule 1 is not breached. But consider `line 3`. Is the function `DisplayString` reentrant? That depends on the code of `DisplayString`, which depends on the user. Unless we are sure that the `DisplayString` function is reentrant (and do this recursively for any functions which may be called directly or indirectly by `DisplayString`), Example 2 is considered to be non-reentrant. So every time a user designs a function, he or she needs to make sure the function is reentrant to avoid errors.

11.6.4 Shared-Data Solutions and Protection

In the previous section, we discussed the problems of using shared data in a RTOS environment. In this section we shall study some methods to protect the shared data. The solutions provided in this section may not be ideal for all applications. The user must judge which solution may work best for the application.

11.6.4.1 Disable Interrupts

One of the easiest methods is to disable the interrupts during the critical section of the task. Disabling the interrupts may not take more than one machine cycle to execute, but will increase the worst case response time of all other code, including other interrupt service routines. Once the critical section, or shared variable section, of the code is executed, the interrupt masking will be restored to its previous state (either enabled or disabled). The user must be cautious while disabling or enabling interrupts, because if interrupts are disabled for too long, the system may fail to meet the timing requirements. See Chapter 9, Using Interrupts with Peripherals, to find out how to disable and restore interrupt masking state. A simple example of disabling interrupts is as follows:

```
1.  #define TRUE 1
2.  #define FALSE 0
3.  static int error;
4.  static int error_count;
5.  void error_counter ( ){
6.      if(error == TRUE){
7.          SAVE_INT_STATE;
8.          DISABLE_INTS;
9.          error_count++;
10.         error = FALSE;
11.         RESTORE_INT_STATE;
12.     }
13. }
```

Disabling and restoring the interrupt masking state requires only one or a few machine cycles. Disabling interrupts must take place only at critical sections to avoid increasing response time excessively. Also, while restoring the interrupt masking state the user must keep in mind the need to enable only those interrupts that were active (enabled) before they were disabled. Determining the interrupt masking status can be achieved by referring to the **interrupt mask register.** The Interrupt mask register keeps track of which interrupts are enabled and disabled.

11.6.4.2 Use a Lock

Another solution is to associate every shared variable with a lock variable, which is also declared globally. If a function uses the shared variable, then it sets the lock variable, and once it has finished process it resets the lock variable. Every function must test the lock variable before accessing it. If the lock variable is already set, the task should inform the scheduler to be rescheduled once the variable becomes available. Since only one variable has to be checked every time before accessing the data, using lock variables simplifies the data structure and I/O devices access. Consider the following example for using a lock:

```
1.  unsigned int var;
2.  char lock_var;
3.  void task_var ( ){
4.     unsigned int sum;
5.     if(lock_var == 0){
6.         lock_var = 1;
7.         var = var + sum;
8.         lock_var = 0;
9.     }
10.    else {
11.        /* message to scheduler to check var
12.        and reschedule */
13.    }
14. }
```

Since it takes more than one clock cycle to check whether a variable is available and use a lock on it, the interrupts have to be disabled. Once again when the lock has to be released, the interrupts should be disabled since locking and releasing the variable is a critical part of the code. Interrupts must be enabled whenever possible to lower the interrupt service response time. If the variable is not available, the scheduler is informed about the lock and the task goes into a waiting state.

Microprocessors such as the Renesas RX support Bit Test and Set instructions can perform a test and set in one atomic machine instruction, and therefore do not require an interrupt disable/enable lock around semaphore usage.

The challenge with this approach is determining what to do in lines 11 and 12 if there is no scheduler support. There may be no easy way to tell the scheduler to reschedule this task when the lock variable becomes available again.

11.6.4.3 RTOS-Provided Semaphore

Most operating systems provide locks to shared variables through the use of semaphores. A semaphore is a mechanism that uses most of the multitasking kernels to protect shared data and to synchronize two tasks. A semaphore is very much similar to the variable lock process explained in the Section 12.4.3. The main difference is that the OS takes care of initializing and handling the locks, so the implementation is much more likely to be correct than if you try to create your own lock.

There are two types of semaphores—binary semaphores and counting semaphores. Binary semaphores take two values, 0 or 1. A counting semaphore takes a value between

0 and $2^N - 1$, where N is the number of bits used for the semaphore. In this book we consider only the binary semaphore. A semaphore usually has three tasks: initialization/create, wait, and signal.

A semaphore used for protecting a resource is initialized with the value 1, to indicate the resource is initially available. At this point no task is waiting for the semaphore. Once a task requires a data, the task performs a wait operation on the semaphore. The OS checks the value of the semaphore; for example, if the semaphore is available (semaphore value is non-zero), the OS changes the value of the semaphore to zero and assigns the semaphore to the task. If the semaphore value is zero during the wait operation, the task that requested the wait operation is placed on the semaphore's waiting list. Once the semaphore becomes available based on the priority of the tasks waiting for it, the OS decides which task to assign to the semaphore.

A task can ask to wait on a semaphore, potentially specifying a time limit for waiting. If the time expires, the RTOS returns an error code to the semaphore-seeking function for the appropriate response. On the other hand, if the function has obtained the semaphore, it can then complete its operation using the shared resource and perform a signal operation, announcing that the semaphore is free. The OS checks if any other task is waiting for the semaphore. If so, that task is notified that it has obtained the semaphore (without changing the semaphore's value). On the other hand, if no task is waiting for the semaphore, the semaphore is incremented to a non-zero number. The wait operation is also referred to as Take or Pend or P and signal operation is referred to as Release or Post or V. The following example shows how wait and signal operations are performed in μC/OS-II.

The example below shows how the semaphore LCD_Sem is used to ensure only one task can access the LCD at a time. The semaphore is initialized with a value of 1 (in line 4) to indicate that the resource is available. Each task must obtain the semaphore through a pend operation (lines 16 and 34) before using the LCD (lines 18 and 36). When the task is done with the LCD, it must release the semaphore with a post operation (lines 19 and 37).

```
1. OS_EVENT * LCD_Sem;
2. void TaskStartup(void * data)
3. {
4.     LCD_Sem = Ossemcreate(1);
5.     if (!LCD_Sem) {
6.         // handle error
7.     }
8. }
9. void Task1(void * data)
10. {
11.     char state = 0, * p;
12.     unsigned counter = 0;
13.     INT8U err = OS_NO_ERR;
14.     for (;;)
15.     {
```

```
16.        OSSemPend(LCD_Sem, 10000, &err); // wait to get LCD
17.        if (err == OS_NO_ERR) {
18.           LCD_Update(data_1);
19.           err = OSSemPost(LCD_Sem);
20.        } else {
21.           // handle LCD semaphore time-out
22.        }
23.        OSTimeDly(MSEC_TO_TICKS(TASK1_PERIOD_MSEC));
24.     }
25. }
26. void Task3b(void * data)
27. {
28.     char state = 0, * p;
29.     unsigned counter = 0;
30.     INT8U err = OS_NO_ERR;
31.
32.     for (;;)
33.     {
34.        OSSemPend(LCD_Sem, 10000, &err); // wait to get LCD
35.        if (err == OS_NO_ERR) {
36.           LCD_Update(data_3);
37.           err = OSSemPost(LCD_Sem);
38.        } else {
39.           // handle LCD semaphore time-out
40.        }
41.        OSTimeDly(MSEC_TO_TICKS(TASK3_PERIOD_MSEC));
42.     }
43. }
```

11.6.4.4   RTOS-Provided Messages

We have seen that an RTOS may provide other mechanisms besides semaphores for allowing tasks to communicate, such as message queues and mailboxes. It may be possible to structure your program to use messages to pass information rather than sharing data objects directly. We leave further discussion of this approach to the many RTOS-oriented books and articles already available.

11.6.4.5   Disable Task Switching

If no other method seems to work, one unattractive option is to disable the scheduler. If the scheduler is disabled, the task switching does not take place and the critical sections or shared data can be protected by other tasks. This method is counter-productive; disabling the scheduler increases response times and makes analysis much more difficult. This is considered bad practice and must be properly justified; hence consider this method as a last resort.

11.7   ANALYSIS OF RESPONSE TIME AND SCHEDULABILITY

So far in this chapter we have seen how allowing (1) dynamic scheduling and (2) preemption of tasks improves a system's responsiveness. In this section we will introduce the basic analytical methods which enable us to predict the timing behavior of the resulting **real-time** systems accurately. There is an abundance of research papers on real-time scheduling theory; two survey papers stand out for their clarity and context and should be consulted as starting points (Audsley, Burns, Davis, Tindell, & Wellings, 1995; Sha, et al., 2004).

We are mainly concerned with two aspects of a real-time system's behavior:

- How long will it take the processor to finish executing all the instructions of a particular task, given that other tasks may disrupt this timing? This is called the **response time.**
- If each task has a deadline, will the system always meet all deadlines, even under the worst case situation? A system which will always meet all deadlines is called **schedulable. A feasibility test** will let us calculate if the system is schedulable or not.

11.7.1   Assumptions and Task Model

We model the computational workload according to the following assumptions and restrictions. Basic fixed-priority real-time scheduling analysis begins with this mathematical model:

- We have a single CPU.
- The workload consists of **n tasks** τ_i. Each task releases a series of **jobs.**
- Tasks **release** jobs periodically at the beginning of their period T_i and the deadline for a job is at the end of the period.
- When a job is **released,** it is ready to run. We would like for the job to **complete** before its **deadline. Hard real-time** jobs **must** meet their deadlines, while **soft real-time** jobs should meet most of their deadlines.
- No task is allowed to suspend itself.
- A task can be preempted at any time. This means this model does not apply to the non-preemptive schedulers we examined earlier.
- The worst-case execution time of each job is C_i. Determining this value is non-

trivial because it depends on both software (the control flow may be dependent on the input data) and hardware (pipelining, caches, dynamic instruction execution). Instead, people attempt to estimate a tight bound which is reasonably close to the actual number but not smaller (which would be unsafe).

■ Overhead such as scheduler activity and context switches take no time.

■ Tasks are independent. They do not communicate with each other in a way which could make one wait for another, and they do not have any precedence relationships.

One aspect of the workload to consider is the **utilization U,** which is the fraction of the processor's time which is needed to perform all the processing of the tasks. Utilization is calculated as the sum of the each individual task's utilization. A task's utilization is the ratio of its computation time divided by the period of the task (how frequently the computation is needed):

$$U = \sum_{i=1}^{n} U_i = \sum_{i=1}^{n} \frac{C_i}{T_i}$$

11.7.2 Fixed Task Priority

We can now examine different scheduling approaches using this foundation as a starting point. One critical question which we haven't answered yet is **how do we assign priorities?** We can assign a fixed priority to each task, or allow a task's priority to vary. The pros and cons for these approaches are discussed in detail elsewhere (Buttazzo, 2005). We first examine fixed-priority assignments.

11.7.2.1 *Rate Monotonic Priority Assignment—RMPA*

The first fixed-priority approach we examine gives **higher priorities** to tasks with **higher rates** (execution frequencies). One very nice characteristic of RMPA is that it is **optimal**— given the above assumptions listed above, there is no other task priority assignment approach which makes a system schedulable if it is not schedulable with RMPA.

Another nice characteristic of RMPA is that for some workloads it is very easy to determine if the workload is definitely schedulable. The **Least Upper Bound (LUB)** test compares the utilization of the resulting workload against a function based on the number of tasks.

$$U = \sum_{i=1}^{n} \frac{C_i}{T_i} \leq n\left(2^{\frac{1}{n}} - 1\right) = LUB$$

- If U is less than or equal to the LUB, then the system is definitely schedulable. The LUB starts out at 1. As n grows, the LUB approaches 0.693. This means that **any** workload with RMPA and meeting the above criteria is schedulable.
- If U is greater than the LUB, then this test is inconclusive. The workload **may or may not** be schedulable with RMPA. We will need to use a different test to determine schedulability.[13]

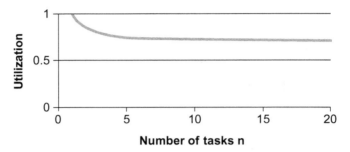

Figure 11.13   Least Upper Bound for RMPA as a function of the number of tasks *n*.

Figure 11.13 plots the rate monotonic least upper bound as a function of the number of tasks *n*. The area below the curve represents workloads which are always schedulable with RMPA. For the area above the curve, the test is inconclusive.

EXAMPLE 1

TABLE 11.1   Sample Workload

TASK	EXECUTION TIME C	PERIOD T	PRIORITY WITH RMPA
τ_1	1	4	High
τ_2	2	6	Medium
τ_3	1	13	Low

[13] Researchers studying a large number of random task sets found that the average real feasible utilization is about 0.88. However, this is just an average. Some task sets with $0.693 < U < 0.88$ were not schedulable, while some with $0.88 < U < 1$ were schedulable.

Let's see how this works for a system with three tasks, as shown in Table 11.1. We first compute the utilization of the workload:

$$U = \sum_{i=1}^{n} U_i = \sum_{i=1}^{n} \frac{C_i}{T_i} = \frac{1}{4} + \frac{2}{6} + \frac{1}{13} = 0.660$$

We compute the RM LUB for n = 3 tasks:

$$LUB = 3\left(2^{\frac{1}{3}} - 1\right) = 0.780$$

Since U < LUB, we know the system is schedulable and will meet all its deadlines.
Let's see what happens if task τ_3 takes three instead of one time unit to execute.

TABLE 11.2   Sample Workload with Longer Task Three

TASK	EXECUTION TIME C	PERIOD T	PRIORITY WITH RMPA
τ_1	1	4	High
τ_2	2	6	Medium
τ_3	3	13	Low

Let's see how this works for a system with three tasks, as shown in Table 11.2. We first compute the utilization of the workload:

$$U = \sum_{i=1}^{n} U_i = \sum_{i=1}^{n} \frac{C_i}{T_i} = \frac{1}{4} + \frac{2}{6} + \frac{3}{13} = 0.814$$

We use the same RM LUB as we still have n = 3 tasks:

$$LUB = 3\left(2^{\frac{1}{3}} - 1\right) = 0.780$$

Since U > LUB, we do not know if the system is schedulable using the LUB test. We will learn about Response Time Analysis in Section 11.7.3 and it will enable us to determine schedulability.

11.7.2.2   *Rate Monotonic Priority Assignment with Harmonic Periods*

If we are able to adjust task periods, we can make RMPA systems schedulable up to utilization of 1. The trick is to make task periods **harmonic:** a task's period must be an exact integer multiple of the next shorter period. We can only shorten the period of a task to make it harmonic, as increasing it would violate the original deadline. The challenge is that as we shorten a task's period, we increase the processor utilization for that task. We need to keep utilization at or below 1 to keep the system schedulable.

EXAMPLE 2

TABLE 11.3   Sample Workload with Longer Task Three and Harmonic Periods

TASK	EXECUTION TIME C	PERIOD T	ORIGINAL UTILIZATION	FIRST HARMONIC PERIOD ATTEMPT MODIFIED PERIOD T	UTILIZATION	SECOND HARMONIC PERIOD ATTEMPT MODIFIED PERIOD T	UTILIZATION
τ_1	1	4	0.250	4	0.250	3	0.333
τ_2	2	6	0.333	4	0.500	6	0.333
τ_3	3	13	0.231	8	0.375	12	0.231
Total			0.814		1.125		0.897
Schedulable			Maybe		No		Yes

Our first attempt at period modification lowers the period of task two to four time units, and that of task three to eight time units. The resulting utilization of 1.125 is greater than 1, so the system is not schedulable. Our second attempt lowers the periods of tasks one and three, with a resulting utilization of 0.897 so the system is now schedulable.

11.7.2.3   Deadline Monotonic Priority Assignment—DMPA

One constraint given above is that a task's deadline D_i must equal its period T_i. If we allow $D_i < T_i$ then RMPA is no longer optimal. Instead, assigning **higher priorities** to tasks with **shorter deadlines** results in optimal behavior. This is another common fixed-priority assignment approach.

11.7.3   Response Time Analysis

We can analyze the response time (the maximum delay between a task's release and completion) for a task set with any fixed priority assignment, and with deadlines which may be shorter than task periods. The equation computes the worst-case response time R_i for task

τ_1 as the sum of that task's computation time C_i and the sum of all possible computation from higher-priority tasks, as they will preempt τ_1 if they are released before τ_1 completes. The tricky part of this equation is that if τ_1 is preempted, then it will take longer to complete (R_i will grow), raising the possibility of more preemptions. So, the equation needs to be repeated until R_i stops changing or it exceeds the deadline D_i. Note that the square half brackets $\lceil x \rceil$ signify the **ceiling function,** which returns the smallest integer which is not smaller than the argument x.

$$R_i = C_i + \sum_{j=1}^{i-1} \left\lceil \frac{R_i}{T_j} \right\rceil C_j$$

EXAMPLE 3

Let's evaluate the response time for the system of Table 11.3 from the previous example (with non-harmonic periods). We will evaluate the response time for the lowest priority task. We begin with a value of 0 for R_i.

$$R_3 = C_3 + \sum_{j=1}^{2} \left\lceil \frac{R_i}{T_j} \right\rceil C_j = 3 + \left\lceil \frac{0}{4} \right\rceil 1 + \left\lceil \frac{0}{6} \right\rceil 2 = 3 + 1 + 2 = 6$$

$$R_3 = C_3 + \sum_{j=1}^{2} \left\lceil \frac{6}{T_j} \right\rceil C_j = 3 + \left\lceil \frac{6}{4} \right\rceil 1 + \left\lceil \frac{6}{6} \right\rceil 2 = 3 + 2 + 2 = 7$$

$$R_3 = C_3 + \sum_{j=1}^{2} \left\lceil \frac{7}{T_j} \right\rceil C_j = 3 + \left\lceil \frac{7}{4} \right\rceil 1 + \left\lceil \frac{7}{6} \right\rceil 2 = 3 + 2 + 4 = 9$$

$$R_3 = C_3 + \sum_{j=1}^{2} \left\lceil \frac{9}{T_j} \right\rceil C_j = 3 + \left\lceil \frac{9}{4} \right\rceil 1 + \left\lceil \frac{9}{6} \right\rceil 2 = 3 + 3 + 4 = 10$$

$$R_3 = C_3 + \sum_{j=1}^{2} \left\lceil \frac{10}{T_j} \right\rceil C_j = 3 + \left\lceil \frac{10}{4} \right\rceil 1 + \left\lceil \frac{10}{6} \right\rceil 2 = 3 + 3 + 4 = 10$$

The estimated response time for task three to complete begins at six time units and grows until it reaches a fixed point at 10 time units. Since this is less than the deadline for task three, we know the system is schedulable and will always meet its deadlines.

11.7.4 Loosening the Restrictions

The assumptions listed in the beginning of the section limit the range of real-time systems which can be analyzed, so researchers have been busy removing them.

11.7.4.1 Supporting Task Interactions

One assumption is that tasks cannot interact with each other. They cannot share resources which could lead to blocking.

Tasks typically need to interact with each other. They may need to share a resource, typically using a semaphore to provide mutually-exclusive resource use. This leads to a possible situation called **priority inversion.** If a low priority task τ_L acquires a resource and then is preempted by a higher priority task τ_H which also needs the resource, then τ_H blocks and cannot proceed until τ_L gets to run and has released the resource. In effect, the priorities are inverted so that τ_L has a higher priority than τ_H.

Priority inversion is prevented by changing when a task is allowed to lock a resource. Two examples of such rules are the Priority Ceiling Protocol and the Stack Resource Protocol. The response time analysis equation listed above can be modified to factor in blocking times.

11.7.4.2 Supporting Aperiodic Tasks

Another assumption is that each task runs with a fixed period T_i. This is quite restrictive, but it is possible to support aperiodic tasks by finding the minimum time between task releases (inter-task release time) and using this as the period T_i. This approach works but overprovisions the system as the difference between minimum and average inter-task release times grows, limiting its usefulness. There are other approaches (e.g., polling servers) which are beyond the scope of this text, but which are listed in the references section.

11.7.5 Dynamic Task Priority

Instead of assigning each task a fixed priority, it is possible to have a priority which changes. We still use all of the assumptions in our model of Section 11.7.1. One simple approach is called *Earliest Deadline First,* which unsurprisingly runs the task with the earliest deadline first. This approach is optimal among preemptive scheduling approaches: if a feasible schedule is possible, EDF will find it.

One nice characteristic of EDF is that it is easy to determine whether a system will be schedulable. Another is that using EDF will result in a schedulable system if the total utilization is no greater than 1. This simplifies system analysis significantly!

$$U = \sum_{i=1}^{n} \frac{C_i}{T_i} \leq 1$$

11.7.5.1 Supporting Task Interactions

Enabling tasks to share resources with dynamic task priorities is different from static task priorities. With EDF, each job of a task is assigned a priority which indicates how soon its deadline is. Priority inversion can still occur, but now job priorities may change. Researchers have developed approaches such as the Stack Resource Policy (SRP), Dynamic Priority Inheritance, Dynamic Priority Ceiling, and Dynamic Deadline Modification.

Let's look at one example—the Stack Resource Policy. SRP assigns a preemption level to each task in addition to its priority. Each shared resource has a **ceiling,** which is the highest preemption level of any task which can lock this resource. The system is assigned a ceiling which is the highest of all currently locked resource ceilings. These factors are used to determine when a job can start executing. Specifically, a job cannot start executing if it does not both (1) have the highest priority of all active tasks, and (2) have a preemption level greater than the system ceiling.

SRP simplifies analysis of the system because it ensures that a job can only block before it starts running, but never after. In addition, the maximum blocking time is one critical section. These factors lead to a simple feasibility test for periodic and sporadic tasks. For each task i, the sum of the utilizations of all tasks with greater preemption levels and the blocking time fraction for this task must be no greater than one.

$$\forall i, \quad 1 \le i \le n \quad \sum_{k=1}^{i} \frac{C_k}{T_k} + \frac{B_i}{T_i} \le 1$$

11.7.5.2 *Supporting Aperiodic Tasks*

Recall that our task model requires each task to be periodic. If a task's period can vary, we need to choose the minimum period and design the system according to this worst-case, which can lead to an overbuilt system. As with fixed-priority systems, there are ways to relax this limitation. For example, the Total Bandwidth Server (TBS) assigns deadlines for aperiodic jobs so that their demand never exceeds a specified limit U_s on the maximum allowed processor utilization by sporadic tasks. The deadline d_k which assigned depends on the current time r_k and the deadline d_{k-1} assigned for this task's previous job. The deadline is pushed farther out in time as the ratio of the execution time of the request C_k and acceptable sporadic server utilization U_s increases.

$$d_k = max(cr_k, d_{k-1}) + \frac{C_k}{U_s}$$

With this approach, we can guarantee that the entire system is schedulable with EDF if the utilization from periodic tasks (U_p) and the TBS (U_s) is no greater than one.

11.7.6 Non-Preemptive Scheduling Approaches

All of the scheduling analysis we just examined depends on being able to preempt any task at any time. Let's consider scheduling when preemption is **not** possible. The processor cannot meet the deadline for a task τ_i with deadline D_i **shorter** than the **duration** of the longest task τ_L plus the actual **computation time** C_i for our task of interest τ_i. This limits the range of real-time systems for which non-preemptive scheduling is suitable to those with deadlines which are longer than the longest task's computation time. This is not a significant limitation if we design our tasks so that they cannot block internally, and take no longer than a certain time to execute. Many embedded systems use non-preemptive schedulers due to their simplicity and limited memory requirements.

11.8   RECAP

In this chapter we have seen how the responsiveness of a program with multiple tasks depends on the ordering of the tasks, their prioritization, and whether preemption can occur. We have seen how the scheduler manages task state based on system behavior, and have examined two types of schedulers. We have also seen that a preemptive scheduler is often built into RTOS to enable event-based mechanisms. We have examined how to protect shared data in a preemptive system. Finally, we have studied how to calculate the worst-case response time and schedulability for some real-time systems.

11.9   REFERENCES

Audsley, N. C., Burns, A., Davis, R. I., Tindell, K. W., & Wellings, A. J.. Fixed Priority Pre-emptive Scheduling: An Historical Perspective. *Real-Time Systems, 8*(3), (1995): 173–198.

Buttazzo, G. C., Rate Monotonic vs. EDF: Judgment Day. *Real-Time Systems, 29,* (2005): 5–26.

Labrosse, J., *MicroC/OS II: The Real-Time Kernel, 2nd Ed.* Lawrence, KS: Newnes (2002).

Renesas Electronics, *RL78 Family User's Manual: Software,* USA: Renesas Electronics, 2011.

Sha, L., Abdelzhaer, T., Arzen, K.-E., Cervin, A., Baker, T., Burns, A., et al., Real Time Scheduling Theory: A Historical Perspective. *Real Time Systems, 28*(2–3), (2004, November-December) 101–155.

11.10   EXERCISES

1. For some task sets, changing from static to dynamic task ordering in a scheduler will provide a major response time improvement for the highest priority task, while for other task sets it will not. Give an example of each and explain the difference.

2. For some task sets, adding preemption to a scheduler will provide a major response time improvement for the highest priority task, while for other task sets it will not. Give an example of each and explain the difference.

3. Write C code to implement run-to-completion dynamic scheduling without interrupts to poll the following tasks:
   a. If switch 1 is pressed toggle the RED LEDs.

      b. If switch 2 is pressed read the temperature value from the onboard temperature sensor and display on LCD.

      c. If switch 3 is pressed read the potentiometer value and display on the LCD.

      d. If no switch is pressed toggle the GREEN LEDs.

4. Write an algorithm which implements the below functionality using run-to-completion dynamic scheduling with interrupts:

      a. Toggle RED LEDs every 0.5 seconds.

      b. Toggle GREEN LEDs every 0.25 seconds.

      c. Read temperature value from onboard temperature sensor and display on LCD every 1.0 seconds.

      d. Read potentiometer value and display on LCD every 2.5 seconds.

5. Write a C code to implement round-robin with interrupts algorithm to perform the following tasks:

      a. Toggle RED LEDs every 0.5 seconds.

      b. Toggle GREEN LEDs every 0.25 seconds.

      c. Read temperature value from onboard temperature sensor and display on LCD every 1.0 seconds.

      d. Read potentiometer value and display on LCD every 2.5 seconds.

6. Fill in the following table to show which tasks the processor will execute and when, as well as scheduler table contents. Assume that timer tick interrupts occur every 1 millisecond, all tasks take 1.2 milliseconds to complete, and initial Timer-Value for tasks A, B, and C are 2, 4, and 5 respectively. Note that the entries in the table in column labeled INITIAL VALUE show each variable's value before the timer tick interrupt occurs. This means that a task will run on the tick when its timer reaches 0 (but show the value after the tick and after the ISR executes). Assume task A has the highest priority, followed by task B, and then C.

TASK NAME		INITIAL VALUE	n	n + 1	n + 2	n + 3	n + 4	n + 5	n + 6	n + 7	n + 8	n + 9	n + 10	n + 11	n + 12	n + 13
A	timer	2														
	run	0														
	enabled	1														
B	timer	3														
	run	0														
	enabled	1														
C	timer	1														
	run	0														
	enabled	1														
	Activity	—														

7. Fill in the table in Exercise 6 if timer tick interrupts occur every 0.5 milliseconds and all tasks take 1.25 milliseconds to complete.

8. Create a six-task workload which is not schedulable under preemptive RMPA, and then modify the task periods so that it is schedulable. You are allowed to decrease but not increase the periods. What is the worst-case response time for each of the tasks?

TASK	C	T		
τ_1				
τ_2				
τ_3				
τ_4				
τ_5				
τ_6				

9. Create a four-task workload which is not schedulable under preemptive RMPA, but is schedulable under EDF. What is the worst-case response time for each of the tasks?

TASK	C	T		
τ_1				
τ_2				
τ_3				
τ_4				

Chapter Twelve

Optimizing for Program Speed

12.1   LEARNING OBJECTIVES

This chapter deals with how to make a program run faster. In particular, it shows how to find the slow parts of a program and address them. There are many guides to optimization which provide a plethora of ways to improve code speed. The challenge is to know **which code** to optimize. This chapter concentrates on finding the slow code and either removing or accelerating it.

12.2   BASIC CONCEPTS

There are many reasons why an embedded program may need to run faster: a quicker response, to free up time for using a more sophisticated control algorithm, to move to a slower or less expensive processor, to save energy by letting the processor sleep longer, and so on.

However, an embedded system is built of many parts, any one of which could be limiting performance. The challenge is to find out **which part** of the system is limiting performance. It is similar to a detective story—there are many suspects, but who really did it?

- Was the architecture a bad fit for the work at hand?
- Is your algorithm to blame?
- Did you do a bad job coding up the algorithm?
- Did the person who coded up the free software you are using do a bad job?
- Is the compiler generating sloppy object code from your source code?
- Is the compiler configured appropriately?
- Are inefficient or extra library functions wasting time?
- Is the input data causing problems?
- Are communications with peripheral devices taking too much time?

Clearly there are many **possible** culprits, but we would like to find the biggest ones quickly to maximize our benefits.

*The real problem is that programmers have spent far too much time worrying about efficiency in the **wrong places** and at the **wrong times;** premature optimization is the root of all evil (or at least most of it) in programming.*

—Donald Knuth

With this in mind, here is an overview of how to develop fast code quickly:

1. Create a reasonable system design.
2. Implement the system with **reasonable** implementation decisions. Good judgment is critical here. However, don't start optimizing too early.
3. Get the code working.
4. Evaluate the performance—if fast enough, then your work is done. If not, then repeat as needed:
   a. Profile to find bottlenecks.
   b. Refine design or implementation to remove or lessen them.

12.2.1 Correctness before Performance

Don't try to optimize too early. Make a reasonable attempt to make good design and implementation decisions early on, but understand that it is essentially impossible for puny earthlings like us to create an optimal implementation without iterative development. So start with a **good implementation** based on reasonable assumptions. This implementation needs to be **correct.** If it isn't correct, then fix it. Once it is correct it is time to examine the performance to determine performance bottlenecks.

Certain critical system characteristics do need to be considered to create a good implementation. In particular, one must consider the MCU's native word size, hardware support for floating-point math, and any particularly slow operations (e.g., multiply, divide).

12.2.2 Reminder: Compilation is Not a One-to-One Translation

There are many possible correct assembly language versions of a single C language program. The compiler will generally create a reasonably fast version, but it is by no means the fastest. Part of your role in optimizing software is to understand if the compiler is generating assembly code which is **good enough.** This requires examining the assembly code and using your judgment[1] to make this decision. Examining the assembly code generated

---

[1] Good judgment comes from experience. Experience comes from bad judgment.

by the compiler is a remarkably effective way to learn how to help the compiler generate more efficient code.

12.3   AN EXAMPLE PROGRAM TO OPTIMIZE

In order to illustrate the long and winding road of optimizations, let's consider a real program. We need to determine the distance and bearing from an arbitrary position on the surface of the earth to the nearest weather and sea state monitoring station.

The US government's National Oceanographic and Atmospheric Administration (NOAA) monitors weather and sea conditions near the US using a variety of sensor platforms, such as buoy and fixed platforms. This information is used for weather forecasting and other applications. NOAA's National Data Buoy Center (http://www.ndbc.noaa.gov/ and http://www.ndbc.noaa.gov/cman.php) gathers information from many buoy-mounted (and fixed) platforms and makes it available online. The locations of these platforms are to be stored in the MCU's flash ROM.

Finding the distance and bearing between two locations on the surface of the earth uses spherical geometry. Locations are represented as latitude and longitude coordinates. We use the spherical law of cosines to compute the distance in kilometers:

$$d = \mathrm{acos}(\sin(lat_1) * \sin(lat_2) + (\cos(lat_1) * \cos(lat_2) * \cos(lon_2 - lon_1))$$

We compute the bearing (angle toward the location) in degrees as follows:

$$a = atan2(\cos(lat_1) * \sin(lat_2) - \sin(lat_1) * \cos(lat_2) * \cos(lon_2 - lon_1),$$
$$\sin(lon_2 - lon_1) * \cos(lat_2)) * \frac{180}{\pi}$$

Further details are available online at http://www.movable-type.co.uk/scripts/latlong.html. This is a mathematically intensive computation with many trigonometric functions, so we expect many opportunities for optimization.

Let's examine the relevant functions needed to do this work. The function Calc_ Distance calculates the distance between two points.

```
1. float Calc_Distance( PT_T * p1,  const PT_T * p2) {
2. //calculates distance in kilometers between locations (represented
   in degrees)
3.     return acos(sin(p1->Lat * PI/180) * sin(p2->Lat * PI/180) +
4.         cos(p1->Lat * PI/180) * cos(p2->Lat * PI/180)*
5.         cos(p2->Lon * PI/180 - p1->Lon*PI/180)) * 6371;
6. }
```

The function Calc_Bearing calculates the bearing from the first to the second point.

```
1. float Calc_Bearing( PT_T * p1,  const PT_T * p2){
2. //calculates bearing in degrees between locations (represented in
      degrees)
3.    float angle = atan2(
4.       sin(p1->Lon * PI/180 - p2->Lon * PI/180) * cos(p2->Lat * PI/180),
5.       cos(p1->Lat * PI/180) * sin(p2->Lat * PI/180) -
6.       sin(p1->Lat * PI/180) * cos(p2->Lat * PI/180)*
7.       cos(p1->Lon * PI/180 - p2->Lon * PI/180)
8.       ) * 180/PI;
9.    if (angle < 0.0)
10.       angle += 360;
11.    return angle;
12. }
```

The function Find_Nearest_Point calculates the distance to each point (in line 15) to find the one closest to the current position. It keeps track of the closest point's distance and index in lines 18–20.

```
1. void Find_Nearest_Point(float cur_pos_lat, float cur_pos_lon,
2.       float * distance, float * bearing,  char  * * name) {
3.    //cur_pos_lat and cur_pos_lon are in degrees
4.    //distance is in kilometers
5.    //bearing is in degrees
6.    int i = 0, closest_i;
7.    PT_T ref;
8.    float d, b, closest_d = 1E10;
9.    *distance = *bearing = NULL;
10.    *name = NULL;
11.    ref.Lat = cur_pos_lat;
12.    ref.Lon = cur_pos_lon;
13.    strcpy(ref.Name, "Reference");
14.    while (strcmp(points[i].Name, "END")) {
15.       d = Calc_Distance(&ref, &(points[i]) );
16.       b = Calc_Bearing(&ref, &(points[i]) );
17.       //if we found a closer point, remember it and display it
18.       if (d<closest_d) {
19.          closest_d = d;
20.          closest_i = i;
21.       }
```

```
22.        i++;
23.      }
24.      d = Calc_Distance(&ref, &(points[closest_i]) );
25.      b = Calc_Bearing(&ref, &(points[closest_i]) );
26.      //return information to calling function about closest point
27.      *distance = d;
28.      *bearing = b;
29.      *name = (char * ) (points[closest_i].Name);
30.  }
```

Note that there are various other functions (e.g., for initialization) in the program, but these three do the bulk of the work. Our main function calls Find_Nearest_Point twice, with locations of Raleigh, NC, and San Francisco, CA.

We examine the default compiler setting for optimization, which turns out to be "Low Optimization." We change this to "High Optimization" and "Optimize for Speed" and build the program. We download it to the MCU and run it. It takes 3.22 seconds to find the closest of all the points for two different test cases. This means that each point's comparison takes about 3.22 sec/(164 points * 2) = 9.82 ms, or roughly 314,000 clock cycles given the clock speed of 32 MHz.

12.4   PROFILING—WHAT IS SLOW?

There must be many opportunities for optimization here, but where and how should we start? We could waste a lot of time speeding up code which doesn't really matter much to the system's overall performance.[2] In order to avoid this, we want to figure out what parts of the program **take up most of its time.** Optimizing those parts first will give us the biggest payback on our development time. **Profiling** a program shows us where it spends its time, and therefore where we should spend our time for optimization.

12.4.1 Mechanisms

There are three basic approaches to profiling a program.

1. We can **sample the program counter** periodically by interrupting the program to see what it is doing by, and then looking up what function (or region, to generalize) contains that instruction address. This approach provides the biggest return on development time effort.

---

[2] You can avoid ten minutes of thinking by instead spending the whole day blindly hacking code.

2. We can modify each function in the program to **record when it starts and finishes executing.** After the program runs we process the function execution time information to calculate the profile. We don't discuss this further, as it requires extensive modification to the program (for each user function and library function). Some compilers or code post-processing tools provide this support.

3. We can use hardware circuitry to **extract an instruction address trace** by monitor the address bus as the program runs. The address trace can then be processed to create the profile. We don't discuss this further, as the address bus is generally inaccessible for single-chip microcontrollers.

We will use the PC-sampling approach here for reasons of practicality. There are commercial and open source profiling tools available, but we will create our own tool.

12.4.2   An Example PC-Sampling Profiler for the RL78

Let's see how to build a PC-sampling profiler for the RL78.

12.4.2.1   Sampling the PC

First we need a way to sample the PC occasionally. During system initialization we configure a timer array unit peripheral to generate interrupts at a frequency[3] of 100 Hz. This interrupt is handled at run time by the service routine shown below.

```
1. volatile unsigned int PC;
2. #pragma vector = INTTM00_vect
3. __interrupt void MD_INTTM00(void)
4. {
5.     /* Start user code. Do not edit comment generated here */
6.
7.     unsigned int s, e;
8.     unsigned int i;
9.
10.    if (!profiling_enabled)
11.        return;
12.
13.    profile_ticks++;
14.
```

---

[3] This is an arbitrary frequency. A higher frequency increases resolution but also timing overhead. A lower frequency reduces resolution and overhead.

```
15.      //Extract low 16 bits of return address
16.      __asm("    PUSH  AX\n"
17.              "    MOVW  AX, [SP+10]\n"
18.              "    MOVW  PC_val_low, AX\n"
19.              "    POP   AX\n");
20.
21.      /* look up function in table and increment counter  */
22.      for (i = 0; i <> NumProfileRegions; i++) {
23.          s = RegionTable[i].Start;
24.          e = RegionTable[i].End;
25.          if ((PC >= s) && (PC <>= e)) {
26.              RegionCount[i]++;
27.              return;
28.          }
29.      }
30.      /* End user code. Do not edit comment generated here */
31. }
```

This ISR needs to retrieve the saved PC value from the stack. Figure 12.1 shows the stack contents upon responding to an interrupt. The address of the next instruction to execute after completing this ISR is stored on the stack in three bytes: PC7–0, PC15–8, and PC19–16. At the beginning of the ISR, they will be at addresses SP + 1, SP + 2 and SP + 3. However, the ISR may push additional data onto the stack so we will need to

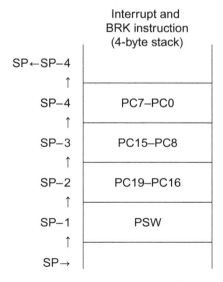

Figure 12.1   Stack contents upon responding to an interrupt.

examine the assembly code generated by the compiler for our ISR before we can defini-
tively identify the offsets from SP. In our case there is additional data allocated on the stack
for local variables, so the high byte of the saved PC (PC19 − PC16) is located at SP + 12
and the low word (PC0 − PC7 and PC8 − PC15) is at SP + 10. The code at lines
16 through 19 in the listing copies the low word of the saved PC value into register AX and
then into local variable PC on the stack. It also saves and restores the previous value of
AX to ensure correctness.

12.4.2.2 Finding the Corresponding Code Region

TABLE 12.1   Region Address Information Table

REGION NAME	START ADDRESS	END ADDRESS	COUNT
foo	0x00001234	0x00001267	0
bar	0x00001268	0x00001300	0

So now we have the saved PC, which shows us what instruction the processor will execute
after finishing this ISR. What program region (e.g., function) corresponds to that PC? Ide-
ally we would like a table of information such as in Table 12.1.

There are various ways to create such a table. One approach is to process the map file
created by the linker. The IAR Embedded Workbench for RL78 generates a **map** file in the
output directory (e.g., debug/your_project_name.map) which shows the size and location
of each function in a human-readable format. Functions are stored in one of three types of
code segment:

- CODE holds program code
- RCODE holds start-up and run-time library code
- XCODE holds code from functions declared with the attribute _far_func.

Here is an example entry from the map file:

```
CODE
    Relative segment, address: 00001238 - 000013C8 (0x191 bytes),
align: 0
    Segment part 11.
        ENTRY                   ADDRESS             REF BY
        =====                   =======             ======
        sim_motion              00001238            main (CG_main)
            calls direct
            CSTACK = 00000000 ( 000000A4 )
    _____
```

It shows that the function *sim-motion* starts at address 00001238 and ends at address 000013c8. We can use this information to create a region table entry for the function. We create a type of structure called REGION_T to hold a region's start address, end address, and label (to simplify debugging). The addresses are stored as unsigned ints (16 bits long) because we wish to save space, and our target MCU's program memory is located within the first 64 KB of the address space. This would need to be changed if we needed to store larger addresses.

```
1. typedef struct {
2.    unsigned int Start;
3.    unsigned int End;
4.    char Name[16];
5. } REGION_T;
```

We will use an awk script to extract function names and addresses and generate a C file which holds two arrays, as shown in the listing below. Some toolchains offer tools for extracting symbols and their information from the object code. For example, gnu binutils provides nm and objdump.

The first array (RegionTable, lines 2–19 holds the start and end addresses of the functions and their names. The ISR MD_INTTM00 accesses it in lines 21 and 22 from previous coding list. The array is declared as a const to allow the compiler to place it into ROM, which is usually larger and less valuable than RAM for microcontrollers.

The second array (RegionCount, line 21) is an array of unsigned integers which count the number of times the region was interrupted by the ISR. This array is initialized to all zeros on start-up. The ISR increments the appropriate array entry in line 26. If we do not find a corresponding region, then no region counter is incremented.

```
1. #include "region.h"
2. const REGION_T RegionTable[] = {
3.    {0x00000A46, 0x00000A79, "AD_Init"},    //0
4.    {0x00000A7A, 0x00000A83, "AD_Start"},    //1
5.    {0x00000A84, 0x00000A87, "AD_ComparatorOn"},    //2
6.    {0x00000A88, 0x00000A95, "MD_INTAD"},    //3
7.    {0x00000A96, 0x00000AAF, "IT_Init"},    //4
8.    {0x00000AB0, 0x00000ABC, "IT_Start"},    //5
9.    {0x00000AD4, 0x00000AE8, "MD_INTIT"},    //6
10.    {0x00000AE9, 0x00000B8F, "main"},    //7

    (many lines deleted)

11.    {0x00000A1D, 0x00000A45, "_matherr"},    //60
12.    {0x00001606, 0x00001710, "sqrt"},    //61
```

```
13.     {0x00001711, 0x0000185C, "__iar_Atan"},    //62
14.     {0x0000185D, 0x00001907, "__iar_Dint"},    //63
15.     {0x00001912, 0x00001964, "__iar_Dnorm"},   //64
16.     {0x00001965, 0x00001B1D, "__iar_Dscale"},  //65
17.     {0x00001B27, 0x00001C66, "__iar_Quad"},    //66
18.     {0x00001C67, 0x00001DC2, "__iar_Sin"},     //67
19.  };
20.  const unsigned NumProfileRegions = 68;
21.  volatile unsigned RegionCount[68];
```

We also have the ISR increment a variable (sample_count) in line 12 preceding to count how many samples we've taken. We need this value to correctly calculate the profile if any of our samples did not hit any regions in our table.

12.4.2.3 Modifications to the Build Process

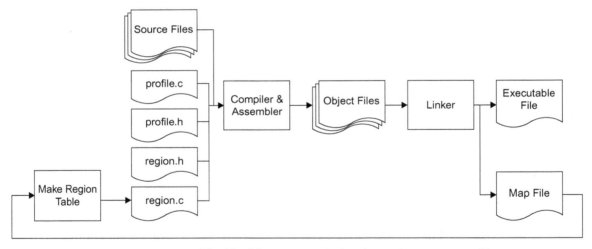

Figure 12.2   Modified build process includes dependency on map file.

Our build process is now more complicated, because the region table depends on the map file, as shown in Figure 12.2. Note that the map file is automatically generated by the linker to describe the contents of the executable file. Because of this we do not edit the map file—our changes would have no effect, and may even introduce bugs into our profiler in this case. The map file is not created until after the program is fully compiled and linked, so we will need to rebuild the program several times. With suitable tools this build process can be automated.

- We first **build** the program using a dummy region.c file, which contains an empty region table. The resulting map file has the correct number of functions, but with addresses which will probably change, so they are wrong.
- We run our tool to **create the region table** from the map file. The region table now has the correct number of entries, but the addresses are wrong.
- We **rebuild** the program. The resulting map file has the correct (final) function addresses.
- We run our tool to **create the region table** from the map file.
- We **rebuild** the program for the final time. The resulting executable program contains a region table with correct address information for each function.

12.4.2.4 Analyzing Results

We can now analyze where the program spends most of its time. We simply find the region with the largest number of profile hits and start looking at that region's C and assembly code. In doing this, we will keep in mind some critical ideas of optimization:

- Measure the performance.
- Avoid run-time work when possible.
- Look at the assembly code the compiler generated.

12.5 EXAMPLE: OPTIMIZING THE DISTANCE AND BEARING CALCULATION _____

12.5.1 First Measurement: 3220 ms

We are now ready to examine how our program spends its time. We recompile the program with the profiling support described above and run it. We look at the execution profile and find that these regions shown in Table 12.2 account for most of the time.

TABLE 12.2   Top Regions in Initial Execution Time Profile

COUNT	REGION NAME	TIME (%)
140	?MOVE_LONG_L06	44%
46	?WRKSEG_PUSH_L09	14%
40	?F_DIV	12%
24	?F_ADD	7%
22	?F_MUL	7%
13	?WRKSEG_POP_L09	4%

What is ?MOVE_LONG_L06? We didn't call it explicitly, so it must be a library function call added by the compiler. We use the debugger to insert a breakpoint in that function and then examine call the function, call stack, or step out of the function to determine which function calls it.[4] It turns out that WRKSEG_POP_L09 calls it. Stepping out of WRKSEG_POP_L09 leads us into F_MUL, which is a floating point multiply operation. We see that F_MUL accounts for 7 percent of the time already, and related functions F_DIV and F_ADD are also significant. WRKSEG_PUSH_L09 is also called by the other floating point library functions.

12.5.2 First Optimization

There is a lot of time spent doing floating point math in software. Let's examine our source code to see how we can reduce the amount of floating point math. Line 16 in Find_Nearest_Point calculates the bearing to each point using the function Calc_Bearing, which uses a lot of floating point math and trigonometric functions. Stepping back and looking at the bigger picture, we don't really need to know the bearing to **every** point, just the **closest** one. And that bearing is calculated in line 25, so we can delete line 16.

Looking at the code further we see a similar recomputation. We recalculate the distance to the closest point in line 24. This distance is already stored in closest_d (assigned in line 19), so we could delete line 24 and replace line 27 with distance = closest_d. We expect that this optimization will give a minor improvement, since it reduces the number of distance calculations by only one. But since it is very easy to implement, we do it. We find that the execution time has fallen to 143 ticks, primarily due to the elimination of most of the Calc_Bearing calls.

12.5.3 Second Measurement: 1430 ms

Let's look at the profile information to see if we should keep working on the floating point math, or if something else is now the biggest problem. The top regions in the profile table are shown in Table 12.3. It's still the same functions, so let's keep working in the same direction.

---

[4] Some profiling tools will identify the calling functions automatically, but our simple scheme here does not, which forces us to use the debugger.

TABLE 12.3 Execution Time Profile after First Optimization Pass

COUNT	REGION NAME	TIME (%)
52	?MOVE_LONG_L06	36%
23	?WRKSEG_PUSH_L09	16%
17	?F_DIV	12%
11	?F_MUL	8%
10	?WRKSEG_POP_L09	7%

12.5.4 Second Optimization

The functions Calc_Distance and Calc_Bearing have many divisions of constants by constants (e.g., PI/180). The compiler should be able to do these divisions at compile-time, right? Let's look at the assembly code for Calc_Distance and find out.

We don't include the two pages of assembly code here, but there are six calls to F_DIV. The C source code has six floating point divides, so it is obvious that the compiler isn't doing that possible optimization. Let's do it by defining PI_DIV_180 to eliminate those divides.

```
1. #define PI_DIV_180 (PI/180)
```

Strangely enough, this is enough to eliminate the divide calls. We do this optimization everywhere we have the PI/180 division, then recompile and analyze the code.

Sometimes compilers are very careful when it comes to optimizations—the "dark corners" of the semantics of the C language probably allow our program to behave in a certain way which would cause the optimized code to be incorrect. So sometimes we need to be explicit to make sure the compiler can generate better code.

12.5.5 Third Measurement: 1300 ms

The execution time falls to 130 ticks with the distribution shown in Table 12.4.

12.5.6 Third Optimization

There is still quite a bit of floating-point math. Let's look at what's in Calc_Distance and Calc_Bearing again. The second parameter to each function is a pointer to a "const"

TABLE 12.4 Execution Time Profile after Second Optimization Pass

COUNT	REGION NAME	TIME (%)
57	?MOVE_LONG_L06	44%
23	?WRKSEG_PUSH_L09	18%
9	__finfws	7%
8	F_DIV	6%
6	F_ADD	5%
6	F_MUL	5%

point—one stored in the array points. These points are defined at compile time and then will not change again until we want to update the list. We could save quite a bit of time by pre-computing in two ways:

- Storing a point's latitude and longitude in radians rather than degrees, avoiding the need to convert at run-time.
- Storing the derived trigonometric values. Calc_Distance and Calc_Bearing both use the sine of latitude and cosine of latitude.

So we will modify the spreadsheet we used to create CMAN_coords.c to precompute these values. We will also need to modify the type definition of PT_T to include the sine and cosine of the latitude. This actually simplifies the code quite a bit, as shown below.

```
2. float Calc_Distance( PT_T * p1,  const PT_T * p2) {
3.    //calculates distance in kilometers between locations
         (represented in degrees)
4.    return acos(p1->SinLat * p2->SinLat +
5.        p1->CosLat * p2->CosLat * cos(p2->Lon - p1->Lon)) * 6371;
6. }

7. float Calc_Bearing( PT_T * p1,  const PT_T * p2){
8.    //calculates bearing in degrees between locations (represented
         in degrees)
9.    float angle = atan2(
10.       sin(p1->Lon - p2->Lon) * p2->CosLat,
11.       p1->CosLat * p2->SinLat -
12.       p1->SinLat * p2->CosLat * cos(p1->Lon - p2->Lon)
13.       ) * 180/PI;
```

```
14.    if (angle < 0.0)
15.       angle += 360;
16.    return angle;
17. }
```

We will also modify the code in Find_Nearest_Point to convert the current location to radians and save the sine and cosine of latitude.

```
1. void Find_Nearest_Point(float cur_pos_lat, float cur_pos_lon, float *
   distance, float * bearing,
2.    char  * * name) {
3.    //cur_pos_lat and cur_pos_lon are in degrees
4.    //distance is in kilometers
5.    //bearing is in degrees
6.
7.    int i = 0, closest_i;
8.    PT_T ref;
9.    float d, b, closest_d = 1E10;
10.
11.    *distance = *bearing = NULL;
12.    *name = NULL;
13.
14.    ref.Lat = cur_pos_lat * PI_DIV_180;
15.    ref.SinLat = sin(ref.Lat);
16.    ref.CosLat = cos(ref.Lat);
17.    ref.Lon = cur_pos_lon * PI_DIV_180;
18.    strcpy(ref.Name, "Reference");
```

12.5.7 Fourth Measurement: 600 ms

TABLE 12.5   Execution Time Profile after Third Optimization Pass

COUNT	REGION NAME	TIME (%)
21	?0EMOVE_LONG_L06	35%
10	?0EWRKSEG_PUSH_L09	17%
8	F_ADD	13%
6	F_DIV	10%
6	F_MUL	10%

Here we see that the execution time has fallen significantly (to 60 ticks), but still we have the same functions dominating the total time. This means that the floating point math should still be our focus.

12.5.8 Fourth Optimization

Looking at the problem some more shows us that most of the time is spent in functions called by Calc_Distance. So we will focus on speeding it up.

In this case, we have over-specified the problem. Calc_Distance in line 4 below multiplies an intermediate result by 6371 to provide a return value which measures the distance in kilometers. We don't need to perform this unit conversion until we find the closest point, at which we can take the intermediate result for that point and then multiply it to get kilometers.

```
1. float Calc_Distance( PT_T * p1,  const PT_T * p2) {
2.    //calculates distance in kilometers between locations
         (represented in degrees)
3.    return acos(p1->SinLat * p2->SinLat +
4.       p1->CosLat * p2->CosLat * cos(p2->Lon - p1->Lon)) * 6371;
5. }
```

So we could instead call the simplified function below to find the closest point, eliminating $N_{\text{Points-1}}$ floating point multiplies.

```
1. float Calc_Distance_in_Unknown_Units( PT_T * p1,  const PT_T * p2) {
2. //calculates distance in kilometers between locations (represented
     in degrees)
3.    return acos(p1->SinLat * p2->SinLat +
4.       p1->CosLat * p2->CosLat * cos(p2->Lon - p1->Lon));
5. }
```

We can take this a step further. The arc cosine function is a decreasing function, as shown in Figure 12.3. So we don't really need to calculate the arc cosine to find the closest point. Instead, we just need to find the point with the *largest* input (*X* value in Figure 12.3) to the arc cosine, as that will result in the *smallest* output. That will give the smallest distance, as it is just multiplied by a scaling constant to convert to kilometers.

The optimized version of Calc_Distance is renamed and shown below, with changes in lines 3 and 4.

```
1. float Calc_Distance_Partially( PT_T * p1,  const PT_T * p2) {
2.    //calculates cosine of distance between locations
```

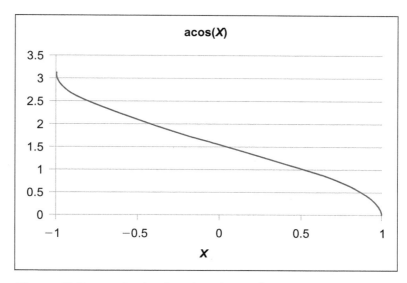

Figure 12.3   Arc Cosine function always decreases as *X* increases.

```
3.      return p1->SinLat * p2->SinLat +
4.          p1->CosLat * p2->CosLat * cos(p2->Lon - p1->Lon);
5. }
```

We need to change Find_Nearest point slightly. First, we need to change various aspects of the code because acos *increases* as distance *decreases*—we want to find the *largest* intermediate result.

- In line 9 we set the closest *d* value to 0.
- In line 23 we look for the *largest* value of *d*.

Finally, we need to compute the actual distance for the point.

- In line 33 we complete the calculation of the distance for the closest point.

```
1. void Find_Nearest_Point(float cur_pos_lat, float cur_pos_lon, float
* distance, float * bearing,
2.     char  * * name) {
3.         //cur_pos_lat and cur_pos_lon are in degrees
4.         //distance is in kilometers
5.         //bearing is in degrees
6.
7.         int i = 0, closest_i;
8.         PT_T ref;
```

```
9.          float d, b, closest_d = 0;
10.
11.         *distance =* bearing = NULL;
12.         *name = NULL;
13.
14.         ref.Lat = cur_pos_lat * PI_DIV_180;
15.         ref.SinLat = MYSIN(ref.Lat);
16.         ref.CosLat = MYCOS(ref.Lat);
17.         ref.Lon = cur_pos_lon * PI_DIV_180;
18.         strcpy(ref.Name, "Reference");
19.
20.         while (strcmp(points[i].Name, "END")) {
21.             d = Calc_Distance_Partially(&ref, &(points[i]) );
22.             //if we found a closer point, remember it and display it
23.             if (d > closest_d) {
24.                 closest_d = d;
25.                 closest_i = i;
26.             }
27.             i++;
28.         }
29.         b = Calc_Bearing(&ref, &(points[closest_i]) );
30.         //return information to calling function about closest point
31.         *distance = acos(closest_d) * 6371;
32.         *bearing = b;
33.         *name = (char *) (points[closest_i].Name);
34. }
```

12.5.9 Fifth Measurement: 230 ms

How well does this work? The resulting code takes 23 ticks, or 230 ms. This translates to an average of 1.4 ms per point, or 44,800 clock cycles. The profile is shown in Table 12.6. The floating point math still dominates.

Table 12.7 summarizes the impact of each optimization. If we wanted to continue with optimizations, we could examine several directions:

- Replace trig functions with lower-precision but faster polynomial approximations.
- Replace floating point math with fixed point math.
- Arrange point data into a two-dimensional array to reduce number of comparisons needed.
- Convert math to use matrix operations on unit circle, avoiding the law of cosines.

TABLE 12.6   Execution Time Profile after Fourth Optimization Pass

COUNT	REGION NAME	TIME (%)
7	?0EMOVE_LONG_L06	30%
5	?0EWRKSEG_PUSH_L09	22%
3	F_ADD	13%
2	?0EWRKSEG_POP_L09	9%
2	__finfws	9%
1	__iar_Dint	4%
1	__iar_Sin	4%
1	?0EFUNC_LEAVE_L06	4%
1	F_MUL	4%

TABLE 12.7   Speed-Ups Resulting from Optimizations

OPTIMIZATION	TICKS	INCREMENTAL	CUMULATIVE
Initial program	322	—	—
Remove extra calls to Calc_Bearing and Calc_Distance	143	2.25	2.25
Help compiler pre-compute PI/180	130	1.10	2.48
Store points in radians, precompute sin & cos of latitude	60	2.17	5.37
Don't compute full distance until essential	23	2.61	14.00

12.6   GUIDANCE FOR CODE OPTIMIZATION

So far in this chapter we have learned three concepts. First, we now know how to profile an application. Second, we have learned that the part of the program which is slowest is often a surprise. In many cases the developer does not realize that the object code for a given operation will be slow, while other times the developer is sloppy and includes extra computations or uses a poor algorithm or data type. Another common problem is that the developer thinks the compiler is performing an obvious optimization when in fact it is not due to possible side effects. Finally, we have seen several optimization methods and approaches. These are just a few of the vast range possible. The best optimization approach is built on understanding two critical system aspects: Where does the program spend most of its time? What object code is the compiler generating? Given this context, we can now move on to examining different optimization strategies.

12.6.1   Your Mileage Will Vary

We need to keep several points in mind as we examine these types of optimizations.

- Each program is structured differently and likely has a different bottleneck.
- There may be several different bottlenecks depending on which code is executing. A system with four different operating modes (or four different input events) may have four different bottlenecks, so be sure to profile the code for a variety of operating modes and input conditions.
- A program's bottleneck may move after an optimization is performed. After all, it is just the slowest part of the code. If it is optimized enough, then another piece of code becomes the slowest.
- Different processor architectures have different bottlenecks. Accessing memory in a deeply-pipelined 2 GHz processor may cost 500 cycles. On the RL78, however, there is generally only a single cycle penalty. Hence optimizations which are effective on one processor architecture may be inconsequential on another.
- Different compilers use different approaches to generate code. Recall that there are many possible assembly language programs which can implement the specification given by a source-level program. One compiler may aggressively unroll loops, while another may not. If you manually try unrolling loops with the first compiler you likely will see no performance improvement. It is valuable to examine the optimization section of the compiler manual (e.g., (IAR Systems AB, 2011)) for guidance and suggestions.

There are many excellent guides to optimizing code; some are listed in the references at the end of the chapter. Here we seek to provide a framework with which to classify the available optimization approaches.

12.6.2   Reduce Run-time Work

There are many different ways to reduce the amount of computation which must be done by the program at run-time. Here are a few high-level approaches which may be helpful.

12.6.2.1   Precompute before Run-time

Take advantage of the compiler's preprocessing capabilities, as well as other tools such as spreadsheets. How much computation can be done ahead of time? In the example program we saved time by storing each coordinate in radians, eliminating the conversion from degrees. We also saved time by pre-computing the sine and cosine of the latitude for each coordinate.

12.6.2.2   Quit Early and Often

If it is possible to use the result of partial computations to make decisions, then do so. In the example program we saved time by not computing the actual distance, but instead making the distance comparison using an intermediate value before it is passed through the arc cosine function.

12.6.2.3   Arrange Data to Minimize the Work

It may be possible to arrange data so that less work is necessary. For example, after the first profiling run we know which regions dominate the execution time of the target program. We could sort the region table to place the most frequently accessed regions at the top. This would dramatically reduce execution time of the ISR and hence profiling overhead.

12.6.3   Do the Remaining Run-time Work Efficiently

After eliminating as much run-time work as possible, we want to do the remaining work as quickly as possible. Here are a few high-level approaches.

12.6.3.1   Use a Better Algorithm

The profiling code could be optimized to reduce the ISR's execution time overhead. The current implementation uses a linear search, starting with the first entry and advancing to the next until it finds a match. If we ensure that the region list entries are sorted by address, then we can use a binary search to find the matching region. This will reduce search time dramatically.

Similarly, the coordinates are stored alphabetically by name. Sorting these by longitude would reduce the number of comparisons required. In fact, sorting the coordinates into a two-dimensional data structure could further reduce the number of comparisons. This latter example is left as an exercise for the reader.

12.6.3.2   Avoid Double-precision Floating Point Math

Many embedded compilers stick to the letter of the law for ANSI C. The functions in the standard math library take double-precision float arguments, perform their operations on double-precision floats, and return double-precision results. This is usually far more precision than is needed for embedded systems. Some compilers offer single-precision versions of functions (e.g., sinf() in addition to sin()). Others allow one to specify that double-precision operations and variables in the source code should be implemented with the corresponding single-precision versions.

Some embedded compilers omit double-precision floating point math, treating it as single-precision. Others support it, but offer a compiler option switch which forces double-precision floating point math to single-precision.

12.6.3.3   Avoid Single-precision Floating Point Math, Too

Unless a microcontroller has a hardware floating point unit, floating point math is emulated in software. It is slow and uses large amounts of memory (for the library routines, your code, and the variables). Instead, it is often possible to use fixed-point math instead. Some references are presented below.

12.6.3.4   Use Approximations

The trigonometric and other math library functions are very accurate—perhaps more accurate than necessary for your application. These functions are typically implemented with numerical approximations. The library designers ensured high accuracy by using a large number of terms or iteration steps in the approximation. Perhaps your application doesn't need as much accuracy, in which case you may benefit from implementing your own reduced-precision polynomial approximations. Jack Ganssle provides excellent explanations in his articles (http://www.ganssle.com/articles/atrig.htm, http://www.ganssle.com/approx.htm).

12.6.4   Use MCU-Appropriate Data

12.6.4.1   Use the Right Memory Model

Compilers for embedded systems typically support multiple memory models, varying in how much memory can be addressed. This is because accessing more data requires longer addresses and pointers, which in turn typically require more instructions and hence memory and execution time. Using the smallest possible memory model can reduce the amount of code needed, speeding up the program and reducing memory requirements.

12.6.4.2   Data Size

Use the smallest practical data size. Data which doesn't match the machine's native word size will require extra instructions for processing. Native data sizes for the RL78 architecture are the bit, byte, and 16-bit word.

12.6.4.3 Signed vs. Unsigned Data

Some ISAs offer uneven performance for signed or unsigned data, so there may be a benefit to using one type or another. The IAR Compiler manual recommends using unsigned data types rather than signed data types if possible.

12.6.4.4 Data Alignment

Some memory systems offer non-uniform access speeds based on alignment. For example, the RL78 has word-aligned memory, so smaller elements (e.g., chars) in a structure may result in padding bytes, wasting memory.

12.6.5   Help the Compiler do a Good Job

12.6.5.1   Basics: ISA Familiarity, Tweak/Compile/Examine/Repeat

How do we know if the compiler is doing a good enough job on your code? To answer this we need to understand enough **assembly language** for the MCU to understand what the compiler has generated. This textbook and the RL78 software reference manual contain more details. We also need to understand **how C concepts and mechanisms are implemented** in assembly code. How are subroutines called? How are arguments passed and returned? How are switch statements implemented? This textbook's chapter on C as implemented in assembly language has more details.

An iterative and experimental approach is the best way to evaluate how well the compiler is doing its job. Tweak the code, recompile the module, and examine the assembly code output. Repeat as necessary.

12.6.5.2   What Should the Compiler be Able to Do on Its Own?

The compiler should do these optimizations at a fine-grain level (assembly-language operations) if you enable optimizations. Don't waste your time on these optimizations, as the compiler should handle them automatically:

- Perform compile-time math operations
- Reuse a register for variables which do not interfere
- Eliminate unreachable code, or code with no effect
- Eliminate useless control flow
- Simplify some algebraic operations (e.g., $x * 1 = x$, $x + 0 = x$)
- Move operation to where it executes less often (e.g., out of a loop)
- Eliminate redundant computations

- Reuse intermediate results
- Unroll loops
- Manually inline functions (instead use macros)

Note that the compiler has a harder time identifying optimization opportunities across more complex program structure boundaries (or when accessing memory), so it may not be able to do as much as expected.

12.6.5.3 *Don't Handcuff the Compiler*

The compiler would like to optimize the code but must be conservative due to possible unsafe side effects. Code should be written to make it clear to the compiler what side effects are impossible. There are many possible issues, but here are a few suggestions:

- Using complete ANSI function prototypes make it possible for the compiler to promote arguments so they are passed to functions by register rather than through the stack.
- Taking the address of an automatic variable may prevent the compiler from promoting it to a register variable.
- Use qualifiers such as const and static when helpful.
- Mixing data types leads to automatic type promotions which are specified by ANSI C. These typically lead to library calls which waste time and memory. As these promotions aren't immediately obvious in the source code, it is valuable to examine the generated assembly code.

This subject is covered in detail in Jakob Engblom's article "Getting the Least out of your C Compiler" (Engblom, 2002).

12.7   RECAP

In this chapter we have seen that determining **which code to optimize** is as important as determining **how to optimize it.** The key tools in the embedded software developer's toolbox are a profiler, an understanding of assembly code, and a creative mind.

12.8   REFERENCES

Engblom, J. *"Getting the Least out of your C Compiler."* San Francisco: Embedded Systems Conference, 2002, http://www.engbloms.se/publications/engblom-esc-sf-2001.pdf.

IAR Systems AB. *IAR C/C_ Compiler Reference Guide for the Renesas RL78 Microcontroller Family.* Sweden: IAR Systems AB, 2011.

Crenshaw, J. Math Toolkit for Real-Time Programming. CMP, 2000, ISBN-1929629095

Kastner, R., Hosangadi, A., Fallah, F. Arithmetic Optimization Techniques for Hardware and Software Design. Cambridge University Press, 2010, ISBN-0521880998

Lemieux, J. Fixed-Point Math in C. Embedded Systems Programming Magazine, April 2001.

Jones, N. Efficient C Code for Eight-bit MCUs. Embedded Systems Programming Magazine, November 1998.

12.9   EXERCISES

1. Write a program and compile it to determine why unsigned data is recommended over signed data. What is the performance impact? What are the differences in the assembly code?

2. Modify the distance calculation program to store the coordinates into a two-dimensional data structure in order to reduce the number of comparisons needed to find the closest point. What is the performance impact of the optimization?

3. Modify the profiling support code and tools to sort the region table to place the most frequently accessed regions at the top of the list. What is the performance impact of the optimization?

Chapter Thirteen

Power and Energy Optimization

13.1 LEARNING OBJECTIVES

This chapter deals with how to make an embedded system use less power or energy.

- We examine the differences between power and energy.
- We evaluate how a digital circuit uses power and then use this to develop basic optimization approaches.
- We examine the clock control mechanisms available in RL78 family MCUs.
- We review the standby states of RL78 family MCUs, in which no instructions execute.
- We explore the power and energy characteristics of the RL78G13 MCU.
- We walk through an example embedded application to optimize energy use, first for the operating lifetime and then for the standby lifetime.

13.2 BASIC CONCEPTS

Let's begin by reviewing the differences between power and energy, which are related but different.

13.2.1 Power and Energy

Power is the product of current and voltage. One Ampere of current flowing across a one Volt drop will dissipate one Watt of power.

Energy is power multiplied by time. Power is an instantaneous value, while energy integrates power over time. One Watt being dissipated for a period of one second represents one Joule of energy.

Do we want to save power, energy, or both?

- In some cases, there is a limited amount of **energy** available. For example, consider a rechargeable NiMH AA cell with a nominal capacity of 2500 mAH, or

2.5 AH. This means the cell can supply 25 mA for one hundred hours. We will assume the average voltage is 1.2 V.[1] Multiplying 1.2 V by 2.5 AH gives the cell energy capacity as 3 Watt-Hours, or 3 * 60 * 60 J = 10800 J.

- In some cases, the power budget is limited. There may be **limited power** available. For example, a photovoltaic panel may produce at most 100 mW, and less when the sky is cloudy. In other applications there is **limited cooling** available. The power dissipated by the circuit heats it above the ambient temperature, based upon thermal resistance and available cooling. In order to keep the circuit from overheating we need to limit the power dissipated.

13.2.2 Digital Circuit Power Consumption

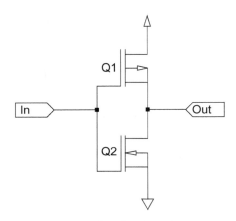

Figure 13.1 Example of a digital inverter circuit.

Let's take a look at how digital circuits use power and energy. The inverter in Figure 13.1 dissipates power in two ways.

- When the **input signal is not changing,** one transistor is on (saturated or active) and the other is off. For example, a low input level will turn on Q1 and turn off Q2. A high input level will turn off Q1 and turn on Q2. In either case, since the transistors are in series, the total resistance is quite large, and only a small amount of current flows from V_{DD} to ground. This current leads to a **static power component** which is proportional to the square of the supply voltage. The power is still dissipated even though there is no switching, so it is independent of the clock frequency.

---

[1] A NiMH cell's voltage is not constant. It depends on the state of charge, load current, and temperature. The voltage is roughly 1.35 V when fully charged, and falls to roughly 1.0 V when mostly discharged.

■ When the **input signal is changing,** then as the input voltage changes from one logic level to another, the transistors will pass through the linear operation mode between off and fully on. In addition, some components in the circuit have capacitance (e.g., gates, wires) which must be charged or discharged in order to change the voltage level of a signal. This current leads to a **dynamic power component** which is proportional to the square of the supply voltage. It also depends on how often the switching occurs (i.e., the frequency of the switching).

The resulting total power dissipated can be modeled as the sum of the static and the dynamic power components:

$$P = S_p V_{DD}^2 + C_p V_{DD}^2 f_{sw}$$

S_p and C_p are proportionality constants representing conductance and capacitance and can be experimentally derived.

13.2.3   Basic Optimization Methods

The power equation gives us some insight into how to reduce the **power** consumption for a digital circuit.

■ Lowering the supply voltage will reduce power quadratically for both terms. For example, cutting V_{DD} to 80 percent of its original value will reduce power to $(80\%)^2 = 64\%$ of its original value.
■ Shutting off the supply voltage for unused circuits will eliminate all of their power.
■ Disabling the clock ("clock gating") for unused circuits will eliminate their dynamic power.
■ Reducing the switching frequency for circuits which are used will reduce their dynamic power proportionately.

Reducing energy is a bit more involved. As we reduce the supply voltage, transistors take longer to switch because when they turn on they are operating closer to the threshold voltage V_{Th}, so they do not turn on as strongly (since a saturated MOSFET's current depends on $(V_{GS} - V_{Th})^2$).

$$f_{max} = \frac{K_P(V_{DD} - V_{Th})^2}{V_{DD}}$$

Looking at this from the point of view of a CPU core lowering the clock frequency means that the processor has to be active longer to complete the same amount of processing work.

Optimizing energy is more complex than optimizing power since it requires us to balance multiple factors. Slowing the clock f_{max} lets us lower V_{DD} and therefore both static and dynamic power. Slowing the clock also raises the computation time, so that power is integrated over a longer time, potentially raising total energy used. If there is a low-power standby mode available, in many cases it turns out that the best approach is to run the processor as fast as possible (at the minimum V_{DD} possible for that frequency) when there is work to do, and put the processor into standby mode otherwise.

13.3   RL78 CLOCK CONTROL

Let's start by looking at how we control the clock frequency and perform clock gating for the RL78 family of MCUs (Renesas Electronics Corporation, 2011.)

13.3.1   Clock Sources

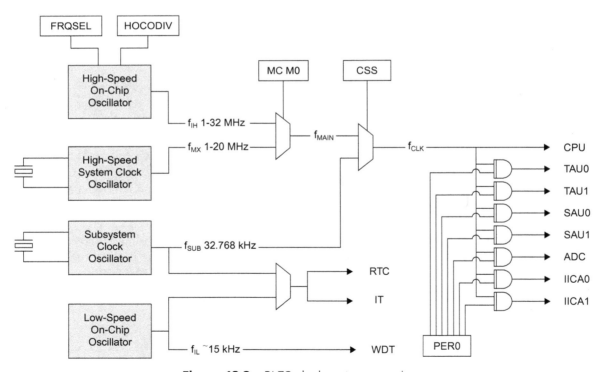

Figure 13.2   RL78 clock system overview.

There are multiple oscillators in an RL78 family MCU, as shown in Figure 13.2. The first three can be used to clock the CPU and most of the peripherals (serial and timer array units, analog to digital converter, I2C interface, etc.).

- The high-speed on-chip oscillator is configurable and generates clock signal f_{IH} at certain frequencies from 1 to 32 MHz. These frequencies are approximate, and the accuracy can be increased by adjusting the value in the trimming register HIOTRM.
- The high-speed system clock oscillator uses an external crystal, resonator, or clock signal to generate the signal f_{MX}, which can range from 1 to 20 MHz.
- The subsystem clock oscillator uses an external 32.768 kHz resonator, crystal or clock signal to generate the f_{XT} signal.

There is a fourth oscillator available as well:

- The low-speed on-chip oscillator generates the f_{SUB} signal at approximately 15 kHz ($\pm$2.25 kHz). This signal can only be used by the watchdog timer, real-time clock, or interval timer.

13.3.2 Clock Source Configuration

There are several registers used to configure the various clocks and how they are used.

- The Clock Operation Mode Control (CMC) register determines critical parameters such as oscillation amplitude and frequency range, and whether external pins are used as crystal connections or input ports. It can only be written once after reset in order to protect it from corruption by abnormal program behavior.
- The System Clock Control (CKC) register selects the CPU/peripheral hardware clock (f_{CLK}) using the CSS bit, and the main system clock (f_{MAIN}) using the MCM0 bit.
- The Clock Operation Status Control (CSC) register controls whether an oscillator is stopped or running. The MSTOP bit controls the high-speed system clock oscillator, the XTSTOP bit controls the subsystem clock oscillator, and the HIOSTOP bit controls the high-speed on-chip oscillator.
- The Peripheral Enable Register 0 (PER0) allows the program to disable the clock signals for unused peripherals in order to save power. The analog to digital converter, and each timer array unit, serial array unit, and IICA unit can be controlled independently.

13.3.3 Oscillation Stabilization

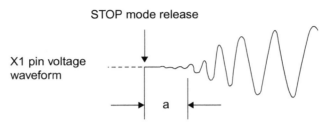

STOP mode release

X1 pin voltage
waveform

a

Figure 13.3 High-speed system clock oscillator start-up time.

There is some time delay between when the high-speed system clock oscillator is started and when it runs at the correct frequency and amplitude, as shown in Figure 13.3. There are two registers associated with controlling and monitoring this time delay.

■ The Oscillation Stabilization Time Select register (OSTS) specifies how long the MCU waits for the X1 clock to stabilize when coming out of stop mode. Delays from 2^8 to 2^{18} X1 counts are possible (i.e., from tens of microseconds to tens of milliseconds).
■ The Oscillation Stabilization Time Counter Status register (OSTC) indicates how much time has elapsed since coming out of stop mode. Each bit is set to one as the time threshold passes and remains at one.

13.3.4 High-Speed On-Chip Oscillator Frequency Selection

The high-speed on-chip oscillator's output frequency f_{IH} can be selected in two ways. First, the FRQSEL bits of option byte 000C2H can be used to specify a speed.

FRQSEL3	FRQSEL2	FRQSEL1	FRQSEL0	FREQUENCY OF THE HIGH-SPEED ON-CHIP OSCILLATOR
1	0	0	0	32 MHz
0	0	0	0	24 MHz
1	0	0	1	16 MHz
0	0	0	1	12 MHz
1	0	1	0	8 MHz
1	0	1	1	4 MHz
1	1	0	1	1 MHz
Other than above				Setting prohibited

Figure 13.4 Oscillator speed selection with option byte 000C2H.

| | | | HIGH-SPEED ON-CHIP OSCILLATOR CLOCK FREQUENCY | |
HOCODIV2	HOCODIV1	HOCODIV0	FRQSEL3 BIT IS 0	FRQSEL3 BIT IS 1
0	0	0	24 MHz	32 MHz
0	0	1	12 MHz	16 MHz
0	1	0	6 MHz	8 MHz
0	1	1	3 MHz	4 MHz
1	0	0	Setting prohibited	2 MHz
1	0	1	Setting prohibited	1 MHz
Other than above			Setting prohibited	

Figure 13.5   Oscillator speed selection with HOCODIV register.

Second, the frequency select register HOCODIV can be used, as shown in Figure 13.5. There are two possible sets of frequencies based on whether the FRQSEL3 bit of option byte 000C2H is set to 1 or 0.

13.4   RL78 STANDBY MODES

In addition to the normal operating mode of executing instructions, the RL78 offers several standby modes in which the processor cannot execute instructions but other portions of the MCU continue to operate. Figure 13.6 presents a state diagram showing the halt, stop, and snooze states and possible transitions among them.[2] Note that the peripherals are functioning in the Halt and Operating states, while most are off in the Stop and Snooze modes. Turning off the peripherals dramatically reduces power consumption.

A circuit's current consumption can be cut significantly by using the standby states: starting at 2.1 mA when executing instructions at 32 MHz, current falls to 540 mA when halted but with clocks running at 32 MHz, and falls further to 0.23 mA when stopped with only the 32.768 kHz subsystem clock running.

Table 13.1 shows which portions operate in the different standby modes. Note that which clock source is used affects which subsystems can operate in HALT mode.

---

[2] Note that this is a simplification of the complete state diagram present in the RL78G13 hardware manual.

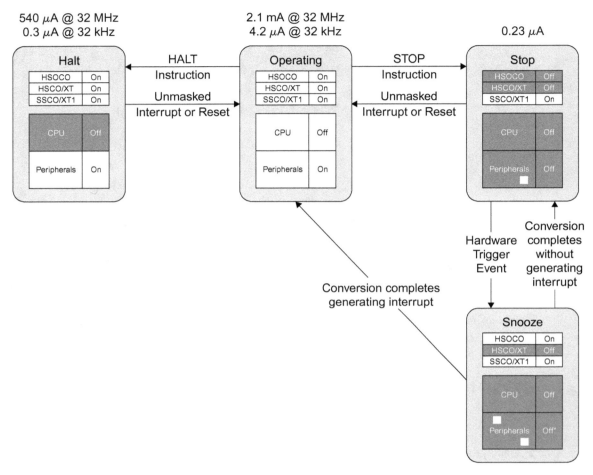

Figure 13.6 MCU operating and standby state transitions with ADC Snooze mode.

Let's examine each of the available standby states next.

13.4.1 Halt

A program executes the HALT instruction to enter the halt mode. The CPU stops executing instructions, but some or all peripherals continue to operate. If the main system clock is used then all peripherals will be able to operate, while if the subsystem clock is used some peripherals will be unavailable.

The MCU exits the halt state if it receives an unmasked interrupt request or a reset signal.

TABLE 13.1   MCU Subsystem Operation in Standby Modes.

SUBSYSTEM	HALT MAIN SYSTEM CLOCK	HALT SUBSYSTEM CLOCK	STOP	SNOOZE
Port	y	y	y	y
Power On Reset	y	y	y	y
Voltage Detection Circuit	y	y	y	y
External Interrupt	y	y	y	y
Key Interrupt	y	y	y	y
Real-Time Clock	y	y	y	y
Interval Timer	y	y	y	y
Clock/Buzzer	y	config.	config.	config.
Watchdog Timer	config.	config.	config.	config.
Serial Array Unit	y	config.	wake to snooze	y
Analog to Digital Converter	y		wake to snooze	y
I²C Array	y		adx. match wake	
Multiplier/Divider/Accumulator	y	config.		
Direct Memory Access	y	config.		
Timer Array Units	y	config.		
General Purpose CRC	y	y		
High-Speed CRC	y			
Illegal Memory Access Detection	y			

13.4.2 Stop

A program executes the STOP instruction to enter the stop mode, which shuts down most peripherals in order to save additional power. The stop mode shuts down the main oscillator (X1 pin). When exiting stop mode, the oscillator must start up again so it incurs the stabilization delay described earlier.

The MCU exits the stop state if it receives an unmasked interrupt request or a reset signal.

13.4.3 Snooze

In order to use the Snooze mode the program must configure the peripheral accordingly, and then the MCU enters the Snooze mode with a STOP instruction. The analog to digital converter and serial array units can be configured to move the processor from STOP to SNOOZE mode when an appropriate trigger condition occurs.

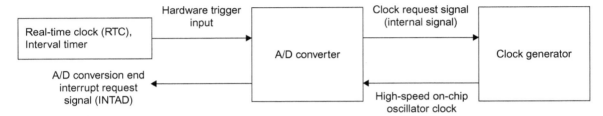

Figure 13.7 ADC and snooze mode operation.

For example, the ADC can be be triggered by the real-time clock or the interval timer, as shown in Figure 13.7. When triggered, the ADC will assert a signal starting up the high-speed on-chip oscillator clock. The clock starts up (and stabilizes for the specified delay) and is fed to the ADC, which uses it to perform the specified conversion(s). After the conversion(s) complete there are two possible actions, based on interrupt signal generation.

  ▦ If no interrupt is generated, the clock stops running and the system goes back into snooze mode.
  ▦ If an interrupt is generated, the clock continues running. The interrupt signal wakes up the MCU from STOP mode so it can execute instructions.

Further details are available in a white paper (Renesas Electronics America Inc., 2011).

13.5   RL78 POWER AND ENERGY CHARACTERISTICS _____

TABLE 13.2 Minimum Supply Voltage vs. Maximum Frequency.

MINIMUM V_{DD}	MAXIMUM FREQUENCY
1.6 V	4 MHz
1.8 V	8 MHz
2.4 V	32 MHz

Let's look at the RL78/G13 hardware manual's electrical characteristics section. As shown in Table 13.2, the minimum voltage required **increases** as the maximum desired frequency **increases.** The transistors need higher voltages to switch faster and support higher clock frequencies.

TABLE 13.3   RL78G13 Energy per Clock Cycle for Various Speeds and Voltages.

FREQUENCY (MHz)	VOLTAGE (V)	CURRENT (mA)	POWER (mW)	ENERGY PER CYCLE (pJ)
0.032768	2	0.0049	0.0098	299.07
8	2	1.3	2.6	325.00
32	3	2.1	6.3	196.88

Next let's examine how much energy is used per clock cycle at various operating points, as shown in Table 13.3. This data was gleaned from the hardware manual and is a good starting point to see how the MCU behaves.

- The **lowest power** operating point runs the clock **as slow as possible** (using the 32.768 kHz oscillator), and therefore can use a low voltage (2 V) to reduce power. The resulting power is 9.8 mW.
- The **lowest energy** operating point on the other hand runs the clock as **fast as possible** (32 MHz with the on-chip oscillator). In this case, the power has risen to 6.3 mW, but the energy per cycle is a mere 196.88 pJ per clock cycle. This is the most energy-efficient of the operating points.

This apparent contradiction makes sense if we consider that static power is wasted from a point of view of computations. The faster we run the clock, the less overhead static power incurs on each computation. In general, the most energy-efficient way to use an MCU is to run at top speed when there is any work to do, and shift into an extremely low-power standby state otherwise.

It is interesting to note that the MCU can operate with lower power or energy than these levels by using a lower operating voltage. Notice that $V_{DD} = 1.6$ V is sufficient for running at 32 kHz (see Table 13.2). This is an optimal operating point: it provides the highest clock frequency which will run at a given voltage. We would expect the power to fall to about $(1.6 \text{ V}/2.0 \text{ V})^2 = 64\%$ of the original value. If we scale all of the power and energy calculations according to the minimum voltages we can predict the minimum power and energy required, as shown in Table 13.4.

TABLE 13.4 Estimated Power and Energy for RL78G13 Running at Optimal Operating Points.

FREQUENCY (MHz)	VOLTAGE (V)	ESTIMATED POWER (mW)	ESTIMATED ENERGY PER CYCLE (pJ)
0.032768	1.6	0.006272	191.41
8	1.8	2.268	283.50
32	2.4	3.744	117.00

The results of the calculations show that the power used for the 32 kHz and 32 MHz cases falls by nearly one half, and the energy falls by about one third. The 8 MHz case sees a smaller increase because the relative voltage drop is smaller (2.0 V to 1.8 V).

13.6 POWER AND ENERGY OPTIMIZATION

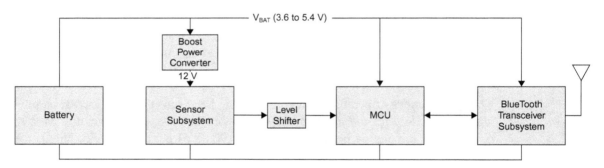

Figure 13.8 Remote sensor block diagram.

Let's see how to put together all of these techniques and factors by examining how to optimize the power and energy use of a remote sensor system shown in Figure 8. We use a sensor subsystem to measure the parameter of interest. The sensor subsystem transmits its measurements through a serial port to the MCU, which relays this information through a Bluetooth wireless transceiver to the rest of the system. The MCU also reports local battery voltage information via Bluetooth so that we can determine when replacements are needed.

- The battery consists of four NiMH AAA cells in series, producing a voltage from 3.6 to 5.4 V. Each D cell has a nominal capacity of 1 AH. If we assume an average voltage of 5 V, the energy capacity is 5 WH = 5 W * 3600 s = 18,000 J.

- The sensor subsystem runs at 12 V, so we use a boost power converter to generate a regulated 12 V supply from the battery voltage.
- The boost converter is only 85% efficient, so it uses some additional power.
- The level shifter uses a negligible amount of power and can safely be disregarded.
- We use an RL78G13 MCU running at 32 MHz with the high-speed on-chip oscillator.
- The Bluetooth transceiver runs internally at 3.3 V, but contains an onboard low-dropout linear voltage regulator which can accept up to 6 V.

13.6.1 Power Analysis

TABLE 13.5 Power Use by System Components.

COMPONENT	VOLTAGE (V)	CURRENT (mA)	POWER (mW)
Sensor	12	60	720
MCU	5	4.6	23
Bluetooth Transceiver	5	30	150
Boost Power Converter			108

We start with a power analysis. We will assume that the battery voltage is 5 V in order to simplify our initial analysis. We multiply operating voltage by current to find the power used by each component, as shown in Table 5. We can see that the majority of the power is used by the sensor subsystem.

13.6.2 Energy Analysis

Next let's look at how the energy is used. If all components are used all the time, we simply multiply power by 24 hours to find daily energy use, which unsurprisingly will show the sensor subsystem dominating the energy use as well.

13.6.2.1 Reducing Sensor Energy Use

What if our system does not need to have all components powered all of the time? Instead, each day the sensor is only activated to perform a reading, for a total of 15 minutes per day. In the remainder of the time the sensor and its power converter are turned off. We can now add duty cycles and daily energy use, resulting in Table 6. We see that the Bluetooth transceiver now dominates energy use. Our 18 kJ battery will power the system for roughly 1.15 days.

TABLE 13.6   Energy use by system components. Battery life is 1.15 days.

COMPONENT	VOLTAGE (V)	CURRENT (mA)	POWER (mW)	HOURS ACTIVE/DAY	DUTY CYCLE	ENERGY (J)
Sensor	12	60	720	0.25	1.0%	648
MCU	5	4.6	23	24	100.0%	1,987
Bluetooth Transceiver	5	30	150	24	100.0%	12,960
Boost Power Converter			108	0.25	1.0%	97
Total						**15,692**

13.6.2.2   *Reducing Bluetooth Power Energy Use*

We can reduce Bluetooth power and energy consumption in a few ways. Let's examine two options.

First, we can reduce the supply voltage of the Bluetooth module. Recall that it has an on-board 3.3V linear regulator. In this case it dissipates $(5 - 3.3V) * 30\,mA = 51\,mW$, or about one third of the Bluetooth module's power. We need to use a switching power converter to perform this conversion, as it will be more efficient than a linear regulator. An added bonus of this approach is that we can reduce the supply voltage for the RL78 as well, reducing its power and energy use. The disadvantage is the circuit will cost more and use more space.

Second, we can reduce the amount of time the Bluetooth module is active, and have it spend the remainder of its time in a lower power mode. This will require some additional configuration of the module. The Bluetooth protocol offers various low-power modes specifically designed to save energy by reducing the duty cycle. When the sensor is turned off we will use this approach (when the sensor is on, we want minimum latency and highest speed). We will use the *sniff* mode, in which this node will keep its radio turned off most of the time, so the current consumption is only 3 mA. Periodically it will turn on the radio for communication, raising the current to 30 mA. We assume a radio on-time of 20 ms and total period of 1.5 seconds, resulting in an average current of 3.36 mA in sniff mode.

By applying both of these approaches we can reduce the daily energy use by a factor of almost five, as shown in Table 7. Our 18 kJ battery will power the system for roughly 5.6 days.

13.6.2.3   *MCU Clock Speed Reduction*

We now see that the MCU dominates the power consumption. There is much room for optimization here because the MCU has a very light processing load. It just needs to sample and log the battery voltage periodically (e.g. every minute) and report on it via Bluetooth (e.g. every hour).

TABLE 13.7   Energy Use After Adding 3.3 V Buck Regulator and Using Bluetooth Sniff Mode. Battery Life is 5.6 days.

COMPONENT	VOLTAGE (V)	CURRENT (mA)	POWER (mW)	HOURS ACTIVE/DAY	DUTY CYCLE	ENERGY (J)
Sensor	12	60	720	0.25	1.0%	648
MCU	3.3	4.6	15.18	24	100.0%	1,312
Bluetooth Transceiver	3.3	3.36	11.088	24	100.0%	958
Boost Power Converter						97
Buck Power Converter						227
Total						**3,242**

There are several approaches to consider: slowing down the clock, using a standby mode and lowering the supply voltage. There is an RL78 application note which goes into detail and is recommended reading (Renesas Electronics America Inc., 2011). Let's take a look at where the energy use data leads us in our continued optimization investigations.

How slowly can we run the MCU clock? This depends upon the amount of processing needed as well as clock speeds needed for serial communications. Given the light processing load we can drop the speed to 1 MHz (generated by the high-speed on-chip oscillator), and the MCU current will fall to 0.72 mA. The resulting energy for the system falls to 2025 J as shown in Table 8. The total battery life rises to 8.9 days. Reducing the MCU current has left the Bluetooth transceiver as the highest energy user.

TABLE 13.8   Energy use after dropping MCU clock rate to 1 MHz. Battery life is 8.9 days.

COMPONENT	VOLTAGE (V)	CURRENT (mA)	POWER (mW)	HOURS ACTIVE/DAY	DUTY CYCLE	ENERGY (J)
Sensor	12	60	720	0.25	1%	648
MCU (1 MHz)	3.3	0.72	2.376	24	100%	205
Bluetooth Transceiver	3.3	3.36	11.088	24	100%	958
Boost Power Converter						97
Buck Power Converter						116
Total						**2,025**

13.6.3 Standby Mode Energy

Let's consider another way this system might be used. What if we keep it powered off most of the time, but we need to use it occasionally? We would like for the MCU to monitor the battery voltage and report it via Bluetooth so we can determine if we need to recharge the batteries. This is similar to the standby battery lifetime measurement used for cellphones.

TABLE 13.9   Energy use in standby mode. Battery life is 14.1 days.

COMPONENT	VOLTAGE (V)	CURRENT (mA)	POWER (mW)	HOURS ACTIVE/DAY	DUTY CYCLE	ENERGY (J)
Sensor	12	60	720	0	0%	0
MCU	3.3	0.72	2.376	24	100%	205
Bluetooth Transceiver	3.3	3.36	11.088	24	100%	958
Boost Power Converter						0
Buck Power Converter						116
Total						**1,280**

Our energy use model has now changed. We only need to examine power when the sensor subsystem is off, as shown in Table 9. Daily energy use falls to 1280 J, so the standby battery life is 14.1 days.

13.6.3.1 Shutting Off Bluetooth When Idle

We see the Bluetooth transceiver uses most of the energy, but in fact we only need for the transceiver to be turned on occasionally to report the battery voltage. Rather than use sniff mode we will shut down the transceiver completely, and power it up once every five minutes. We assume it will take about two seconds to start up, connect, transmit its data, and shut down. The resulting energy use has fallen by a factor of about five, as shown in Table 10. The battery life is now 62.4 days.

13.6.3.2 Halt Mode

The MCU is now the largest consumer of energy, but it has very little computing to do. We can put the MCU into halt mode when it is idle. All of the oscillators will continue running, so we will not need to change much code. The MCU current will fall to 0.260 mA. We estimate that the code will need to run about 100 μs every minute. In this time the program will wake up the MCU, sample the ADC, evaluate the conversion result, and go back to sleep. Every five minutes the MCU will need to also power up the Bluetooth transceiver

TABLE 13.10 Energy use in standby mode with Bluetooth turned off except when needed. Battery life is 62.4 days.

COMPONENT	VOLTAGE (V)	CURRENT (mA)	POWER (mW)	HOURS ACTIVE/DAY	DUTY CYCLE	ENERGY (J)
Sensor	12	60	720	0	0%	0
MCU	3.3	0.72	2.376	24	100%	205
Bluetooth Transceiver	3.3	3.36	99	0.16	1%	57
Boost Power Converter						0
Buck Power Converter						26
Total						**289**

and send the data, taking two seconds. Hence the duty cycle for the MCU in operating mode can be calculated as:

$$D = \frac{100 \ \mu s}{60 \ s} + \frac{2 \ s}{60 * 60 \ s} = 0.6668\%$$

For the remaining 99.3332% of the time the MCU will be in halt mode.

TABLE 13.11 Energy Use with 1 MHz On-Chip Clock and Halt Mode. Battery life is 146.9 Days.

COMPONENT	VOLTAGE (V)	OPERATING CURRENT (mA)	OPERATING POWER (mW)	HALT CURRENT (mA)	HALT POWER (mW)	DUTY CYCLE	ENERGY (J)
Sensor	12	60	720			0.0000%	0.0
MCU (1 MHz)	3.3	0.72	2.376	0.26	0.61776	0.6668%	54.4
Bluetooth Transceiver	3.3	30	99			0.6667%	57.0
Boost Power Converter							0.0
Buck Power Converter							11.1
Total							**122.6**

The resulting energy use from these optimizations appears in Table 11. The MCU energy use has fallen 54.4 J. Total daily energy consumption is 122.6 J, so standby battery life soars to about 147 days.

13.6.3.3 Stop Mode

For our last round of optimization we will make two changes to cut energy use for both the MCU and the Bluetooth. First, we will reduce the Bluetooth activity by updating the battery voltage only once per day, which is reasonable for a system in a deep standby mode. This results in a duty cycle of two seconds per 24 hours.

Second, we will put the processor into stop mode rather than halt mode. The halt mode enables the MCU to wake up immediately, but this is not essential for our application. A more energy-efficient choice is to use the stop mode, which uses less power but requires slightly more time to resume (due to the oscillator start-up delay). We will use the 32.768 kHz subsystem clock to drive the system while in stop mode.

The energy used plummets, reaching only 0.275 J per day as shown in Table 12. Battery life has risen enough (to nearly 180 years) that its self-discharge is the limiting factor.

TABLE 13.12   Energy use with 1 MHz on-chip clock, 32.768 kHz subsystem clock and stop mode. Battery life is limited by self-discharge rather than load circuit.

| COMPONENT | VOLTAGE (V) | OPERATING | | STOP | | DUTY CYCLE | ENERGY (J) |
		CURRENT (mA)	POWER (mW)	CURRENT (mA)	POWER (mW)		
Sensor	12	60	720			0.0000%	0.000
MCU (1 MHz)	3.3	0.72	2.376	0.00023	0.000546	0.0023%	0.052
Bluetooth Transceiver	3.3	30	99			0.0023%	0.198
Boost Power Converter							0.000
Buck Power Converter							0.025
Total							**0.275**

13.7 RECAP

In this chapter we have seen how voltage and switching frequency determine the amount of power used by a digital circuit. We have also examined the relationship between power and energy. We have investigated the RL78 MCU family's design features for reducing power and energy use. Finally we examined how to estimate power and energy consumption for an embedded application and then used them to guide our energy optimization activities.

13.8   REFERENCES

Renesas Electronics America Inc., *White Paper—RL78 Microcontroller Family: Using the Snooze Mode Feature to Dramatically Reduce Power Consumption* (2011).

Renesas Electronics Corporation, *RL78/G13 16-Bit Single-Chip Microcontrollers User's Manual: Hardware* (2011).

13.9   EXERCISES

1. Estimate the battery life of a voice recorder with the following parameters. State and justify your assumptions.
    - 20 kHz audio sample rate
    - 3 V 2500 mAH battery
    - Input amplifier which draws 1 mA when powered
    - Output amplifier which draws 3 mA when powered
    - LCD which draws 0.8 mA
    - Assume a 3% recording duty cycle and a 2% playback duty cycle.

2. Consider replacing the battery of the previous problem with a 1 F supercapacitor charged to 5 V. How long will the system operate before the voltage drops below 2 V?

3. Consider the sensor system presented above. Create functioning code using the halt mode with the techniques described and an 8 MHz clock rate. The authors estimated the MCU would need to spend 100 ms out of halt mode. What is the time for your code? What are the resulting energy use and standby battery life?

4. Experimentally determine the minimum voltage needed to run an RL78G13 MCU at each of the following frequencies: 32 kHz, 1 MHz, 2 MHz, 4 MHz, 8 MHz, 16 MHz and 32 MHz. Measure the current drawn at each frequency and calculate the power used and energy per clock cycle. What is the most power-efficient operating point? What is the most energy-efficient operating point?

5. Processor Vendor X advertises that their microcontroller uses only 80 nJ per clock cycle at 32 MHz, compared with the (expected) 117 nJ for the RL78G13.Similarly, Vendor Y admits their processor uses 160 nJ per clock cycle. Discuss and prioritize what other factors you will need to consider before determining which MCU will lead to minimal energy use for your application.

Index

www.ingramcontent.com/pod-product-compliance
Lightning Source LLC
LaVergne TN
LVHW062302060326
832902LV00013B/2009